Approaches to American Cul

Approaches to American Cultural Studies provides an accessible yet comprehensive overview of the diverse range of subjects encompassed within American Studies, familiarizing students with the history and shape of American Studies as an academic subject as well as its key theories, methods, and concepts.

Written and edited by an international team of authors based primarily in Europe, the book is divided into four thematically organized sections. The first part delineates the evolution of American Studies over the course of the twentieth century, the second elaborates on how American Studies as a field is positioned within the wider humanities, and the third inspects and deconstructs popular tropes such as myths of the West, the self-made man, Manifest Destiny, and representations of the President of the United States. The fourth part introduces theories of society such as Structuralism and Deconstruction, Queer and Transgender Theories, Border and Hemispheric Studies, and Critical Race Theory that are particularly influential within American Studies.

This book is supplemented by a companion website offering further material for study (www.routledge.com/cw/dallmann). Specifically designed for use in courses across Europe, it is a clear and engaging introductory text for students of American culture.

Antje Dallmann teaches North American literature and culture at Humboldt-Universität zu Berlin and at Leipzig University in Germany. She is the author of *ConspiraCity New York* (2009) and co-editor of *Envisioning American Utopias* (2011), *Picturing America* (2009, both with Reinhard Isensee and Philipp Kneis), and *Toward a New Metropolitanism* (2006, with Günter H. Lenz and Friedrich Ulfers).

Eva Boesenberg is the author of *Money and Gender in the American Novel, 1850–2000* (2010) and *Gender – Voice – Vernacular: The Formation of Female Subjectivity in Zora Neale Hurston, Toni Morrison, and Alice Walker* (1999), and co-editor of *American Economies* (2012, with Martin Klepper and Reinhard Isensee). She teaches North American literature and culture at Humboldt-Universität zu Berlin.

Martin Klepper teaches North American literature and culture at Humboldt-Universität zu Berlin. He is the author of *Pynchon, Auster, DeLillo: Die amerikanische Postmoderne zwischen Spiel und Rekonstruktion* (1996) and his latest books include *The Discovery of Point of View: Observation and Narration in the American Novel 1790–1910* (2011) and *Rethinking Narrative Identity: Persona and Perspective* (2013, co-edited with Claudia Holler).

Approaches to American Cultural Studies

Edited by
**Antje Dallmann, Eva Boesenberg, and
Martin Klepper**

Routledge
Taylor & Francis Group

LONDON AND NEW YORK

First published 2016
by Routledge
2 Park Square, Milton Park, Abingdon, Oxon OX14 4RN

and by Routledge
711 Third Avenue, New York, NY 10017

Routledge is an imprint of the Taylor & Francis Group, an informa business

British Library Cataloguing in Publication Data
A catalogue record for this book is available from the British Library

Library of Congress Cataloging in Publication Data
Names: Dallman, Antje, contributing editor. | Boesenberg, Eva,
contributing editor. | Klepper, Martin, 1963- contributing editor.
Title: Approaches to American cultural studies / edited by Antje Dallman,
Eva Boesenberg and Martin Klepper.
Description: New York, NY : Routledge, 2016. | Includes bibliographical
references and index.
Identifiers: LCCN 2015042648| ISBN 9780415720823 (hardback :
alk. paper) | ISBN 9780415720854 (pbk. : alk. paper) |
ISBN 9781315624013 (ebook)
Subjects: LCSH: United States--Civilization--Study and teaching. |
United States--Intellectual life--Study and teaching. | United States--Study
and teaching--History. | National characteristics, American--Study and
teaching. | Popular culture--United States–Study and teaching.
Classification: LCC E169.1 .A67 2016 | DDC 973.0071--dc23
LC record available at http://lccn.loc.gov/2015042648

ISBN: 978-0-415-72082-3 (hbk)
ISBN: 978-0-415-72085-4 (pbk)
ISBN: 978-1-315-62401-3 (ebk)

Typeset in Times New Roman
by Taylor & Francis Books
Printed in Great Britain by
Ashford Colour Press Ltd, Gosport, Hants

Contents

Contributors

Mita Banerjee is Professor of American Studies at the University of Mainz, Germany, as well as speaker of the Center for Comparative Native and Indigenous Studies (CCNIS). Her research interests include postcolonial literature, ethnic American literature and culture, the American Renaissance (*Ethnic Ventriloquism: Literary Minstrelsy in Nineteenth-Century American Literature*, 2008), and issues of naturalization and citizenship (*Color Me White: Naturalism/Naturalization in American Literature*, 2013). She is co-speaker of the research training group "Life Sciences, Life Writing: Boundary Experiences of Human Life between Biomedical Explanation and Lived Experience," which is funded by the German Research Foundation.

Georgiana Banita is Assistant Professor of American literature and media at the University of Bamberg, Germany. She studied and worked at the University of Konstanz, Yale, and the University of Sydney. She is the author of *Plotting Justice: Narrative Ethics and Literary Culture after 9/11* (2012) and editor of the volume *Electoral Cultures: American Democracy and Choice* (ed. with Sascha Pöhlmann, 2015). She has published widely on literature after 9/11, narratives of terror, North American visual culture, energy aesthetics across media (literature, film, photography, comics), and Canadian Studies.

Eva Boesenberg teaches North American literature and culture at Humboldt-Universität zu Berlin, Germany. Among her research interests are Gender Studies, Critical Race and Critical Whiteness Studies, African American literature and culture, South Asian North American literature, literature and economics, graphic novels, and the cultural politics of sports, particularly basketball. She has published *Gender – Voice – Vernacular: The Formation of Female Subjectivity in Zora Neale Hurston, Toni Morrison and Alice Walker*, as well as *Money and Gender in the American Novel, 1850–2000*, and co-edited *American Economies* (with Martin Klepper and Reinhard Isensee).

Antje Dallmann teaches North American literature and culture at Humboldt-Universität zu Berlin and at Leipzig University. In her dissertation, she analyzed contemporary urban literature with a focus on New York City (*ConspiraCity New York*, 2009). She has co-edited *Envisioning American Utopias* (2011), *Picturing America* (2009, both with Reinhard Isensee and Philipp Kneis), and *Toward a New Metropolitanism* (2006, with Günter H. Lenz and Friedrich Ulfers). In her current project, she discusses the intersection of medical, literary, and sentimental discourses in Civil War America. Her research interests include the representation and symbolization of medicine and the "medical romance," urban literature and culture, visual cultures, politics and fictional narration, and the representation and metaphorical appropriation of the American family.

Bart Eeckhout is Professor of English and American literature at the University of Antwerp, Belgium. His books include *Wallace Stevens and the Limits of Reading and Writing* (2002) and, as co-editor, *The Urban Condition: Space, Community, and Self in the Contemporary Metropolis* (1999), *Post Ex Sub Dis: Urban Fragmentations and Constructions* (2002), *Wallace Stevens across the Atlantic* (2008), and *Wallace Stevens, New York, and Modernism* (2012). He has been editor of *The Wallace Stevens Journal* since 2011. He also specializes in Queer Studies and publishes in his double role as an academic and an activist in the Belgian LGBTQ movement.

Marcel Hartwig is an Assistant Professor for English and American Studies at the University of Siegen, Germany. In his PhD thesis, he discussed cultural representations of both 9/11 and the attacks on Pearl Harbor as national traumata (*Die traumatisierte Nation?: "Pearl Harbor" und "9/11" als kulturelle Erinnerungen*, 2011). Currently he is working on a post-doctoral project in the field of Transatlantic Studies ("Transit Cultures: Early Medical Discourses in England and the New World"). His research interests include Media Studies, Television Studies, Literary Criticism, Gender Studies, and popular culture.

Martin Klepper is Professor for American literature and culture at Humboldt-Universität zu Berlin, Germany. He has published *Pynchon, Auster, DeLillo – Die amerikanische Postmoderne zwischen Spiel und Rekonstruktion* (1996), has co-edited books on modernism, cybercultures, and American economies, and has written several essays on postmodernism, visuality and nineteenth-century American literature, American cinema, and critical narratology. His latest books are *The Discovery of Point of View: Observation and Narration in the American Novel 1790–1910* (2011) and *Rethinking Narrative Identity: Persona and Perspective* (ed. with Claudia Holler, 2013).

Philipp Kneis is Assistant Professor at the Political Science Department and Assistant Director of the Public Policy Graduate Program at Oregon State University, USA. He is the author of *(S)aged by Culture: Representations of Old Age in American Indian Literature and Culture* (2013) and *The Emancipation of the Soul: Memes of Destiny in American Visual Culture*

(2010). His research interests include poetry, Visual and Media Studies, seriality, Age Studies, and representations of politics.

Uwe Küchler is Junior Professor for Teaching English as a Foreign Language (TEFL) at Rheinische Friedrich-Wilhelms-Universität Bonn, Germany. In his doctoral dissertation he pursued questions of intercultural learning and teaching in the context of higher education (*Interkulturelle Hochschullehre*, 2007). His research interests comprise skills/multiple literacies as well as the teaching of literature, film, and media in EFL. Currently, he is working on a book project that explores ecological issues in TEFL teaching.

Zuzanna Ladyga is Assistant Professor at the Department of American literature, University of Warsaw, Poland, where she teaches Critical Theory and twentieth-century literature. Her research interests include the relation between ethics and politics, Marxist theories, Affect Studies, and the aesthetics of new media. She is the author of *Rethinking Postmodern Subjectivity: Emmanuel Levinas and Ethics of Referentiality in the Work of Donald Barthelme* (2009).

Dorothea Löbbermann teaches North American literature and culture at Humboldt-Universität zu Berlin, Germany. Her book publications are *Memories of Harlem: Fiktionale (Re)Konstruktionen eines Mythos der zwanziger Jahre* (2002), *Other Modernisms in an Age of Globalization*, co-edited with Djelal Kadir (2002), and *CinematoGraphies: Visual Discourses and Textual Strategies in 1990s New York City*, co-edited with Günter H. Lenz and Karl-Heinz Magister (2006). Her research interests are representations of urban space, theories of "race" and gender, and discourses of nature.

Jodi Melamed is Associate Professor of English and Africana Studies at Marquette University in Milwaukee, USA. She is the author of *Represent and Destroy: Rationalizing Violence in the New Racial Capitalism* (2011). Her essays have appeared in interdisciplinary journals and edited collections including *American Quarterly, American Literature, Social Text, African American Review, Strange Affinities: The Sexual and Gender Politics of Comparative Racialization* (2011), and *Keywords for American Cultural Studies*, Second Edition (2014). Her current book project investigates the financialization of racial capitalism globally since the 1980s and emergent forms of "co-resistance" arising out of concurrent social movements.

Christina Meyer is an Assistant Professor in American Studies and Research Associate in the English Department at the Leibniz University of Hannover, Germany. Her dissertation is titled *War & Trauma Images in Vietnam War Representations* (2008). Presently, she is working on a book project titled "Series of Multimodal Forms of Narration: The Yellow Kid Newspaper Comics of the Nineteenth Century." Christina Meyer has co-edited *New Perspectives on American Comic Books and Graphic Novels* (a special issue of *Amerikastudien/American Studies*, 2011) and *Transnational Perspectives* *on Graphic Narratives: Comics at the Crossroads* (2013). Her research interests include popular culture, Seriality Studies, visual culture, mass culture, Comics Studies, narratology, and trauma theory.

Matthias Oppermann is a Senior Research Associate at the Center for New Designs in Learning and Scholarship (CNDLS) at Georgetown University, USA, and teaches English and geography at Diltheyschule in Wiesbaden, Germany. He has published *American Studies in Dialogue: Radical Reconstructions between Curriculum and Cultural Critique* (2010). In the past, Oppermann coordinated the American Studies Crossroads Project and held a position as Associate Director of the Forum for Inter-American Research (FIAR). He also served on the International Committee of the American Studies Association (ASA) and on the Advisory Board of the International Association of Inter-American Studies (IAS). His current research situates itself at the intersection of American Studies, curriculum design, and student learning.

Gabriele Pisarz-Ramirez is Professor of American Studies and Minority Studies at Leipzig University, Germany. Her research focuses on the role of "race" and ethnicity in the United States, migration, Latino/a cultures, and Inter-American Studies. She received her PhD from the University of Leipzig with a study on the translation of Stephen Crane texts and her Habilitation with a book on Mexican American cultural productions (*MexAmerica: Genealogien und Analysen postnationaler Diskurse in der kulturellen Produktion von Chicanos/as*, 2005). Pisarz-Ramirez has taught at the universities of Göttingen, Bielefeld, Bayreuth, and Groningen (Netherlands) and was a Guest Professor at the Center for Comparative Studies in Race and Ethnicity at Stanford University in 2009. She has co-edited the 2008 *American Studies/Amerikastudien* special issue "The Americas in the Nineteenth Century: Inter-American Perspectives on US Literature" and the volume *Transmediality and Transculturality* (2013).

Michael J. Prince is an Associate Professor of American literature and culture at the University of Agder in Kristiansand, Norway. He was formerly a Lecturer and Associate Professor at the Royal Norwegian Naval Academy in Bergen, Norway in the International Politics/Military Studies Department. He has given numerous courses at undergraduate and graduate level involving cultural myth. His other research interests include music, popular culture, satire, comics, film adaptations, and Beat poets.

Katja Schmieder received her doctorate in American Studies from the University of Leipzig, Germany, where she now teaches American literature and Cultural Studies. Her research interests include popular culture, such as (medical) crime fiction, as well as science and literature in the Anglo-American world. She has published on the reception of American popular culture in Germany and on gender in the TV shows *Bones* and *Crossing Jordan*. She is engaged in the field of medical humanities, from which her recent project on nineteenth-century discourses about reproduction evolved.

Jan Stievermann is Professor of the History of Christianity in the US at Heidelberg University and director of the Jonathan Edwards Center Germany. He has written and edited books and essays on a broad range of topics in the fields of American religious history and American literature, including a comprehensive study of the theology and aesthetics of Ralph Waldo Emerson (2007). He co-edited *A Peculiar Mixture: German-Language Cultures and Identities in Eighteenth-Century North America* (2013) and *Religion and the Marketplace in the United States* (2014). His most recent publications are the edition of volume 5 of Cotton Mather's *Biblia Americana* (2015) and a book-length study of this hitherto unexplored source entitled *Prophecy, Piety, and the Problem of Historicity: Interpreting the Hebrew Scriptures in Cotton Mather's* Biblia Americana (2016). For the *Biblia*-project as a whole (10 volumes) he also serves as the executive editor.

Simon Strick is a Post-doctorate Fellow at the Graduate Research Group "Automatisms" at Paderborn University, Germany. He is the author of *American Dolorologies: Pain, Sentimentalism, Biopolitics* (2015) and has published widely on the intersection of questions of masculinity, gender discourses, media representations, and technology. His fields of research include Gender and Queer Studies, Media Studies, and Disability Studies.

Justine Tally is Emerita Professor of American Literature at the University of La Laguna, Spain, where she has specialized in African American literature and culture. She is author of Paradise *Reconsidered: Toni Morrison's (Hi)stories and Truths* (1999), *The Story of* Jazz*: Toni Morrison's Dialogic Imagination* (2001), and *Toni Morrison's* Beloved*: Origins* (2009). She has edited the *Cambridge Companion to Toni Morrison* (2007) and co-edited with Walter Hölbling *Theories and Texts* (2007, 2009), with Shirley A. Stave *Toni Morrison's* A Mercy*: Critical Approaches* (2011), and with Adrienne Seward *Toni Morrison: Memory and Meaning* (2014).

Christina Wald is Professor of English Literature at the University of Konstanz, Germany. Her research focuses on contemporary drama, performance, film, and TV; early modern drama and prose fiction; gender and feminist theory. She is the author of *Hysteria, Trauma and Melancholia: Performative Maladies in Contemporary Anglophone Drama* (2007) and *The Reformation of Romance: The Eucharist, Disguise and Foreign Fashion in Early Modern Prose Fiction* (2014), and has co-edited several books, most recently *The Literature of Melancholia: Early Modern to Postmodern* (2011) and *English and American Studies: Theory and Practice* (2012).

Introduction

Eva Boesenberg, Antje Dallmann, and
Martin Klepper

In a curious move, Thomas Pynchon's epic novel *Gravity's Rainbow* (1973) chooses to introduce its main protagonist (or: anti-protagonist) Tyrone Slothrop not by way of description, characterization, dialog, or action but through a depiction of his desk in an office that he shares with his colleague Tantivy in war-ravaged London. "Tantivy's desk is neat, Slothrop's is a godawful mess. It hasn't been cleaned down to the original wood surface since 1942," the text declares.

> Things have fallen roughly into layers, over a base of bureaucratic smegma that sifts steadily to the bottom, made up of millions of tiny red and brown curls of rubber eraser, pencil shavings, dried tea or coffee stains, traces of sugar and Household Milk, much cigarette ash, very fine black debris picked and flung from type-writer ribbons, decomposing library paste, broken aspirins ground to powder. Then comes a scatter of paperclips, Zippo flints, rubber bands, staples, cigarette butts and crumpled packs, stray matches, pins, nubs of pens, stubs of pencils of all colors including the hard-to-get heliotrope and raw umber, wooden coffee spoons, Thayer's Slippery Elm Throat Lozenges sent by Slothrop's mother, Nalline, all the way from Massachusetts, bits of tape, string, chalk ... above that a layer of forgotten memoranda, empty buff ration books, phone numbers, unanswered letters, tattered sheets of carbon paper, the scribbled ukulele chords to a dozen songs including "Johnny Doughboy Found a Rose in Ireland" [...]. (20)

Pynchon's strategy, as many commentators have pointed out, is not accidental, even though the desk may look like an accident. The depiction has often been read as a miniature (or *mise-en-abyme,* to use the scholarly term) of the entire novel. Not only does Slothrop's predicament consist in the attempt to keep up with or run after the seemingly insignificant things that surround him: the little bits and pieces of material and symbolic culture that make up and nourish his life and that existed before him and will exist after him. He also makes a valiant effort to extract some sort of meaning and orientation from the ominous order of physical and mental bric-a-brac around him. But the failure of this effort also leads to his impulse to ignore or run away from these things. However, short of disappearing from the fictional world altogether (which he actually does in the end), he cannot escape the detritus from his hopelessly overdetermined social world of solid, fluid, textual, oral, and spiritual products. These things define him, they bring into being his very existence, they are part of him – just as culture is part and parcel of the life of every reader who happens to read this Introduction.

Spontaneously, students of American culture may well prefer Tantivy's neat desk to Slothrop's "godawful mess." Especially, beginning students may long for an orderly arrangement. What is (American) culture? How does it work? How do we read it? How did it evolve? And how can one systematize cultural products – what is important, what is not? Perhaps, one could parse Slothrop's belongings into print products, food products, music, personals, and trash. But at which point does something qualify as trash? And what do we make of the "buff ration books," booklets with coupons that allotted food to the British population during World War II: Do they belong to the print or the food products? Perhaps we need an altogether different approach: After all, Slothrop's desk and office are snooped into because there is a hint that Slothrop may be a security risk for the military establishment in London. Suspicious and unsuspicious items, then?

Literary scholar Susanne Rohr has pointed out that the analogy between Slothrop's desk and *Gravity's Rainbow* at large consists in the existence of a mass of overbearing coincidences that allow for a potentially endless plurality of systems of order. The individual parts could be arranged in ever new patterns according to ever new rules. Whichever order one chooses, part of this mass are relics of broken structures and/or past systems of representation (254). Critic Richard Poirier has suggested that in order to understand the novel and Slothrop's desk one has to explore the various ways and forms in which life is expressing itself.

> These include not only Science and pop culture but the messages sent out by those who usually escape the notice of either, the lost ones, those not "framed," not in the design of things. The signs of their existence are to be found in the waste along the highway, the litter in the trunks of cars, the stuff in the bureau drawer. (64)

Anishinaabe/Chippewa writer Louise Erdrich's *The Bingo Palace* (1994) also offers an exploration of the messages from those usually not in the design of things – albeit one quite different from the perspective of a white (male) European American writer like Pynchon. In fact, Erdrich's opening explicitly raises the questions of perspective, of seeing, of the object(s) of seeing, and of being seen, questions that may confound students of American Studies just as much as the question of systematization:

> On most winter days, Lulu Lamartine did not stir until the sun cast a patch of warmth for her to bask in and purr. She then rose, brewed fresh

coffee [...]. [...] We know her routine – many of us even shared it – so when she was sighted before her usual get-up time approaching her car door in the unsheltered cold of the parking lot, we called on others to look. Sure enough, she was dressed for action. [...] From the hill, we saw her pass into the heart of the reservation. [...]

[F]rom there, we relied on Day Twin Horse to tell us how Lulu entered the post office beneath the flags of the United States, the Great Seal of North Dakota, and the emblem of our Chippewa Nation [...].

Day Twin Horse watched her, that is, until she turned, saw him looking, and set confusion in motion. First she glared a witch gaze that caused him to tape a finger to the postal scale. The tape seemed to have a surprising life all of its own so that, as he leaned over, extracting the finger, balling up the tape, Day Twin Horse became more and more agitated. [...] [He] was unable to keep an eye on Lulu [...]. (1–2)

This passage points to ways of "making meaning," of reading codes no less confusing, but quite distinct from Slothrop's mound of detritus. The collective narrative voice, internally differentiated, emphasizes the communal dimensions of producing culture – a venture that, despite the lightness of the tone, is firmly placed in the historical context of settler colonialism, the continued appropriation of Native American land and cultures by European Americans. The text achieves this, quite economically, by mentioning "the flags of the United States, the Great Seal of North Dakota, and the emblem of our Chippewa Nation" displayed at the post office – insignia of state institutions with decreasing amounts of power. At the same time, the term "Chippewa *Nation*" contests the authority of the United States, at least symbolically.

With its own self-reflexive emphasis on seeing and observing, this text engages one of the central issues of Cultural Studies: From which vantage point, from which position does one perceive and reflect on culture? This is a social as much as a visual and epistemological issue (that is, one concerned with specific ways of knowing), for our *positions* are never merely individual – they are very much shaped by our place in social hierarchies based on gender, "race"/ethnicity, class, sexuality, ability, and so on. These categories are central for any understanding of culture. With its focus on gender as well as ethnicity, *The Bingo Palace* also notes how these hierarchies interact or *intersect* with each other – they do not operate in isolation. Further, the text asks what happens when the gaze, a form of power, is returned – when the character looked at (by other Anishinaabe, but also by the reader) refuses to be a mere object of other people's gazes, but looks back. In many cultures, women were and sometimes are not supposed to look actively in this way. But perhaps this is different in Anishinaabe culture? How can we as European readers know? And perhaps we are not even the primary audience the text is addressed at. How, then, do we relate to the novel?

Choosing Erdrich's novel as a point of departure for examining US-American culture will highlight aspects not found on Slothrop's desk. Among other things, it will remind us that the diversity characteristic of North American cultural landscapes, which may be one of their most impressive features, emerged (and continues to develop) through processes of cultural exchange taking place in the context of severe, sometimes traumatic power imbalances.

Furthermore, the passage from *The Bingo Palace*, focusing on Lulu Lamartine's movement in space, also leads us away from the idea that a culture could be represented by the sum of its artifacts; unordered, confusing, and contradictory as they might appear on Slothrop's desk. As a symbol, in fact, a desk signals order as well as stability. It evokes its owner's capability to think, read, and write in relative peace and tranquility. A desk also symbolizes power: It might matter a lot on what side of it you sit; whether you are the one who answers letters (or leaves them unanswered) and approves of (or rejects) applications, or whether you are the one on the other side, applying for a grant, for a job, for financial support, for the right to stay in a country.

The two literary examples above, in their opposition, can be read as drawing attention to fundamental dynamics of culture, which always intertwines permanence and stability with ongoing change and movement. At the same time, they highlight that the seemingly neutral position of ordered (or orderless) stability is one of inherent power: A power to define and to approve of what does and what does not belong on a desk read as a cultural archive in miniature.

If a culture is solely reconstructed through material, physical evidence, the history/ies of those who own little or nothing, who do not leave too many traces, remain unwritten. Yet even if material evidence of those who are on the wrong side of the desk is more sparse, American literature, and culture at large, have been tremendously influenced by texts that give expression to experiences of flux, of disrootedness, of hybridity. Told by emergent voices, these narratives often inspect culture from the perspective of someone who does not own a ration book, let alone a desk.

The perspectives of the marginalized that have vitalized and diversified American culture and literature throughout its history include those of people not born and raised in the United States of America. In a recent novel, Nigerian American Teju Cole's 2012 *Open City*, the protagonist Julius, a young Nigerian graduate of psychiatry who interns in a New York clinic, roams the big city. He strikes up a friendship with his former university mentor, Professor Saito, whom he visits regularly, describing the older man's apartment as

> dense with its various collections: [...] the several months' worth of daily newspapers stacked on the table and near the door, the overstuffed bookshelves, from which hundreds of volumes called out for attention, the little figurines and puppets crammed on the desk facing the entryway. All that was missing, it occurred to me, were photographs: of family members, of friends, of Professor Saito himself. (170)

In Cole's book, it takes Julius's outsider perspective to perceive what is missing on his friend's crowded desk, and to draw conclusions as to the significance of this absence. For us as students of culture, this third example helps to understand American culture's complexity, the uses of looking from different perspectives, but also the contradictory meanings of seemingly very ordinary literary – and cultural – objects like, for instance, desks.

***

American Studies as an academic discipline started out at the beginning of the twentieth century as a coalition between dissident scholars from English Literature and from American History (see Chapter 1). Scholars from the English departments strove to broaden the canon through the inclusion of American texts; scholars from History wished to transcend the narrow confines of political history toward a more culturally oriented inquiry. Thus, the pioneers of the young field, V.L. Parrington, Perry Miller, and Henry Nash Smith among others, created a distinctly American history of ideas. This dynamic subject soon began to include other disciplines – art history, sociology, architecture, psychology, to name but a few. In the context of the Myth and Symbol School of the 1950s and 1960s, they (Smith himself, Leo Marx, Richard Slotkin, and others) also began to embrace "the waste along the highway, the litter in the trunks of cars, the stuff in the bureau drawer."

In the late 1960s and 1970s, these earlier Americanists began to be criticized for transporting the idea of an American Exceptionalism, the assumption that there is something unique and visionary in American culture that distinguishes North America from all other cultures. This rather ethnocentric view was attacked with the exploration of transnational concerns, postcolonial migrations, and globalization – and the critique of internal colonizations, which Erdrich, among others, tackles in her novels. Moreover, Critical Race Theory, Gender Studies, Queer Theory, Age and Disability Studies addressed the overwhelming whiteness, male dominance, heteronormativity, and ableism of research in this field. Increasingly, those previously "not 'framed,' not in the design of things" asserted their voices in discussions of American culture, or rather American *cultures*.

While it was clear that Slothrop's desk (to stay in the picture) needed indeed to be sifted from various perspectives, positions of speaking, and according to various different systems of making sense in order to detect broken or past as well as emergent or present patterns, Tantivy's neighboring desk with its neatness and structure at first seems to uphold the promise of providing a well-assorted toolbox of Cultural Studies methodologies. Perhaps one could find a magnifying glass there. After all, students of American Studies (just like Tyrone himself) are in dire need of some tools to make sense of the "godawful mess" of culture. However, even a single collection of possible definitions of culture would not have enough space on Tantivy's desktop.

The conundrum of Cultural Studies is not only that every piece of waste found along the highway generates its own definition of culture, but that every definition of culture also brings to light more litter in the trunks of cars. In other words, Cultural Studies are *themselves* part of culture. Tantivy's desk turns out to be an inverted version of Slothrop's desk – let's say a more repressed, a more authoritarian one. This is why Slothrop's attempt to run from his desk does not get him away from the enigmatic coincidences of his collected smegma; there is no way to escape from the detritus of his life. At best, he manages to drift from one cultural context into another; he is forever lost in cultures.

Smegma is actually a physiological term for a secretion that forms as a byproduct of sexuality. This allusion draws attention to the circumstance that cultural creations – whether literary monuments or pop cultural songs, food products or forgotten memoranda, paperclips or cultural theories – are deeply informed by desire. So is the gaze that follows Lulu Lamartine on all of her ways. Culture, in fact, structures desire, it directs desire into specific channels, and it is itself a byproduct of desire. Western romances or icons of masculinity and femininity are merely obvious examples of this. Much of Cultural Studies, then, is an attempt to decipher the specific desires of cultural texts.

Evidently, on the way to desire, other forces are involved. Slothrop's coloring pencils, his throat lozenges, ration books, type-writer ribbons, unanswered letters, desks, and Lulu's counter-gaze touch on many aspects of existence: "race" and ethnicity, class, power, visuality, and language, to give just a few examples. American Cultural Studies attempt to make these forces readable, always mindful of the fact that they also implicate the scholar and the inquiry involved.

In this volume we aim to show – rather than tell – how cultural scholars might proceed. In other words, cognizant of the fact that a systematic formal explanation of theories and methodologies may obscure the involved, self-reflexive, and probing nature of American Cultural Studies, the authors of the chapters in this book have usually started from concrete examples (texts, TV serials, movies, paintings) and have developed a line of argument that fore-grounds a specific productive method. You may call this "grounded theory"; it has the advantage that the reader obtains a token of a particular theoretical orientation rather than a recipe – an approach that is particularly valuable for beginning students.

The tokens that we present employ theoretical and methodological tools that have proven beneficial for a sifting of the "godawful mess" of culture: Marxism and Post-Marxism, Structuralism and Deconstruction, psychoanalysis and Social Theories, Gender, Queer and Age Studies, postcolonialism, Ethical Studies, Critical Race and Critical Whiteness Studies. We have prefaced these readings with reflections on the discipline that go into more detail than this Introduction. Part I (American Studies as a Discipline) gives the reader some background on the history and pedagogy of the field; Part II (American Studies and Cultural Studies) uses particular examples to show the reader what the difference between Literary Studies, British Cultural Studies, and Popular Culture Studies might look like.

While these first two sections may still smack of Tantivy's desk (with all the advantages and disadvantages), Part III jumps right into some of the entangled and messy narratives with which American Studies scholars have traditionally tried to explain processes of nation building: the myth of the West, the self-made man, God's own country, family and community, the city and the country, and tales of political heroism. All of these need to be addressed critically, or deconstructed, in light of more recent scholarship in Settler Colonialism Studies, Critical Whiteness Studies, Queer Theory, Transgender Studies, etc. Some of the critical paradigms that are useful for this endeavor are introduced in Part IV (Theories in American Studies). With its exemplary readings, this part aims at helping students to focus on the "things" on Slothrop's desk or the exchanges around Lulu's reservation and at illuminating their connotations, innuendos, relations, and contexts.

Is a focus on Cultural Studies the end of literature? No, it helps illuminate literature. Just as literature remediates and re-negotiates songs, letters, paper clips, gazes and the like, songs, letters, paper clips and even looks in their turn remediate and re-negotiate literature. There is nothing wrong with American Studies as Literary Studies (or, for that matter, American Studies as Art History, as Visual Studies, etc.). Only: Literary scholarship and Art History have slightly different foci. They may be more interested in the development of textual strategies or the changing compositions, forms, and tones of iconographies. American Cultural Studies are fascinated by the ominous patterns, power hierarchies, forms of desire, narrative appearances, and counter narratives of representation. In terms of theory and method, American Cultural Studies may be more multifaceted than Literary Studies or Art History. This is one of the reasons why we are convinced there is a real need to teach these methods. And American Cultural Studies have much to give – not least to the neighboring disciplines.

By way of conclusion, have a look at the image on the cover of this book. Street Artist Eduardo Kobra is a Brazilian painter whose specialty is huge murals; the one you see is located on West 25th Street and 10th Avenue in New York City. At first sight, Kobra's painting is quite different from Slothrop's desk or Lulu's itinerary. It shows a street scene (the mural extends further than the segment we have represented on the cover: There are more cars, a streetcar, and more buildings on the other side of the street). When you approach the wall, it appears that you could walk right into the scene, into a sort of parallel world. Kobra's murals frequently present parallel worlds – sometimes he inserts famous vistas or well-known people into the paintings, sometimes he simply represents mundane street scenes. But there is a difference: Quite often Kobra, as in this case, creates nostalgic pictures; we walk into a scene that is, historically, not so far away from Pynchon's. Moreover, Kobra works with a specific, almost rainbow-like color scheme and a checkered patterning – the world we enter seems at the same time familiar and de-familiarized.

It is very well possible that the spectator in the street attempts to make sense of this scene. What does it have to do with me? How would it feel to live in this world? The girl on the left seems quite happy, the man crossing the street appears rather annoyed and suspicious. Perhaps, Tyrone and Lulu are in there, someplace, too. Is it a world that would work for me, as a queer or gender-nonconforming person, as a queer or trans woman, a white person, an Anishinaabe/Chippewa, Asian American or African American? Is it the land over the rainbow? Does it house a wonderful wizard of Oz? And, on a different note, is this the way we imagine the 1940s or '50s? (Kobra, in fact, uses documentary photographs to base his murals on.) Does it simply remind us of the past existence of the very place in which we are now standing? Does it emphasize our existence on top of relics of broken structures of the past or past systems of representation?

Murals are significant cultural texts in America. In the 1930s, at the time of the Depression, the federal government sponsored the creation of murals all over the United States. They had a triple function: Firstly, they were supposed to present scenes of hope and optimism in order to uplift the morale of the population; secondly, they aimed at depicting scenes of local life so that the spectators would develop a feeling of belonging, patriotism, and community; and thirdly, they transported the benevolent, albeit patriarchal and white-dominated ideology of the common man, which the New Deal championed. While Kobra also uses the medium of public art, he does something different: He confronts the spectators with their own imaginations, their visual memories, and their nostalgia.

Kobra's paintings are enjoyable (like reading *Gravity's Rainbow*, *The Bingo Palace*, or *Open City*). On one level, they simply beautify a particular street scene – or make it more interesting. On a more implicit level, they also make us wonder about the world around us and about our perception of it. Who are these people? Why do they look the way they look? Why is this world rainbow-colored and structured in cubistic geometrical forms? What is the relation of this imaginary world to the here-and-now? If this represented world is based on documentary photographs, what will become of our world? Will it also be represented like this, sometime in the future? How will transformed under-standings of gender, racial, and ethnic identities, forms of value and distinction, of space and community change representations of us and our world in the future? Whatever the answers may be, it is evident that walking into Slothrop's cubicle, Day Twin Horse's post office, and Julius's or Kobra's New York streets confronts us with the strange patterns of represented lives – and then, with our own lives as students, scholars, consumers of culture. And this is what American Cultural Studies are all about. At the same time, as our literary and visual examples indicate, there are multiple approaches to per-ceiving the cultural world that surrounds us and of interpreting it, that depend on the complex ways in which we as observers are situated in it. Clearly, many perspectives and interpretative methods are still missing in this volume. The dominance of white, middle-class, able-bodied, gender-conforming positions in academia is visible in our book as well, even if we have tried to address it critically.

Our gratitude for invaluable support in planning, editing, and completing this volume goes to Eve Setch and Amy Welmers of Routledge. And, of course, to the authors of the chapters, who bring to scholarship what counts: Enthusiasm, curiosity, care, and competence. Thank you!

References

Cole, Teju. *Open City*. New York: Random House, 2012. Print.
Erdrich, Louise. *The Bingo Palace*. 1994. New York: Perennial, 2001. Print.
Kobra, Eduardo. Untitled. 2012. Street mural based on vintage black-and-white photograph. West 25th Street and 10th Avenue, New York City.
Poirier, Richard. "Rocket Power." *The Saturday Review* (3 Mar. 1973): 59–63. Print.
Pynchon, Thomas. *Gravity's Rainbow*. Toronto: Bantam Books. 1973. Print.
Rohr, Susanne. *Wahrheit der Täuschung: Wirklichkeitskonstitution im amerikanischen Roman, 1889–1989*. München: Fink. 2004. Print.

Part I
American Studies as a discipline

1 History of American Studies

From its emergence to transnational American Studies

Matthias Oppermann

American Studies is a field of teaching and research that is primarily concerned with the interdisciplinary study of American cultures. People "do" American Studies in schools and universities, in museums and libraries, at national historic sites and in independent community projects. American Studies scholars examine rare manuscripts or viral videos, they write books or code databases, they create maps, collages, or performances. And when two or more practitioners meet, there is often very little agreement about what precisely they mean by "American," and by "cultures," and what an appropriate object of study may be, and which methods one should use.

Unfortunately, I cannot offer you a comprehensive history of American Studies as a transnational field of inquiry that would do justice to all of the specific political, economic, cultural, or historic conditions that have influenced the development of American Studies in very diverse national, regional, and local configurations. So in lieu of such a brief history of everything American Studies everywhere, I will concentrate on the development of academic American Studies in the United States. This limited focus does not suggest that the ways in which American Studies have developed in the United States are somehow exceptional or unique, but that their history in the United States is a particularly significant part of the many other cultural and institutional histories that continue to shape our current understanding of American Studies across a wide range of international and institutional landscapes.

In the United States, the development of American Studies as an academic field is often traced back to the 1920s when professors of English began to offer individual courses that combined the study of (US-)American literature and (US) history. It is important to note that at the time, these two subjects were not considered equals: The study of US-American history was already well established in academia, but the literature of the United States was just beginning to receive scholarly attention in English departments where it had thus far been considered a subordinate category of English literature (for an institutional history of American Literature Studies, see Renker; Graff and Warner). However, during World War I English departments began to emphasize the "American quality of American literature" (Crane 13), and the first courses appeared under the label "American Civilization" — a label you

can still find in the name of certain university programs or course descriptions. World War I also made it very difficult for faculty to go on research
visits to continental Europe or Britain, and so scholars increasingly focused
on research dedicated to genuinely "American" subjects.

These developments coincided with a creative output (fiction, drama,
poetry) that highlighted the progress of "civilization" in North America, and
so the quality of American literature (almost exclusively by white male
authors) became an indicator for the achievements of American culture. Still,
by the end of the 1920s, only four percent of all literature courses dealt with
texts from the United States; in English departments, more attention was
given to Milton and Chaucer than to all US-American authors combined
(Nuhn 329).

The economic disaster of the Great Depression and Franklin D. Roosevelt's
New Deal in the 1930s led a number of scholars to engage in curricular
experiments and new modes of research that consciously crossed disciplinary
boundaries. They approached questions about potential reasons for the social
crisis from multiple angles, and they stressed the practical value of knowing
about their nation's cultural history in order to come up with practical solutions
to the problem (see Cowan). The introduction of "regional courses" – the
combination of American literature and history on a regional basis – was
celebrated as a curricular innovation of the 1930s (Crane 19). A focus on
regional histories and literatures promised to make the teaching of American
literature more effective and more interesting to students. It also included
internationalist (although almost exclusively European) perspectives and
consciously moved beyond the restrictions of disciplinary conventions in
English or history (Flanagan 517). Newly developed courses and programs in
American Civilization at Harvard, Yale, or New York University equally
moved beyond purely philological approaches to literature and offered students
instruction in history, sociology, and fine arts to arrive at a more complete
understanding of American culture. Here, the term "civilization" indicated
not only a defense against criticism from the classicist disciplines that considered
American culture to be inferior to their own objects of study. It also implied an
outspoken dedication to specific US national literatures and cultural traditions,
and it signaled the beginnings of interdisciplinary institutional arrangements
out of which American Studies in US academia were to develop.

The 1940s, and especially the 1950s, saw a sharp increase in American
Civilization programs, with twenty-eight established in the 1940s and forty-eight
in the 1950s (Bassett 306). As the academic establishment began to declare the
"universal principles of democracy" as an official learning goal shortly before
the United States entered World War II, knowledge about the national cultural
past gained ideological relevance (Gleason 348). Subjects like American
literature and American history were needed, Robert Spiller claimed in 1942,
to "define the American way, tell its history," and to distinguish it from "the
way of dictatorship" (295). Spiller argued that the study of American culture
did not only deserve the same academic rigor as the emerging Foreign Area

Studies, but should become the center and guiding principle of liberal education in the United States (269).

The availability of substantial financial support after World War II and the political and cultural climate of the Cold War are often seen as the primary catalysts for the growth of American Studies programs in the United States. However, American Studies after World War II were still a rather marginal subject area in US academia. In 1948, around sixty undergraduate programs were in existence, and no more than fifteen of those programs also offered graduate courses (McDowell 26). Most programs were so small that by the early 1950s, only five programs had more than one professor who taught special courses in American Civilization (Grier 182). Most of the newly institutionalized inter-departmental programs, which now also began to appear under the name American Studies, depended almost entirely on voluntary contributions from traditional departments like English or history.

American Studies courses of the 1950s were dedicated to a homogenous national consensus culture that continued to neglect the contributions of women and ethnic minorities (Harders). At the same time, many American Studies faculty saw internationalist and comparative approaches to the study of literature, music, and art as an effective teaching strategy against the dangers of national chauvinism. In a widely read article of 1952 entitled "The Study of American Civilization: Jingoism or Scholarship," Arthur Bestor claimed that "any serious attempt to understand our national life must carry the student into investigations of things happening far outside our geographical boundaries and long before the beginning of our separate chronology" (Bestor qtd. in Turpie 520). For students, American Studies could thus function as a "door" to foreign backgrounds – "a door opening outward upon the universe of human endeavor" (521). This points to an understanding of the complexities of American cultures that goes beyond national borders and transgresses an isolationist notion of national history. In this sense, Bestor's position could be read as a harbinger of the post-nationalist research agendas that became very influential for American Studies more than four decades later.

The development of American Studies from the early 1950s until the 1970s is closely linked to the work of the so-called Myth and Symbol School (Oppermann 75–85). The group of scholars commonly associated with this school includes R.W.B. Lewis (*The American Adam: Innocence, Tragedy, and Tradition in the Nineteenth Century*, 1955), Leo Marx (*The Machine in the Garden: Technology and the Pastoral Ideal in America*, 1964), John William Ward (*Andrew Jackson: Symbol for an Age*, 1955), Alan Trachtenberg (*Brooklyn Bridge: Fact and Symbol*, 1965), and Henry Nash Smith. Smith's *Virgin Land: The American West as Symbol and Myth* (1950) is generally considered a milestone for American Studies and for the development of the Myth and Symbol School in particular. *Virgin Land* is a study of the imaginary aspects of the "Western Frontier" and of the effects of these myths and symbols for an American national identity and culture.

The premises of *Virgin Land* are symptomatic for approaches of American Studies scholarship during the 1950s: National cultures (and especially US-American national culture) are unique and all expressions of a national culture share a common basis. Myths and symbols are an expression of a national culture's ideals and values; at the same time, they strongly influence the behavior of all Americans who recognize dominant myths as part of their national ideal. In other words: The national culture consists of an – albeit heterogeneous – community of consensus whose identity is firmly based in common myths and symbols. To study this national culture, Myth and Symbol scholars focused primarily on symbols in literary texts and cultural artifacts and brought these to bear on each other in the context of larger national myths. In hindsight, this approach has since been criticized for methodological shortcomings, for neglecting categories like "race," class, and gender, and as an example of American Exceptionalism.

In the early 1970s Bruce Kuklick argued that the direct link between social experience and literary symbols was theoretically unsound and that Myth and Symbol research focused primarily on the literary work of white males. Throughout the next decade, scholars like Annette Kolodny also criticized the male bias of the pastoral ideal in American Studies and made gender a central category of analysis.

In the 1960s and 1970s, quantitative growth in the number of programs and students coincided with a large number of theoretical publications that expressed a growing concern about methodological uncertainties. Americanists grappled with the question of how adequately texts could be used as evidence for cultural processes. Expertise in American Studies was located somewhere between anthropology, literary criticism, and a general humanities skill set. An "inclusive principle of operation" (a unifying method for an emerging discipline), which Roy Harvey Pearce (179) and others had still hoped for in the late 1950s, was certainly not on the horizon.

By the early 1960s, one hundred undergraduate American Studies programs and twenty graduate programs were in existence (Cohen 550). During a decade of rapid expansion, this figure would double to two hundred undergraduate programs until the early 1970s – roughly the same number of programs exist today (Bassett 308). Students chose courses from various departments and "core seminars" in American Studies. In theory, these core courses employed interdisciplinary methodologies and introduced students to various culture concepts and their possible applications in American Studies scholarship. In practice, even core courses usually retained a bipolar literature–history concentration and operated with a holistic concept of a homogenous and unique national culture.

During the 1960s, diverse social movements and identity politics demanded to be recognized as integral parts of the cultural fabric of the United States and radically challenged the notion of a holistic and homogenous US national culture that was dominated by white, heterosexual, protestant men. The political, social, and cultural climate of the 1960s led to vibrant debates about traditional subject matter and methodologies in American Studies and had a genuinely transformative effect on the field. Informed by political agendas and social activism of the late 1960s, a new generation of Americanists of the 1970s insisted that practitioners in the field should take a much more politically committed and critical stance toward the dominant culture in their teaching and scholarship (see Robert Merideth's pamphlet "Subverting Culture: The Radical as Teacher," 1969, qtd. in Wise 185). At many universities, younger faculty rejected the role of professors as politically neutral transmitters of knowledge, and graduate students successfully pressed for representation in the national council of the American Studies Association (Cowan; see Chapter 13, 150–52).

In the late 1970s, newly institutionalized interdisciplinary programs and sub-fields emerged in the academy. Programs and curricula like Women's Studies, Queer Studies, Asian American Studies, African American Studies, Chicano and Chicana Studies, Ethnic Studies, or Postcolonial Studies contributed to a new understanding of American society and culture that emphasizes various dimensions of cultural difference in terms of "race," class, ethnicity, or gender. Despite differences in degree and direction, these projects were concerned with critical interventions into racist or sexist societal structures and modes of representation, and brought subject matters to the fore that had been largely neglected by American Studies in more traditional configurations.

The critiques of social movements and emerging interdisciplinary programs broadened the subject matter of American Studies and challenged core epistemologies: American society could not be sufficiently analyzed if culture was understood as the "realm of artistic and intellectual activity" (Klein 160) or the "complexities of everyday behavior" (Shank 101). In the multicultural realities of the United States, culture was a site of conflict and struggle, and power was unevenly distributed. Marginalized groups and minority subject positions revealed dynamic dimensions of difference in American society and culture.

The influences of various intersecting and overlapping programs and research agendas continued to transform the American Studies project during the 1980s. European critical theory and the success of British Cultural Studies played a crucial role in re-locating American Studies in a force-field between more strictly academic work and a commitment to progressive politics and social change (Pease 23). Since then, American Studies have continued to build on the work of minority discourses and interdisciplinary programs and have responded to the challenges that Critical Theory and Cultural Studies posed to earlier concepts of an imaginary national consensus culture.

Throughout the past three decades, so-called "New Americanists" have been a dominant group of critics working within American Studies, among them Robyn Wiegman, Donald Pease, and John Carlos Rowe. New Americanists have situated the work of the field at the conjuncture between progressive social movements and the academy, have actively challenged national meta-narratives, and highlighted the explicitly dialogic, international, and comparativist nature of American Studies. In the mid-1990s, the German American Studies scholar Günter H. Lenz formulated a vision for an "American Culture Studies" that foregrounded the importance of "border discourses" and "contact zones" (Pratt) as two key discursive formations that are central to more comparative versions of multicultural critique. For Lenz, the dialogic contact zones that are involved in the historical construction of multicultural communities of difference must take precedence over the traditional centrality of isolated and representative literary works, authors, periods, or events. Also in the mid-1990s, Lenz's US-American colleague Rowe called for the creation of "comparative US cultures courses" that should be based on a canon of social situations (rather than texts) in order to fully realize the theoretical and pedagogical implications of Pratt's concept of the contact zone and Lenz's notion of the dialogics of American Culture Studies qua border discourses (Rowe, "A Future"). Within this framework, African American cultures, Chicana/mestiza communities, or Asian American communities can be understood in terms of the liminal spaces, exchanges, and hybridizations that have been markers of their historical constructions (Rowe, *The New American Studies* 15). As a consequence, the study of American culture should no longer gravitate around a stable set of representative literary texts, but focus on the ways in which different cultures interact and are transformed by contact with each other. This approach allows for a more processual, performative, and conflictual understanding of culture that goes beyond the pluralism of stable, territory-based national cultures, yet neither erases differences based on "race," ethnicity, class, and gender nor dismisses the existence of very real borders around nation states.

New work in American Studies that recognizes the importance of "multi-directional flows" (Fishkin) of people and goods across national borders is necessarily comparative and transnational in focus. As Joel Pfister has pointed out, this "ongoing transnationalization" of American Studies is paramount to the development of the field because power and culture "aren't neatly divided into nations" and because "America's impact and significance have never been confined solely to the space within its porous borders" (16–17). While the actual borders of the United States where immigration is controlled are not porous at all (as anyone who has ever tried to enter the country as a non-US citizen knows), the cultural sources of American power and domination cannot be sufficiently explained without taking into consideration the dynamics of global power relationships as well as processes of cultural translation and cross-cultural exchange, such as the cultural work of multi-national "American" companies like Facebook or Google or the ways in which the United States has used institutions like the International Monetary Fund to influence social and political policies in many Latin American countries. Comparative and transnational versions of cultural critique promise to expose the constructedness of national myths and borders (Rowe et al. 3), to challenge notions of American Exceptionalism and a fixed national consensus culture (Fluck 74) and to address the role of the United States as a (neo-)imperial power more effectively than earlier approaches. The influences of minority discourses and Cultural Studies remain relevant for evolving research agendas of American Studies because they underscore the political significance and comparative nature of academic work that is transnational in scope and yet specific to different historical and cultural situations.

Recent scholarship in American Studies that encourages multicultural perspectives and transcends national borders also calls for poly- and postlingual approaches to the study of American cultures that draw on a variety of media and a broad range of cultural expressions. The social situations of contact zones are not exclusively contained in monolingual (mostly English) literary texts, but are condensed in cultural productions in different languages and in all shapes and genres, including novels, movies, computer games, podcasts, ads, images, music, dance, or performances. Both Rowe and Paul Lauter have been insistent on the need to expand the traditional concept of textuality that still dominates much of American Studies scholarship to explicitly include "nonliterary modes of social and cultural expression" (Rowe, *The New American Studies* 12; see also Lauter 23). According to Rowe, American Studies in the academy must "identify in particularly effective ways the sites of social confrontation and negotiation that have defined US history and are likely to confront students in the future" (*The New American Studies* 12).

It is quite remarkable in this respect that the innovative research, which has emerged from New Americanist circles since the early 1990s, has almost completely neglected the cultural and political work of digital media. While much of our cultural archive has been transformed into a database, and social networking sites have become genuine contact zones for political negotiations and cultural critique, New Americanist scholarship remains dominated by the paradigm of print texts. This exposes a tension between current processes of cultural translation and appropriation in the light of digital media and (tacit) assumptions about the prioritization of certain media that still undergird American Studies scholarship. Digital media are clearly highly relevant to those categories of representation and their potential for social and political change that have informed the New Americanist project throughout the past decades. In this respect, the current growth of the digital humanities creates exciting opportunities to move beyond a false dichotomy between the digital and the analog and to engage in transformative methods of cultural critique with new tools and across a broad range of media types.

Despite the obvious heterogeneity of current American Studies scholarship, and despite the incompleteness and non-continuousness that characterizes the development of the field, it seems to me that there may be three signature convictions that – although certainly not unique to American Studies – somehow distinguish the field from other, related academic projects. First, there is the strong belief in interdisciplinary methodologies (Bauerlein 38; Bronner) and a constant insecurity about what these should look like in practice. Second, there is the centrality of the concept of "culture" in all of its generative definitional varieties. Finally, there is an intense affective engagement that American Studies practitioners develop with their research. Such an affective dimension does not resonate with more traditional notions of academic work in many other fields where research is understood as something distant, objective, and abstract. In contrast, as DeWitt Douglas Kilgore has pointed out, "foregrounding the very personal nature of a project" has almost become a "necessary strategy" for expert cultural critics in American Studies (35). With reference to the work of Jay Mechling, Richard P. Horwitz, Doris Friedensohn, or Barry Shank, Kilgore explains that to display a high degree of personal involvement with one's topic is neither a "disavowal of serious intellectual effort" nor "done in a spirit of apology, but in recognition of the partial, incomplete and always vested nature of any history or interpretation" (36). Thus, the personal investment that characterizes many research projects in American Studies suggests that academic work is not external to, but embedded in, personal or historical events and that the affective dimensions of American Studies are not opposed to serious cultural critique, but paramount to making the leap from description and interpretation to critical intervention.

Works cited

Bassett, Charles W. "Undergraduate and Graduate American Studies Programs in the United States: A Survey." *American Quarterly* 27.3 (1975): 306–30. Print.

Bauerlein, Mark. "The Institutionalization of American Studies." *REAL* 19 (2003): 37–47. Print.

Bronner, Simon J. "The ASA Survey of Departments and Programs, 2007: Findings and Projections." *ASA Newsletter* 31.1 (2008): 11–19. Print.

Cohen, Henning. "American Studies and American Literature." *College English* XXIV.7 (1963): 550–4. Print.

Cowan, Michael. "American Studies: An Overview." *Encyclopedia of American Studies.* Ed. Simon Bronner. Baltimore, MD: Johns Hopkins UP, 2014. Web.

Crane, William G. *American Literature in the College Curriculum.* Chicago, IL: National Council of Teachers of English, 1948. Print.

Fishkin, Shelley Fisher. "Notes from the Editor." *Journal of Transnational American Studies* 1.1 (2009). Web. 25 Feb. 2009.

Flanagan, John T. "American Literature in American Colleges." *College English* 1.6 (1940): 513–19. Print.

Fluck, Winfried. "Theories of American Culture (and the Transnational Turn in American Studies)." Special Issue "Transnational American Studies." Ed. Winfried Fluck, Stefan Brandt, and Ingrid Thaler. *REAL* 23 (2007): 59–77. Print.

Gleason, Philip. "World War II and the Development of American Studies." *American Quarterly* 36.3 (1984): 343–58. Print.

Graff, Gerald, and Michael Warner, eds. *The Origins of Literary Studies in America: A Documentary Anthology.* New York: Routledge, 1989. Print.

Grier, Edward F. "Programs in American Civilization." *Journal of Higher Education* 25.4 (1954): 179–90. Print.

Harders, Levke. *American Studies: Disziplingeschichte und Geschlecht.* Stuttgart: Steiner, 2013. Print.

Kilgore, DeWitt Douglas. "Undisciplined Multiplicity: The Relevance of an American Cultural Studies." *American Studies* 38.2 (1997): 31–40. Print.

Klein, Julie Thompson. *Humanities, Culture, and Interdisciplinarity: The Changing American Academy.* Albany: State U of New York P, 2005. Print.

Kolodny, Annette. *The Land before Her: Fantasy and Experience of the American Frontiers, 1630–1860.* Chapel Hill: U of North Carolina P, 1984. Print.

---. *The Lay of the Land: Metaphor as Experience in American Life and Letters.* Chapel Hill: U of North Carolina P, 1975. Print.

Kuklick, Bruce. "Myth and Symbol in American Studies." 1972. *Locating American Studies: The Evolution of a Discipline.* Ed. Lucy Maddox. Baltimore, MD: Johns Hopkins UP, 1999. 71–86. Print.

Lauter, Paul. "Reconfiguring Academic Disciplines: The Emergence of American Studies." *American Studies* 40.2 (1999): 23–38. Print.

Lenz, Günter H. "Toward a Dialogics of International American Culture Studies: Transnationality, Border Discourses, and Public Culture(s)." *American Studies/ Amerikastudien* 44.1 (1999): 5–23. Print.

McDowell, Tremaine. *American Studies.* Minneapolis: U of Minnesota P, 1948. Print.

Nuhn, Ferner. "Teaching American Literature in American Colleges." *American Mercury* 13 (1928): 328–31. Print.

Oppermann, Matthias. *American Studies in Dialogue: Radical Reconstructions between Curriculum and Cultural Critique.* Frankfurt am Main: Campus, 2010. Print.

Pearce, Roy Harvey. "American Studies as a Discipline." *College English* 18.4 (1957): 179–86. Print.

Pease, Donald E. "The Place of Theory in American Cultural Studies: The Case of Gene Wise." Special Issue. Ed. Winfried Fluck and Thomas Claviez. *REAL* 19 (2003): 19–35. Print.

Pfister, Joel. "Transnational American Studies for What?" *Comparative American Studies* 6.1 (2008): 13–36. Print.

Pratt, Mary Louise. "The Art of the Contact Zone." *Profession* 91 (1991): 33–40. Print.

Renker, Elizabeth. *The Origins of American Literature Studies: An Institutional History.* Cambridge: Cambridge UP, 2007. Print.

Rowe, John Carlos. "A Future for 'American Studies': The Comparative US Cultures Model." *American Studies in Germany: European Contexts and Intercultural Relations.* Ed. Günter H. Lenz and Klaus J. Milich. Frankfurt am Main: Campus, 1995. 263–78. Print.

---. *The New American Studies.* Minneapolis: U of Minnesota P, 2002. Print.

Rowe, John Carlos et al. Introduction. *Post-Nationalist American Studies.* Ed. John Carlos Rowe. Berkeley: U of California P, 2000. 1–21. Print.

Shank, Barry. "The Continuing Embarrassment of Culture: From the Culture Concept to Cultural Studies." *American Studies* 38.2 (1997): 95–116. Print.

Spiller, Robert E. "Higher Education and the War." *Journal of Higher Education* 13.6 (1942): 287–97. Print.

Turpie, Mary C. "American Studies at the U of Minnesota." *American Quarterly* 22.2 (1970): 518–27. Print.

Wise, Robert. "'Paradigm Dramas' in American Studies: A Cultural and Institutional History of the Movement." 1979. *Locating American Studies: The Evolution of a Discipline.* Ed. Lucy Maddox. Baltimore, MD: Johns Hopkins UP, 1999. 166–210. Print.

2 The learning and teaching of American Studies

Uwe Küchler

The subject of this chapter, as straightforward as it might initially appear, must be complicated by several preliminary considerations. To start with the most obvious: What, actually, is American Studies all about? Then: What should learning and teaching be like in this discipline? And: Who is it who does the learning and teaching? Obviously, to complicate matters further, these three questions are interdependent and interrelated: The answers given to one will shape the definitions of the others.

Academic subjects are complex and dynamic (even if they are sometimes given the appearance of being monolithic and fixed). To teach and to learn in any complex field always means to find approaches that suit both one's own contexts, as a student and as an instructor, and one's research interests. Such approaches are like access roads you take from where you are to where you would like to be.

In terms of teaching and learning, this means that a useful approach to a subject meets you as close as possible to "where you are": working with what you already know, acknowledging your own cultural, social, linguistic situatedness within a complex world. It will, in fact, endorse your knowledge and experience as a valuable contribution to or complication of an academic subject's initial assumptions.

At the same time, however, the spatial metaphor, which compares a teaching and learning approach to an access road, already ends here. While there are many roads to take to access a field like American Studies, there is no one fixed point, no "Rome," they are all leading to. Not only is American Studies not about one fixed destination (an essential truth); the different and often contradictory "truths" American Studies is interested in take shape through the questions posed; questions that are sensitive to changing cultural preconceptions.

As perplexing as these preliminary remarks might appear, they have already transported us some way nearer to a perception of what teaching and learning within American Studies is about. If a class should bring learners closer to an understanding of American Studies as a discipline, then in which ways can it acknowledge their particular interests, their individual contexts, and their social situatedness? Let's turn to this question first.

Learning and teaching approaches: from where to start?

At European universities, American Studies are often taught in English departments, which traditionally entails a heightened interest in Literature (with a capital "L"), within the disciplinary context of Area Studies with a research agenda that is particularly indebted to the social sciences, and often within contexts of language acquisition. While American Studies productively relate to all of these diverse teaching and learning traditions, it might still sometimes be difficult to make sense of their panoply of methods, theories, and subjects.

In order for you to determine your own place – of learning, of teaching – within this field, I suggest you take a long step back first to locate yourself within the broader academic traditions of your country and of your university. Then, step forward and look closely: What is the pedagogical agenda in the specific class you are attending?

To be sure, learning should not be about passively consuming what is offered. Classes are not simply about receiving units of set knowledge. Instead, for learning to be productive and truly transformative, learners need to engage in the learning process actively and inquisitively. Consequently, learning should never be one-directional and teaching should turn out as always grounded in learning, and vice versa.

Over the last decades, in fact, a shift from the theorization of teaching to that of learning has occurred that derives its potential from the idea that meanings require negotiation and communicative validation. To put it differently: Teaching is increasingly understood to be a context-sensitive form of learning, an exchange rather than a one-sided offer. Work in class, therefore, is likely to be governed by a re-construction, re-positioning, and re-negotiation of disciplinary knowledge – the multitude of methods, theories, and subject matters that constitute what we think of as American Studies – in dialogue with the prior knowledge, experiences, and perspectives of the learner (see Küchler 130).

Teaching is learning precisely because academic topics and research foci, thematic turns and the expansion and revision of "canons," as well as the instructors' and learners' ongoing research translate into subjects discussed in class. For instance: You will perhaps be familiar with the analytic categories "race," class, and gender, which have found a central place within American Studies research efforts over the last decades. More recent analytic concepts, such as place, space, bioregion, or environment, have become influential in the last years and need to be related to the former (I will return to them later in this chapter). These recent topics inspired the development of new critical fields, such as bioregionalism or, most recently, the sustainable or environmental humanities (Branch et al.; Cronon; Lemenager and Foote; Nixon). The way seminars are structured, which methods and approaches are chosen depends on the initial choice of subject matter in interplay with analytical categories such as the ones just mentioned.

Being actively involved in the process of learning, you as learners should pay critical attention to a seminar's topical and teaching agenda and, as a future instructor, you should also encourage learners to do so. Your own "readings," your engagement with these "texts" (be they books, comics, films, or music, to give but a few examples) can and should inform what goes on in class. Your learning, in fact, both in class and outside, should be governed by several questions: What similarities can be uncovered between different genres or modes of expression? What shared (cultural) patterns of perception or representation and what layers of meaning can be discovered by reading a photo, a narrative text, and a movie side by side? This last question can be flipped around by focusing on the unique perspective each mode allows: What can be expressed by means of visual art that a verbal narrative cannot capture? What can be expressed by literary non-fiction that a factual, scientific account cannot convey? In order to apply these questions in a productive way, you should always link them to a critical interrogation of your own position within a cultural spectrum, which will allow you to perceive of your knowledge as subjective and situated instead of trying to generalize it as objective and universal.

The American Studies tradition: where it takes us

In the previous chapter, Matthias Oppermann has outlined American Studies' history from its academic beginnings in the early twentieth century to the Myth and Symbol School, which set out to study what was believed to be a homogeneous American culture, leading to critical disciplinary self-reflections initiated in particular by the works of scholars who have become known as New Americanists. Addressing the question of how cultural consent, which earlier students of American culture had taken for granted, is culturally produced and how hegemonic cultural positions (e.g., white, middle-class, male, able-bodied, cis-positions) are normalized, more recent discussions in the field of American Studies critically reflect on the conflictual construction of cultural identities and, by the same token, on the diversity – instead of consensual uniformity – of American culture.

"American Studies pedagogy," Americanist Eric Sandeen emphasizes, "cannot be extricated from the practices of teaching, the position of the American Studies classroom within the contemporary university, and the history of our field." This interest also indicates the field's attention to self-evaluation and self-revision, not least in respect to its methodology. One of the most pertinent points of criticism launched against the earlier Myth and Symbol School had pertained to its methodological shortcomings: its engagement in the "state fantasy of American exceptionalism" (Pease, *The New American Exceptionalism* 163), leading New Americanists to put an emphasis on transnational perspectives – of studying the United States in a historical as well as contemporary context of global interdependence that earlier scholarship had often neglected (see Kroes; Fishkin; Lenz; Rowe; Hannerz).

One of the most obvious ways in which New Americanists have revisited their field of research and teaching, furthermore, is in the ongoing debate over its "canon": the "texts" and topics deemed worth studying. While earlier Myth and Symbol scholars believed in a cultural consensus concerning a canon of outstanding, aesthetically particularly valuable – literary – texts, constituted by a number of what they understood as masterpieces (incidentally mostly authored by white, male, middle-class – WASP – writers), New Americanists have engaged in "revisionist interventions into the canon," as Donald E. Pease calls it ("Revisionist Interventions"). American Studies today analyze popular culture and different media as well as contributions by authors of color and by women who had been marginalized by earlier scholarship together with critical re-readings of canonized "classic" (WASP) American literature from Herman Melville to Nathaniel Hawthorne, from Washington Irving to Edgar Allan Poe, or from F. Scott Fitzgerald to John Updike. New Americanists, furthermore, also reflect upon their own stake in an always ongoing process of canon-(re)formation and canon-revision.

Contemporary American Studies, in contrast to the earlier Myth and Symbol School, thus rely on a semiotic understanding of culture and make use of a broad concept of what a "text" is: Cultural artifacts as well as narrative forms and genres, the arts, social institutions, and even individual or collective behaviors can be read as signs or as symbolizations with regard to different layers of meaning or the cultural work they are doing (see Geertz; Tompkins). American culture, as documented by the variety of "texts" of which it is constituted, is not unified, isolated, or exceptional but, instead, is internally diverse and located in an international context, and is shaped by transnational cross-references, exchanges, and impacts.

American Studies' broad understanding of what can be considered a text worth studying is borrowed from Cultural Studies. From its inception, in fact, American Studies have fervently transgressed disciplinary boundaries. Ethnologist and Americanist Simon J. Bronner points out:

> An enterprising as well as provocative promise of American Studies at its early twentieth-century founding was that it would reform instruction, and institutions in which it occurs, by connecting learning across fields and offering a problem or paradigm centered rather than overly specialized or method-driven approach.

What has started as concatenation of the subjects of History and American Literature has developed into a multi-, inter-, and transdisciplinary research sphere, going beyond traditional philological interest in "Literature" and addressing the cultural work and relevance of a broad variety of texts. In this, American Studies scholars use a vast apparatus of critical theories – from sociology to historiography, from economics to political sciences to Law Studies, or from philosophy to Literary Studies – to come to terms with a broad array of questions posed to texts, both fictional and non-fictional. In the following chapters, Christina Wald, Christina Meyer, and Martin Klepper turn to the close thematic, institutional, disciplinary, and methodological ties research in American Studies has forged, for instance, to Cultural Studies, to Visual Studies, or to Media Studies.

American Studies, in this sense, mirror at the level of disciplinary self-reflection what we have identified as important for you – and indeed: us all – as students engaged in a productive learning and teaching process. This is not a coincidence. As American Studies scholar Jay Mechling emphasizes, American Studies can best be understood as a "way of thinking," as "a cognitive style" characterized by the ability to "step outside [one's] taken-for-granted reality [...] and engage in reflexive analysis," to "play [...] with ideas and perspectives," to know about different disciplinary methods and ideas, and to be "willing to generalize, understanding that generalizations are always tentative, emergent, and subject to change." American Studies, according to Sandeen, privilege "lifelong autodidactic [learning], of adapting [...] to new bodies of knowledge and changing cultural analyses." It thus allows one to productively merge the positions of student and teacher: American Studies effectively demonstrate that there is no end to learning.

Beyond this (re-)orientation of American Studies as a field of transdisciplinary research, one of its hallmarks is, furthermore, its critical investment in regard to questions of social justice. The field's interest in power relations and their deconstruction as well as in its students' social and cultural situatedness translate into an awareness of the necessity to go beyond the narrow confines of the Ivory Tower of academia and to value social and political engagement, outside and also within the university. Keeping this in mind means that American Studies classes should be spaces of critical and conflictual discussion that take seriously individual experiences of marginalization and exclusion and that force students and instructors alike to keep rethinking their own positionalities.

Questions of teaching and learning, as discipline, method, or practice, however, have not yet caught full attention within American Studies. As Oppermann deplores:

> Whereas visual arts, music or psychoanalysis seem compatible with the American Studies research agenda, the attempt to introduce teaching as scholarship easily leads to the question of whether this is pedagogy, education or curriculum theory, or still "genuine" American Studies. It seems that teaching is where interdisciplinarity ends. (325)

This is a boundary American Studies have yet to transgress (see Bach and Donnerstag; Freese), and the discussion above indicates that we can in fact understand better what American Studies are all about by looking at them through a lens of teaching that is always also learning. It not only illustrates a fluidity of positions – it also hints at a spiral way of approaching a field through a set of sometimes overlapping, sometimes antagonistic theories and methods. American Studies could best be understood as an "ecology of knowledge," Sandeen argues (who quotes Gregory Bateson through Jay Mechling). If this is the case, then the ecocritical case study, which I offer in the following section as an example, should be particularly suited for introducing teaching and learning in American Studies: Its focus on the interrelation between human culture and nature, in fact, not only offers an approach that fits into the American Studies agenda of critical engagement with the world outside academia. It might also be read as the very example of how American Studies as an "ecology of knowledge" works.

Looking closely: the environment in American Studies

An interest in questions of nature and the relationship between mankind and its environment is not new: Nature (or the environment) has been an important theme, as well as a complex and problematic symbol, in American culture since the "discovery" and appropriation of this continent. Within an emerging ideology of settler colonialism, the reference to "untouched nature" allowed European Americans to imagine the continent as uncivilized, awaiting colonization, and thus to efface the existence of the continent's native population.

In the late eighteenth and nineteenth centuries, landscape and nature became crucial features of white American literature and culture. The imagining of the North American continent as "the new world," as "virgin land," resonated with the transatlantic Romantic impulse and its fascination with pastoral, untouched beauty and the natural sublime. At the same time, this perception of North America as untamed wilderness contributed central ideas and ideals to an emerging discourse of nation-building that imagined the United States as "nature's nation" (Hebel 310–12).

"The term 'environment' in its broadest sense indexes contested terrains located at the intersections of political, social, cultural, and ecological economies. In its narrowest sense, it refers to the place of nature in human history," Vermonja R. Alston explains. Accordingly, the ways in which scholars today engage in studying the relation between the environment and culture differ greatly. "In American studies and cultural studies," Alston continues, "'environment' has undergone a renewal among scholars and activists, owing in part to resistance to the bracketing of 'nature' and 'wilderness' as privileged sites of national identity and its acceptance as a shorthand for research on ecosystems and diverse environmental movements." Publications such as Cheryll Glotfelty and Harold Fromm's *Ecocriticism Reader* (1996), *American Indian Literature, Environmental Justice, and Ecocriticism* by Joni Adamson (2000), *American Studies, Ecocriticism, and Citizenship* (edited by Joni Adamson and Kimberly Ruffin in 2012), or *The Anticipation of Catastrophe* (edited by Sylvia Mayer and Alexa Weik von Mossner in 2014) document the growing importance of Ecocriticism and concerns of environmental justice as subjects within American Studies.

In many respects, the examination of the "environment" reflects the conversation of a multiplicity of approaches typical of American Studies classrooms and of American Studies in general: as a threatened material reality (deep ecology); as a gendered discourse (environmental justice; ecofeminism) driven by a "masculinist impulse to imagine and experience the land as feminine [...] situat[ing] nature, women, and ethnic minorities as passive 'others' against which the Anglo-American male constructs himself" (Alston), or as a politically and socially activist movement. Environmental concerns, in this sense, are very much part of the "ecology of knowledge" characteristic of the learning and teaching of American Studies.

In the middle of the twentieth century, when the consequences of industrialization and mass production could no longer be overlooked, the genre of nature writing, a literary non-fiction genre that combines observation and reflection on the relationship between humans and their environment (see Slovic), became increasingly important. One of its proponents is the US-American writer Annie Dillard.

In Dillard's short narrative "Total Eclipse" (1982), which I have chosen for a close reading, the narrator gives a seemingly inconspicuous account, as a first-person recollection and reflection, of how she witnessed a total solar eclipse in western Oregon. What initially may appear to be an unfiltered observation turns out to be a deep, existential reflection about life. It triggers thoughts about the ways in which we perceive and read the world that surrounds us and that we shape and harm. It may guide us as readers to critically reflect not only on our attitudes toward this world (a deep ecologist approach), but potentially also on our social, gendered, and racialized positionality within it, as it is shaped by hegemonic discourses (an ecofeminist approach). Possibly, it may move us to transgress discursive binaries by taking an activist position.

A narrative, such as "Total Eclipse," allows readers to closely follow its narrator through a personal experience. In this, it invites comparison to the ways in which learners themselves perceive and construct, and perceive as constructed, their relation to the world and the environment that surrounds them. If, in class, learners and instructor work out the potentially diverse reactions Dillard's narrative triggers, this makes room not only for speculation on how narrative forms work; it also highlights how diverse backgrounds privilege specific forms of knowledge while suppressing others.

The narrator and her husband travel several hours to arrive at a range of hills from where they hope to have a perfect view of the solar eclipse. The narrative skillfully describes a motel, people watching TV, also the commuters in the valley who, forced to ignore the eclipse, hurry to work. Dillard's narrator observes her surroundings closely, and one is tempted to ask what the information will be good for and how it is related to the description of a solar eclipse.

> The hotel lobby was a dark, derelict room, narrow as a corridor, and seemingly without air. [...] On the broad lobby desk, lighted and

bubbling, was a ten-gallon aquarium containing one large fish; the fish tilted up and down in its water. Against the long opposite wall sang a live canary in its cage. Beneath the cage, among spilled millet seeds on the carpet, were a decorated child's sand bucket and matching sand shovel. (11–12)

Using a strategy that cultural anthropologist Clifford Geertz has famously termed "thick description," Dillard makes sense of the environment she describes by paying close attention to detail and facets. In terms of narrative theory, Dillard's strategy could be described as privileging the mode of "showing" over that of "telling." As students, we should ask: What are the consequences of this mode of narration? How can we relate to the experiences described? Which methods should we adopt; which structures "decode"? And, importantly, how does this story relate to the field not only of American Studies, but also of Ecocriticism? Before I give my own interpretation, arguably one of many, let us look at another extract from Dillard's story.

Distance blurred and blued the sight, so that the whole valley looked like a thickness or sediment at the bottom of the sky. [...] The sun was up [...] a piece of the sun went away [...] in its place we saw empty sky [...]. Now the sky to the west deepened to indigo, a color never seen. [...] [T]he alpenglow was upon it [...]. The sky was navy blue. My hands were silver. [...] My mind was going out; my eyes were receding the way galaxies recede to the rim of space. (13–17)

As the eclipse progresses, the narrator sees her surroundings in an ever more disturbing light, the world is no longer tinted in color but in shades of silver and blue. The effect is scary: The people around her seem far away, dead or zombie-like. At this decisive point, the narrator "shifts senses" and begins to describe the world of sounds.

In suspense movies, dramatic (background) music indicates the upcoming crucial thrill. Dillard achieves a similar effect by echoing sounds to be heard during the climax of the eclipse: "From all the hills came screams" (17). Later on, the narrator puts the details observed into perspective and, when trying to contextualize the seemingly black sun during this total eclipse, comes to the conclusion: "Seeing this black body was like seeing a mushroom cloud. The heart screeched. The meaning of the sight overwhelmed its fascination. It obliterated meaning itself" (19).

How, then, is "Total Eclipse" about our human relation to the natural environment? Is it not simply a representation of a fascinating natural pheno-menon that has nothing threatening about it? My answer is that, arguably, it is both. The way Dillard presents the experience of the solar eclipse, in fact, is double-coded. From the beginning, a sense of danger and threat lurks just beneath the surface of representation: dark and deserted hotel lobbies; a pet fish tilting in its aquarium, probably dead; toys on the floor, children nowhere to be seen. A canary sings, making the scene even more eerie, uncanny: This short narrative, clearly, reminds me of the setting of a post-apocalyptic story, a dystopian narrative in which the world as we know it has disappeared.

The description of the solar eclipse itself takes up this motif: A "piece of the sun" goes away; the sky is of a "color never seen"; the narrator's "mind goes out." People scream, as in pain, instead of shouting out in admiration. And, eventually, the sun is like "a mushroom cloud": the symbolic epitome of nuclear apocalypse.

By pulling us as readers into close observation, narratives like Dillard's might make us aware of and ultimately change our ways of perceiving and of learning about the material, textual, and discursive worlds in and around us. We are informed that "[w]hat you see in an eclipse is entirely different from what you know. [...] Usually it is a bit of a trick to keep your knowledge from blinding you" (15). The story's title, thus, not only refers to a fascinating natural phenomenon, but also to the danger of the world's apocalyptic "total eclipse." The extraordinary event of the apocalypse momentarily allows the observer, and the reader, to "see" differently, to de-contextualize and re-contextualize the everyday, to alienate observer/reader from everyday experiences and to allow him or her to interpret them differently.

My analysis of "Total Eclipse," in this sense, not only illustrates that environmental concerns are often central in American texts: It also indicates how the interrelation of different interpretative strategies (for instance, Cultural Studies, narratology, and Film Studies) together with a close awareness of social positionalities, of "ways of seeing," allows for unearthing textual layers and webs of meaning.

Ecocriticism shares with American Studies an interest in a broad array of critical approaches (see also Heise, "Ecocriticism"; "The Hitchhiker's Guide"). Both Ecocriticism and American Studies have in common a critical, activist agenda, and in its research foci, the latter more and more often take up ecocritical aspects. This is how research, and political insight, affect subject choices in American Studies – subjects that are implemented in individual curricula with methods of both close scrutiny and theoretical reflection, as I intended my discussion of Dillard's work to demonstrate. For students of American Studies, including myself, it remains vitally necessary to accept the challenge of diversity this field offers. Not as a threat of incalculable multi-plicity and (to stay in the spatial metaphor introduced above) as a way of arriving at a definitive and unquestionable point of destination, a point of undisputed superior knowledge and truth. But rather as a means of keeping travelling: to continue learning to deal with ambiguity and ambivalence while dedicating one's efforts to matters of, not only environmental, justice.

Works cited

Adamson, Joni. *American Indian Literature, Environmental Justice, and Ecocriticism: The Middle Place.* Tucson: U of Arizona P, 2000. Print.

Adamson, Joni, and Kimberly N. Ruffin, eds. *American Studies, Ecocriticism, and Citizenship: Thinking and Acting in the Local and Global Commons.* London: Routledge, 2012. Print.

Alston, Vermonja R. "Environment." *Keywords for American Cultural Studies.* Ed. Bruce Burgett and Glenn Hendler. Keywords.nyu-press.org. Web. 13 May 2015.

Bach, Gerhard, and Jürgen Donnerstag. "Introduction: Teaching American Studies in the Twenty-First Century." *Amerikastudien/American Studies* 52.3 (2007): 315–20. Print.

Branch, Michael P. et al. eds. *Reading the Earth: New Directions of the Study of Literature and Environment.* Moscow: U of Idaho P, 1998. Print.

Bronner, Simon J. Introduction. *EAS Forum.* "EAS Forum 3: Teaching American Studies: Four Perspectives." Web. 20 Apr. 2015.

Cronon, William, ed. *Uncommon Ground: Rethinking the Human Place in Nature.* London: Norton, 1996. 69–90. Print.

Dillard, Annie. "Total Eclipse." *Teaching a Stone to Talk: Expeditions and Encounters.* New York: HarperPerennial, 1982. 9–28. Print.

Fishkin, Shelley Fisher. "Crossroads of Cultures: The Transnational Turn in American Studies – Presidential Address to the American Studies Association, 12 Nov. 2004." *American Quarterly* 57.1 (2005): 17–57. Print.

Freese, Peter. "American Studies and EFL-Teaching in Germany: A Troubled Relationship." *Amerikastudien/American Studies* 50.1–2 (2005): 183–229. Print.

Geertz, Clifford. "Thick Description: Toward an Interpretive Theory of Culture." *The Interpretation of Cultures: Selected Essays.* New York: Basic Books, 1973. 3–30. Print.

Glotfelty, Cheryll, and Harold Fromm, eds. *The Ecocriticism Reader: Landmarks in Literary Ecology.* Athens: U of Georgia P, 1996. Print.

Hannerz, Ulf. *Transnational Connections: Culture, People, Places.* London: Routledge, 1996. Print.

Hebel, Udo J. *Einführung in die Amerikanistik/American Studies.* Stuttgart: Metzler, 2008. Print.

Heise, Ursula K. "Ecocriticism and the Transnational Turn in American Studies." *American Literary History* 20.1–2 (2008): 383–404. Print.

---. "The Hitchhiker's Guide to Ecocriticism." *PMLA* 121.2 (2006): 503–16. Print.

Kroes, Rob, ed. *Straddling Borders: The American Resonance in Transnational Identities.* Amsterdam: VU UP, 2004. Print.

Küchler, Uwe. *Interkulturelle Hochschullehre: Internationalisierung am Beispiel der Amerikanistik.* Münster: LIT, 2007. Print.

Lemenager, Stephanie, and Stephanie Foote. "The Sustainable Humanities." *PMLA* 127.3 (2008): 572–78. Print.

Lenz, Günter H. "Toward a Dialogics of International American Culture Studies: Transnationality, Border Discourses, and Public Culture(s)." *The Future of American Studies.* Ed. Donald E. Pease and Robyn Wiegman. Durham, NC: Duke UP, 2002. 461–85. Print.

Mayer, Sylvia, and Alexa Weik von Mossner, eds. *The Anticipation of Catastrophe: Environmental Risk in North American Literature and Culture.* Heidelberg: Winter, 2014. Print.

Mechling, Jay. "Teaching American Studies and the Problem of Cognitive Style." *EAS Forum*. "EAS Forum 3: Teaching American Studies: Four Perspectives." Web. 20 Apr. 2015.

Nixon, Rob. *Slow Violence and the Environmentalism of the Poor.* Cambridge, MA: Harvard UP, 2011. Print.

Oppermann, Matthias. *American Studies in Dialogue: Radical Reconstructions between Curriculum and Cultural Critique.* Frankfurt am Main: Campus, 2010. Print.

Pease, Donald E. "Revisionist Interventions into the Canon." *boundary 2* 17.1 (1990): 1–37. Print.

---. *The New American Exceptionalism.* Minneapolis: U of Minnesota P, 2009. Print.

Rowe, John Carlos. *The New American Studies.* Minneapolis: U of Minnesota P, 2002. Print.

Sandeen, Eric. "Questions of Teaching American Studies: Looking Back, Looking Ahead." *EAS Forum*. "EAS Forum 3: Teaching American Studies: Four Perspectives." Web. 20 Apr. 2015.

Slovic, Scott. "Nature Writing and Environmental Psychology." *The Ecocriticism Reader: Landmarks in Literary Ecology.* Ed. Cheryll Glotfelty and Harold Fromm. Athens: U of Georgia P, 1996. 351–70. Print.

Tompkins, Jane. *Sensational Designs: The Cultural Work of American Fiction, 1790–1960.* New York: Oxford UP, 1986. Print.

Part II
American Studies and Cultural Studies

3 Kulturwissenschaft, British Cultural Studies, American Cultural Studies

Perspectives on *Mad Men*

Christina Wald

The success of the TV series *Mad Men* is part of the rise of so-called "quality TV" in the United States. The term itself is interesting, as it suggests that a certain quality is unusual or even new to television, something that has to be emphasized (and marketed) by this novel label. Robert Thompson's study *Television's Second Golden Age: From* Hill Street Blues *to* ER (1996) has specified twelve characteristics of quality TV; most of these features still apply to *Mad Men*, others do not (for instance, the script has not been written by one "auteur" who used to work for the "higher" art form cinema).

Whether or not *Mad Men* and other recent series should be considered quality TV is not the concern of this chapter. What is more relevant is the value judgment inherent in the term "quality TV," as it suggests a hierarchy from popular entertainment to something that is closer to "high," elitist culture. And indeed, when we consider the distribution form of quality TV, we can at least say that a number of these series typically aim at affluent, educated audiences, as they are produced and distributed by cable networks and streaming providers for which customers have to pay. Therefore, *Mad Men* and the label "quality TV" raise questions that are at the heart of Cultural Studies: What can be considered "culture" and is it hence worthy to be studied? Does the term refer to established, "high" art forms only or does it also include popular culture? Who defines "high" and "low," "elite" and "pop" culture? Can we perceive a relation between the economic and the intellectual and artistic cultural elite? And, more specifically, one may ask about *Mad Men*: What does a successful, critically acclaimed TV series tell us about US-American culture? Why and in which respects is a look back to the 1960s relevant for contemporary audiences?

Cultural Studies: genealogies

I will in the following briefly trace the development of Cultural Studies before returning to the case study of *Mad Men*. Prior to its rise in US academia, a particular form of Cultural Studies had become prominent in Great Britain from the 1950s. Several decades earlier, German academics had developed an approach to culture that has been called "Kulturwissenschaft" (cultural science). In the late nineteenth and early twentieth centuries, individual German scholars began to establish a new form of cultural analysis, among them Georg Simmel, Karl Lamprecht, Aby Warburg, Walter Benjamin, Siegfried Kracauer, and Ernst Cassirer. The work of these predominantly Jewish scholars was suppressed by the Nazi regime in the 1930s and 1940s, and re-emerged only later in the century. What was characteristic of the thought of these critics was a concern with the historical contexts in which particular cultural products were produced, distributed, and consumed. They also extended the scope of the objects of analysis: Not only literary texts and the visual arts were of interest, but also social, religious, and ethnic rituals, life styles, non-artistic material cultural objects, etc. (see Böhme). Further, they acknowledged the significance of technology, in particular of the media, which according to these critics did not only deliver, but also shaped the cultural content. Thus, they implicitly aimed at nothing less than a reformation of the entire discipline of Literary Studies.

At German universities, Literary Studies belong to the field of "Geisteswissenschaften," which is similar to the Anglo-American humanities. However, the term Geisteswissenschaften emphasizes the importance of the mind or the spirit (Geist) and hence implies the relevance of the individual, artistic creator of cultural products. Quite on the contrary, the cultural theorists focused on the social, economic, and medial structures in which a cultural product was produced and received, and they hence departed from the traditional Geisteswissenschaften. Programmatically, the German media theorist Friedrich Kittler (who had been trained as a literary scholar) edited an essay collection in 1980 entitled *Exorcizing the Spirit from the Humanities (Austreibung des Geistes aus den Geisteswissenschaften)*. According to Kittler, "Geist" should be replaced by discourse networks – an approach that was shared by post-structuralist theory and its deconstruction of the logos as well as by the Toronto School that argued that cultures are shaped by their media.

In Great Britain, Cultural Studies as an academic discipline was shaped from the 1950s onwards by a group of literary scholars who had studied at Cambridge University where the influential professor F.R. Leavis, in line with the state of Literary Studies at the time, taught a rather formalist approach to canonical literary texts that reflected an elitist concept of "high" culture. Influenced by Marxist thought, his students came to disagree with this conception of culture and instead turned to popular mass culture as a more relevant object of analysis.

Raymond Williams, Edward Thompson, Richard Hoggart, and Stuart Hall at the Centre for Contemporary Cultural Studies at Birmingham University established a form of Cultural Studies that has also been called the "Birmingham School." The Centre was founded in 1964 and first run by Richard Hoggart; with its later director Stuart Hall, it moved to the department of Sociology. They shared the basic assumption of Kulturwissenschaft that culture needs to be understood as material and symbolic practices rather than the sum of individual creations (see Böhme). In his programmatic study *Culture and Society* (1958),

Williams accordingly defined culture as "a whole way of life" (xviii) and established the anthropological, inclusive notion of culture that is at the heart of British Cultural Studies. Accordingly, just like Kulturwissenschaft, Cultural Studies has to be transdisciplinary.

Further, the Birmingham School focused on the economic conditions of cultural practices; they understood culture not as "the embalmed heritage of a national tradition but the arena in which socials groups fought for power, money, recognition and prestige" (Assmann 20). Therefore, cultural products have to be studied in their political and economic contexts, and they offer insight into social mechanisms just as much as into aesthetic practices.

This form of Cultural Studies proved highly attractive to scholars who represented groups formerly excluded from the elitist canon, for instance women, immigrants, and the working class. More recently, before its shutdown in 2002, the work of the Centre for Contemporary Cultural Studies developed a new focus on the role of mass media; another concern that they share with Kulturwissenschaft, even if the specific interest in how media contribute to hegemonic culture is characteristic of the British strand of Cultural Studies.

The inclusive notion of culture established by the Birmingham School was also attractive for the US-American context and its concern with questions of "race" and gender. At the same time, it shared the foundational concepts of two other growing fields in US-American academia, namely New Historicism and Postmodern Theory. While the former approach, just like Cultural Studies, emphasizes the importance of the political and economic context for the study of literary texts, the latter, akin to Cultural Studies, declares the end of a specific aesthetic norm indebted to modernism. What is more, the study of culture had been at the heart of American Studies from the very beginning in the 1930s. Other than the focus on literary texts promoted by New Criticism, American Studies always favored an approach to culture that takes the historical context into account while at the same time appreciating the specific mode of cultural expression (Fluck 287). The first generation of scholars (now called the Myth and Symbol School) concentrated on myth and symbol as central concepts to explore American culture. While "myth" was understood as a foundational narrative that has shaped American identity (for instance, the idea of the "land of the free" or the assumption that hard work will be rewarded), "symbols" were defined as semantically open images that can be adapted to specific circumstances. In the eyes of these scholars, the investigation of central myths and symbols was a way to critical self-analysis of American culture and thus opened up avenues of ideological and social change. The Myth and Symbol School implicitly adhered to a notion of high culture, because they assumed that literary texts of the canon challenge the dominant ideology by laying bare hidden conflicts and because they saw a connection between the aesthetic value of a text and its usefulness for cultural analysis (Fluck 289; see also Campbell and Kean 9–10).

Soon, however, American Studies (in contradistinction to the Myth and Symbol School) extended the scope of analysis to popular culture, thus also including literary genres that had been discounted as inferior before. An even more important point of objection against the Myth and Symbol School was its conception of American culture as homogenous. Concomitant with second-wave feminism and the Civil Rights Movement, Cultural Studies came to acknowledge the diversity of American culture, now paying close attention to the representation of "race," sex, and gender. In contrast to British Cultural Studies, the identity category of class tends to play a more marginal role in American cultural analysis.

To sum up, the main differences between the transdisciplinary approaches of Kulturwissenschaft and Cultural Studies are that the former is an academic project whereas the latter is directly involved in socio-political movements. Cultural Studies understand culture as an arena of identity politics, they have a focus on popular culture, reconstruct the canon, and are concerned with promoting the concerns of social minorities. The academic project of Kulturwissenschaft critically examines and contextualizes symbolic representations from the whole range of high and popular culture, and it is interested in cultural memory and diachronic examination (see Assmann 28; Nünning 263). Whereas British Cultural Studies are clearly indebted to a Marxist approach, Kulturwissenschaft is more pluralistic in its theoretical assumptions. Generally, German Kulturwissenschaft as much as the British and American forms of Cultural Studies has to be distinguished from the study of culture that can be practiced in Literary Studies independent of the theoretical and political dedications of Kulturwissenschaft and Cultural Studies. The differences between the national forms of Cultural Studies show that the study of culture (as much as of literature) is a cultural practice that has to be seen in its local and historical context. Genuinely transnational Cultural Studies have not yet been developed (Nünning 261).

Mad Men and Cultural Studies

To illustrate the outlined approaches, the second part of this chapter will look at the series *Mad Men* from the perspectives of Kulturwissenschaft as well as British and American Cultural Studies. From the viewpoint of Kulturwissenschaft, it is interesting to consider the representation of media in *Mad Men*, which is of course itself a medial product. The serial chronicles the professional and private lives of a number of characters who work for an advertising agency in New York City. The serial's protagonist Don Draper is a good-looking, successful ad man who is haunted by secrets from his past. Set in the early 1960s, the first season depicts a time when the medium of TV was slowly rising; in the agency, a very small TV department is set up, but advertisements are mainly still placed in print media and the radio. In a famous scene toward the end of the first season, Don Draper elegantly masters his task to develop a marketing strategy for a new product by Kodak: a slide projector that arranges the slides in a wheel and can hence effortlessly present a series of photographs without interruption. In his sales pitch for the Kodak representatives, Don outlines his strategy to create a "sentimental bond" with the projector. Showing photographs from his own family life, he presents the wheel as a "time machine," which can take you to "a place where we ache to go again [...;] back home again, to a place where we know we are loved." He suggests renaming the product as carousel, because of its nostalgic association with childhood.

This focus on the Kodak carousel is significant in several respects. First, it offers a self-reflexive device, a comment on how media can help us to travel to a past that makes us feel comfortable – the very effect that *Mad Men* arguably had on audiences cherishing the presumably simpler, more straightforward world of the 1960s (while at the same time feeling at ease with the superior knowledge and more advanced awareness of the 2000s). Secondly, the scene also demonstrates how media form our personal and collective perceptions. Photographs and videos are frequently seen as the quintessential form of personal memory, of family history, of a longing for presumably happy childhood days – to the point that we sometimes can hardly tell actual memories and photographs or videos that we saw apart. What is more, when trying to represent memories, cultural products often use slightly outdated media; for example, black-and-white videos or a super 8-film in a color movie – or, indeed, slides in a TV series. Thus, quite clearly, these devices are not only the media that transport memories, they also shape memories and have become representative of a quality of "being remembered."

What is interesting about Don Draper's slide show is that it is left open whether he shares the sentimental longing that he evokes. Does he yearn for the depicted happy days of his picture-perfect family life, such as the wedding, the pregnancy of his wife, and the birth of his children? Or does he tactically exhibit these private yet iconic images to persuade his clients? Do the images anticipate or supersede his memories, that is, did Don select Betty and build his family life to come closer to iconic images of a happy, beautiful family? Are the images a projection in both the technical and the psychological sense? Is the place where we seemingly "ache to go again" a place where we, or at least Don, actually never were, an imagined place that we know from the cultural memory fed by advertisements rather than from our own, personal memory? Don suggests as much in another scene in season one, when he explains to one of his lovers that love is a feeling invented by ad men to sell nylons. Thus, the examination of media in *Mad Men* lets us gain insight into the formative influence that media have on culture – an insight that, in a self-reflexive gesture, also applies to the series itself.

As established above, British Cultural Studies are characterized by an emphasis on issues of economics, politics, and social power. From this per-spective, the depicted world of advertising on New York City's Madison Avenue in the 1960s is particularly interesting with regard to capitalism and social hierarchies. *Mad Men* is cautious in its judgments of the depicted characters and issues, as we hardly ever are given a clear-cut "message"; instead, audiences have to make up their own minds. This general approach, which is one of the main attractions of the show, also applies to its portrayal of advertisements, which Williams has called "the official art of modern capitalist society" ("Advertising" 421). Are we meant to take a critical view of the frequently ruthless advertisement campaigns, for instance when they deliberately try to conceal the harmful impact of cigarettes? Or are we contrarily invited to support, possibly even to admire the cynical, self-centered men working for the agency? Is consumerism presented as a shallow preoccupation that attempts to make up for personal and social insecurities, but ultimately fails to do so? Or does *Mad Men* offer a nostalgic representation of a phase of capitalism before it grew as aggressive, abstract, and anonymous as today? Can the show itself, which painstakingly recreates and celebrates the look of the 1960s, be understood as an advertisement campaign for the fashion, furniture, cars, etc. of the decade – an effect that it definitely had on a number of spectators? The vogue for the clothes and décor of the 1960s, the marketing of trips to New York City, the fan-sites that offer *Mad Men* avatars, and the dress-up parties that were celebrated by fans of the series would themselves be interesting objects of a cultural analysis of *Mad Men* (see Stoddart 5–8).

The detailed recreation of the look of the 1960s, the inclusion of TV footage of the time, and recurring allusions to the historical and political circumstances of the decade have led some viewers and scholars to the assumption that *Mad Men* presents a historically "accurate" version of the period. Other scholars have called attention to the fact that even if *Mad Men* presented a historically plausible story, it only provides one of many possible histories; a history of the affluent, white, urban, predominantly Christian members of the agency Sterling Cooper. The series hardly ever includes Black characters, and if it does so, they are presented as servants or secretaries who work for the white protagonists. We never learn more about their private lives and preoccupations. Thus, *"Mad Men's* account of the past uses demographic realism: [...] the show documents the actions of characters through the lens of white society, from a vantage point resonant with contemporary logics of whiteness" (Ono 300–1). The opening scenes of the first two episodes, set in 1960, demonstrate this white perspective. At the very beginning of the series, Don Draper is introduced smoking and drinking in a bar, where he ponders on a possible new advertisement strategy for Lucky Strike. When Sam, a Black waiter, lights his cigarette, Don tries to engage him in a conversation about his smoking habits. They are immediately approached by the white supervisor of the bar who asks Don whether the Black waiter "is bothering" him. The very opening of the series thus informs audiences about the separation of Black and white people at the time and about the clear hierarchy between them. When Don reprimands the supervisor that he tries to have a conversation and sends him away to fetch another drink, audiences might assume that Don tacitly protests against the racist politics of the bar. As Kent Ono has pointed out, however, this would mean that we ascribe to Don a post-civil rights perspective on racism (307).

This is another appeal of the series: Audiences watch the events of the 1960s with hindsight while witnessing (and possibly identifying with) characters who lack this awareness; thus, the series "generate[s] anticipation via retrospection" (White 153). By means of the resulting dramatic irony, we often know more than the characters themselves and can recognize their wrong assumptions, gaps of knowledge, or old-fashioned attitudes immediately. When audiences get to learn more about Don Draper and his situation, they might also consider a second layer of his conversation with Sam: Don tries to develop a marketing strategy by doing field research. By interviewing Sam, Don brings him into a very uncomfortable and risky situation, just because he pursues his own professional, capitalist concerns. From this perspective, we can say that Don exploits Sam's intellectual labor without compensation or acknowledgment – a behavior that is far from a proto-egalitarian protest against racial segregation (see Ono 308).

The second episode of the first season once again opens in a restaurant, and it is interesting with regard to the issues of "race" and gender that are important for both British and American Cultural Studies. This time, Don and his wife Betty are having dinner with Roger Sterling and his wife Mona. The conversation at the table is about the Black nannies who raised the three middle- to upper-class characters. (Don's childhood remains a mystery at this point; audiences learn later that he is the child of a prostitute and that he had been physically abused by his working-class father and stepmother.) While Roger and Betty acknowledge how important their respective nannies had been for their education, none of the characters deduces a more egalitarian stance regarding "race" politics from this fact.

When Mona and Betty retreat to the ladies' room, the camera focuses on their fashionable purses, jewelry, nail polish, make-up, and hair styles in a series of close-ups. It thus highlights accessories and techniques of femininity. From the perspective of post-structuralist Gender Theory, we can argue that the short scene emphasizes the performative quality of gender identity, which is produced by the iterative embodiment of a culturally constructed norm. As we see throughout the series, advertisement campaigns play a decisive role in constructing and promoting these ideals; for example, in the episode "Maidenform," a campaign for Playtex bras presents Jackie Kennedy and Marilyn Monroe as the two competing feminine ideals of 1960s' American femininity (and suggests that a woman can incorporate both of these ideals by wearing the respective underwear). The scene in the ladies' room shows how Betty is unable to re-apply her lipstick because of a tremor in her hands; she asks Mona for help and begins to confess how uneasy she feels in her position as wife and mother.

Once again, Betty's uneasiness, which she can hardly articulate and instead converts into physical symptoms, is easily understandable for audiences watching the show in the 2000s. The depicted world is on the verge of second-wave feminism, which will take inspiration from Betty Friedan's *The Feminine Mystique* (1963). The book's first chapter, entitled "The Problem that has No Name," opens with a diagnosis that aptly characterizes Betty's situation:

> The problem lay buried, unspoken, for many years in the minds of American women. It was a strange stirring, a sense of dissatisfaction, a yearning that women suffered in the middle of the twentieth century in the United States. Each suburban housewife struggled with it alone. As she made the beds, shopped for groceries, matched slipcover material, ate peanut butter sandwiches with her children, chauffeured Cub Scouts and Brownies, lay beside her husband at night – she was afraid to ask even of herself the silent question – "Is this all?" (15)

Audiences witness Betty's everyday preoccupations, her isolation, boredom, and dissatisfaction throughout the season, and they learn that she studied before she met Don. They can thus more easily identify her problems than Betty herself who tries to convince herself that her suburban affluent life with two children and a handsome, successful husband is the fulfillment of her dreams. Nor does the psychiatrist whom she begins to see understand her situation. Instead, he secretly reports back to Don, who in turn compares Betty to a car that needs to be fixed; for him, she quite clearly is a status symbol rather than a companion. Whereas he is able to move between the exciting city and the calm suburb, between the professional and private spheres, between countless affairs and family life, Betty is confined to her domestic role.

Friedan's book was an eye-opener for many women living in situations comparable to Betty Draper's, but it was later also criticized because it focused only on a small group of white, heterosexual, affluent women while ignoring the plights of other women. The scene in the ladies' room obliquely refers to the multiplicity of female problems at the time. When Betty – on the verge of tears – tells Mona that she recently lost her mother, Mona does not reply. Instead, we hear a voice saying "I am sorry," the phrase that audiences would have expected to come from Mona. The camera then switches to two female Black lavatory attendants in the background, who ask Mona and Betty to let other ladies use the mirror. The attendants are dressed in shapeless yellow uniforms and wear neither make-up nor elaborate hairstyles; quite clearly, they are excluded from the ideal of white femininity. When Betty and Mona leave without tipping the attendants, one of them wryly remarks: "If their purses get any smaller, we're gonna starve," thus implicitly comparing the white fashion craze to their own urgent question of survival. Even though they are not confined to the domestic sphere and certainly do not suffer from *ennui*, as working-class women of color they are even further away from the rights and opportunities of white men than Betty and Mona. Thus, from the perspective of Cultural Studies, the brief scene is interesting with regard to its representation of "race" and gender, and it gains complexity from its double perspective that connects the situation in the 1960s to the awareness of the 2000s.

This chapter has sought to provide students with an introduction to the genealogies of Cultural Studies. It has also offered some examples of how the perspectives of the competing forms of Cultural Studies can be applied to a cultural text: It has discussed the role of media from the perspective of Kulturwissenschaft, the connections of capitalism, class, and power in the light of British Cultural Studies, and the representation of "race" and gender from the point of view of American Cultural Studies. Of course, many more aspects of *Mad Men* would lend themselves to an investigation from the perspectives of Kulturwissenschaft as well as British and American Cultural Studies.

Works cited

Assmann, Aleida. *Introduction to Cultural Studies: Topics, Concepts, Issues*. Berlin: Schmidt, 2012. Print.

Böhme, Hartmut. "Kulturwissenschaft." *Reallexikon der deutschen Literaturwissenschaft*. Vol. II. Berlin: de Gruyter, 2000. 356–59. Print.

Campbell, Neil, and Alasdair Kean. *American Cultural Studies: An Introduction to American Culture*. Second ed. New York: Routledge, 2006. Print.

Fluck, Winfried. "American Cultural Studies." *English and American Studies: Theory and Practice*. Ed. Martin Middeke et al. Stuttgart: Metzler, 2012. 287–300. Print.

Friedan, Betty. *The Feminine Mystique*. New York: Dell, 1963. Print.

Kittler, Friedrich. *Austreibung des Geistes aus den Geisteswissenschaften: Programme des Poststrukturalismus*. Paderborn: Schöningh, 1980. Print.

Mad Men. Season One. Writ. Matthew Weiner et al. Lionsgate Television, 2007. DVD.

Nünning, Ansgar. "Transnational Approaches to the Study of Culture." *English and American Studies: Theory and Practice*. Ed. Martin Middeke et al. Stuttgart: Metzler, 2012. 261–70. Print.

Ono, Kent. "*Mad Men*'s Postracial Figuration of a Racial Past." *Mad Men, Mad World: Sex, Politics, Style, and the 1960s*. Ed. Lauren M.E. Goodlad, Lilya Kaganovsky, and Robert A. Rushing. Durham, NC: Duke UP, 2013. 300–19. Print.

Stoddart, Scott F. Introduction. *Analyzing Mad Men: Critical Essays on the Television Series*. Ed. Scott F. Stoddart. Jefferson, NC: McFarland, 2011. 1–11. Print.

Thompson, Robert. *Television's Second Golden Age: From* Hill Street Blues *to* ER. New York: Continuum, 1996. Print.

White, Mimi. "Mad Women." *Mad Men: Dream Come True TV*. Ed. Gary Edgerton. London: Tauris, 2011. 147–58. Print.

Williams, Raymond. "Advertising: The Magic System." *The Cultural Studies Reader*. Ed. Simon During. Second ed. London: Routledge, 1999. 410–23. Print.

---. *Culture and Society: 1780–1950*. London: Chatto & Windus, 1958. Print.

4 Visual culture, popular culture
Reading the Brinkley Girls

Christina Meyer

Introduction

As Literary and Cultural Studies students enrolled in a degree program situated in the interdisciplinary field of American Studies, you may have wondered how such (everyday) practices as watching television, reading magazines, watching video clips, listening to popular music, or playing video games might tie into the curriculum of your academic discipline. You may have grappled with questions of how to read and analyze "non-traditional" texts such as films, comics, print advertisements, TV commercials, and others. More importantly still, you may have asked yourselves which of the tools – that is: methods, concepts, and theories – might be useful when it comes to analyzing those "other" texts.[1]

This chapter invests in providing some answers to these questions and seeks to point out a number of directions and perspectives in the two intersecting areas of research and fields of activity: visual culture and popular culture. It will address questions such as: What are the issues, concepts, and materials that you will be dealing with when you engage with visual culture and popular culture? From which theoretical angle(s) do you approach non-literary texts?

Before I explain the focus and the structural organization of this chapter, I need to formulate two cautionary reminders. For one thing, all the aforementioned aspects are examples that relate to "our" contemporary world – whoever this "us" may be. This does not mean, however, that past centuries were devoid of visual/popular practices and products. In terms of visual artifacts in America before the twentieth century just think of (colored) engravings, fashion plates, Civil War photography, song sheet covers, and theater posters. Or think of the numerous magazines and illustrated newspapers, the widespread and widely read popular yellowbacks (cheap novels), or the diverse other forms of mass entertainment (the nickelodeons, dime museums, newspaper comics, or vaudeville shows). For another thing, the aspects listed above relate to a Western, industrialized technological context; in this regard, one should not forget that there are, of course, many different (yet oftentimes mutually influencing, interfering, or cross-fertilizing) visual cultures and popular cultures around the globe (with local and regional specificities).[2]

Having said this, here is what you can expect in this chapter: In regard to visual culture, I will take a number of scholarly essays as a starting point for my discussion of what I consider important areas of concern. With respect to popular culture, I will take a slightly different path: I will present some of the re-conceptualizations of popular culture (brought forward through different "schools") and the ways in which these re-theorizations have changed the understanding and relevance of popular culture. In the final section of this chapter, I aim to show you how you might productively read a text that stands at the interface between visual and popular culture: a graphic newspaper serial from the early twentieth century, titled *"Golden Eyes" and Her Hero, Bill,* penned and written by the American artist Nell Brinkley in 1918/19. Yet, instead of one exemplary analysis, I will delineate a selection of interpretive angles from which you might examine a visual/popular text.

Approaching visual culture – an overview

Let me begin this section with two very general statements: First, the idea or understanding of what constitutes culture has changed considerably especially during the past two centuries (Barker; Storey; see also Chapter 5). The re-theorizations throughout the centuries of what makes and defines a culture are also reflected in the complex *conceptual* histories of visual culture and of popular culture, as I attempt to demonstrate in the following two sections (see Mitchell, "Showing Seeing"; Storey).

Second, "the visual" is studied in all kinds of disciplines in the humanities, medical sciences, architecture, engineering, social and political sciences. It is thus hardly surprising that to answer what constitutes visual culture or to define the scope of what is meant by the term is quite a complicated task. W.J.T. Mitchell, one of the pioneers of Visual Studies, called for the "rediscovery of the picture as a complex interplay between visuality, apparatus, institutions, discourse, bodies, and figurality" (*Picture Theory* 36). The "pictorial turn," as Mitchell called it, has not only led to a new interest in the communicative force of pictures and their relations to texts (*Iconology*; *Picture Theory*). On a less innocent note, it was accompanied by what has come to be called "the war of images," the dissemination of (mostly photographic) pictures by governments, insurgents, or media for political reasons. Mitchell and Susan Sontag have "covered" this aspect of visual culture in several books (Sontag; Mitchell, *What Do Pictures Want?*; *Cloning Terror*).

Wondering whether "visual culture" is still a useful term considering this extension of the subject, Michael Wilson writes that it "refer[s] to any number of phenomena: a particular range of images, or the image as such, or relations between icons and ideas, or the social process of visual perception, or a mode of criticism and analysis" (27). In comparison, Vanessa Schwartz and Jeannene Przyblyski suggest that visual culture "has a particular investment in *vision* as a *historically specific experience*, mediated by new *technologies* and the individual and social *formations* they enable" ("Visual Culture's History" 7, emphases added; see also Mitchell, "Showing Seeing," esp. 166 and 171).

Schwartz and Przyblyski argue that visual culture "identifies and underscores the status of the visual as a *sensory experience* that is itself conditioned by a historical understanding of *physiology, optics*, and *cognitive science*" ("Visual Culture's History" 7, emphases added). Irit Rogoff, on the other hand, claims that to limit visual culture to the field of vision and images is too short-sighted. Instead, she proposes that visual culture should be considered "an arena in which cultural meanings get constituted" and to "anchor [...] to it an entire range of analyses and interpretations of the audio, the spatial, and of the psychic dynamics of *spectatorship*" (24). Finally, Ella Shohat and Robert Stam contend that visual artifacts are

> touched by other texts and discourses, and imbricated in a whole series of apparatuses – the museum, the academy, the art world, the publishing industry, [and other legal, institutional, etc., agencies/agents] which govern the production, dissemination, and legitimation of artistic production. (55)

To study visual culture thus means that you will attempt to carve out, among other things, meaning-making processes, that is "structures of meaning" and schemes of interpretation offered by visual artifacts, and unravel how they are legitimated and perpetuated by public and scholarly discourses (Rogoff 25). It could also entail examining the ideologically inflected aesthetic modes of visual representation and articulation, for instance what and how something is depicted and for whom; what/who is present and visible, what/who is excluded and absent (Mirzoeff, "The Subject of Visual Culture"). Or, it could involve investigating the historical, economic, technological, and political conditions of producing and consuming visual culture, and the means of distribution and circulation of visual culture artifacts.

Such an engagement demands both an extension and a transformation of the conventional tools of literary and cultural analysis. You can take diverse paths and pursue different lines of argumentation, and you have various lenses with which you can read and analyze specific subjects, practices, or products. Theories (i.e., analytical perspectives) and methods (i.e., the procedures or ways to reach a goal) that have influenced the study of visual culture have come from such disciplines as art history, psychology and psychoanalysis, or philosophy to name but a few here; concepts that scholars have dealt with in the past and that have impacted the study of visual culture include the (male) gaze and the conceptions of the observer and observed (see Traube). As Silverman and Rader claim,

> one might examine a particular image, such as the couch [...] in *Friends*, or Lisa Simpson's pearls in *The Simpsons*, [...] one could write an entire paper on the border of the beach and the forest as a means of understanding the complexities, fears, and tensions of *Lost*. (27)

But you need to realize: This variability and openness for interpretation does not mean that you have unlimited possibilities. Ask yourself: If you analyze the couch in *Friends*, then why and to what end? What is the purpose, what is the precise aim, the ultimate goal? What explanatory and epistemological interests lie behind the analysis?

Usually, the material itself prompts questions to which you then set out to find answers. Instead of mere descriptions, you should examine, for example, how certain values and beliefs are conveyed or how meanings are inscribed into the material at hand. You could also find out about the ideologically inflected ascriptions along the lines of "race," class, gender, age, and sexuality and how modes of identification are produced or invented and become dominant through such categories of difference. Similarly, you could try to tease out the visually mediated allocations and negotiations of power (for instance explicate the techniques of exclusion/absence by means of perspective, positioning, or the gaze). In the final section of this chapter I will relate some of these frames of analysis to Brinkley's graphic newspaper serial. For the moment I would like to focus on popular cultural practices, phenomena, objects, and artifacts.

A few notes on studying popular culture

The first point I wish to make in this section concerns popular culture as an intellectual field in the humanities. While popular culture has been discussed by intellectuals throughout the past centuries, it took a while until it was finally instituted in Literary and Cultural Studies programs and disciplines such as American Studies. As Ulla Haselstein, Berndt Ostendorf, and Peter Schneck note, texts, practices, phenomena, and objects in the realm of popular culture "[have] become [...] privileged [areas] of research in American Studies" from the 1960s onwards (331). Yet it took another twenty years for them to actually become visible in the curricula and publications, first in the form of anthologies and edited volumes of essays in the 1980s and later more often in the form of undergraduate and graduate courses.

Secondly, when it comes to defining what popular culture is, we face a problem that is even bigger than the problem of delimiting visual culture. Popular culture, as Holt N. Parker writes, "is like pornography – in, oh, so many ways: we may not be able to define it, but we know it when we see it" (147). This difficulty of defining is, as Storey rightly points out, due to "the implied *otherness* which is always absent/present when we use the term 'popular culture.'" That is, whenever we attempt to define what popular culture is and what it does, it "is always defined, implicitly or explicitly, in contrast to other conceptual categories: folk culture, mass culture, dominant culture, working-class culture, etc. A full definition must always take this into account" (1).

The objects of study, the relevance of studying popular culture, the questions the study of popular culture raises, and the ways of approaching and "fix[ing] the meaning of popular culture" are "islands" that intellectuals have time and again navigated throughout the years – with quite diverse outcomes (Storey 4). Even though I cannot reproduce all of the theories of popular culture here, it is clear that

> popular culture is not a historically fixed set of popular texts and prac-tices, nor is it a historically fixed conceptual category. The object under theoretical scrutiny is both historically *variable*, and always in part con-structed by the very *act of theoretical engagement*. (Storey 11, emphases added)

Against this backdrop, I will – in a generalizing and decontextualized manner – point out two traditions of theorizing popular culture that I consider important.

A number of prominent attempts to define popular culture link the field to the "[t]heories of mass culture (that were dominant in American and European sociology in the 1930s and 1940s)." Many of these "tended to situate popular culture in relation to industrial production, and in opposition to folk culture" (Edgar and Sedgwick 191) and tended to foster a linear top-down model of power relations and manipulation of a passively receiving crowd of consumers. In these approaches to popular culture we see a stronger focus on the side of *production* than on the side of reception or *consumption* (see Kelleter 13–17).

Twentieth-century Marxist theorists, many of whom were and indeed are linked to the British Birmingham School (see Chapter 3), played a key role in re-conceptualizing popular culture. They highlighted the aspect of active – and some would say resistant forms of – consumption (see Hall) and put a stronger emphasis on popular culture as a field of expression and representation, in particular for socially marginalized groups (see Mayer, "Populärkultur" 536).

In recent years, new input has emerged from a group of scholars who work on questions of popular seriality and who bring into dialogue, one might say, both "sides" of popular culture mentioned above (production on the one hand and consumption on the other). The overall goal is

> to do justice to the market orientation of industrially produced narratives by describing popular seriality as a form of standardization and schema-tization that, precisely *because of* its reproducibility and broad base of appeal, continually generates novel possibilities for formal and experi-ential variation and continuation. (Research Unit Popular Seriality n.p., emphasis added; see also Kelleter)

What I find particularly interesting and helpful for students and scholars focusing on popular culture is that this research highlights aspects that have heretofore only marginally been addressed in both Cultural and Literary Studies: reading options, tensions, and recursive processes. They emphasize the possibilities created in serial narratives by repetition, variation, and continuation and the mutual dependency between formal/aesthetic structures and ideological negotiations. For example, as Ruth Mayer has pointed out, "popular narratives are complicated and multifariously entangled in larger political, economical [!], and technical structures that do play instrumental roles in the narratives' progression." Consequently, an

> investigation of the workings of ideology in [...] popular culture [...] needs to account for more than only individual agency on the side of production or reception. Such investigation has to target the modalities, exigencies, and formats of such interactions in their constitutive function. (*Serial Fu Manchu* 125).

In light of these observations, I will now show how the approaches and aspects mentioned might help to make sense of a visual-popular serial narrative: Brinkley's *"Golden Eyes" and Her Hero, Bill.*[3]

Visual-popular culture: a graphic newspaper serial[4]

As I aim to show in the following pages, Brinkley's World War I graphic serial raises a host of interrelated issues about materiality, seriality, and aesthetics, which allow for a number of different theoretical framings. It is a popular visual artifact that lends itself to multiple analyses not only in regard to the topics addressed and the discourses raised, but also concerning its artistic devices, its form (a colored, visual-verbal narrative with recurrent characters, which was printed weekly in full-page size in William Randolph Hearst's syndicated newspapers; see Meyer 1539) or with respect to the consuming practices suggested by the narrative.

At the center of this serial is the heroine, Golden Eyes, a white, heterosexual, blonde curly-haired, slim-figured woman. A collie named Uncle Sam and a pudgy, curly haired angel called Love accompany her. The serial has a clear narrative structure, with a beginning, a middle, and an end, and with a number of cliffhangers (see Lambert) between the respective installments. The story unfolds in fifteen consecutive episodes that are chronologically arranged, and that are geared toward closure, even though each episode can be read and enjoyed without the previous installment. The end of the serial frames the fairy-tale trope of lovers overcoming a series of obstacles toward achieving the middle-class Victorian social ideal: marriage (Meyer 1547–8).

Let me present to you a number of possible approaches: For one thing, what I find fascinating about Brinkley's World War I saga, and thus worthy of close scrutiny, is the way in which the respective episodes, and the graphic narrative at large, visually as well as verbally negotiate the roles of women in the war, and the way in which Brinkley interconnects questions about womanhood in the early twentieth century with questions of nation, citizenship, war, and heroism. The visual representation of the farewell of the two main characters Golden Eyes and Bill in the first installment of the serial, for example, is framed in conventions of sentimental fiction, chivalric romance, and the fairy-tale – the implications of drawing on such gendered literary genres is certainly worthwhile studying. Brinkley adapts, or revives, the medieval idea of chivalry to modern everyday life. Even though the story begins with a rupture, a separation of two people, their reunion, the happy-ending, is implied from the outset. Brinkley uses this overarching premise to establish narrative continuity between the episodes. The opening page blends the discourse of patriotism and questions of citizenship with fairy-tale conventions (triumph over oppressions, closure), a structure that is replicated in the following installments as well.

You may start out by focusing on the artistic techniques, which means you would deal with the question of how the text mediates what it depicts in both words and pictorial elements such as lines, color, typography, or spatial arrangements, etc. – this would be a text-based reading. From there you could delve into the question outlined above, namely of how the serial addresses the discourse of patriotism and questions of citizenship and how these are blended with generic conventions of chivalric romances, sentimental fiction, and fairy-tales.

Another approach would be to situate your analysis of the serial's formal specificities and internal dynamics in the larger context of the modes and means of production and dissemination. You would thus pay attention to the graphic serial as a *form of narrative* and examine how the reading options that are inscribed into this form hinge on prevalent material, economic, technological, and political conditions. Innovations in printing, the rise and distribution of national newspapers, and the debates about new models of womanhood, for instance, significantly influenced the development of this comic form.

If you were interested instead in questions of knowledge formation your focus would, again, be slightly different: Another way to approach the serial would be to read the text as one discursive "player" among many. You would thus pay close attention to the ways in which the serial intersects with, borrows from, or reacts to other materials and media formats of this specific historical time. In order to find out how meanings proliferate and how knowledge is formed in the texts, you need to consider a text, Stephen Greenblatt would argue, not as an immutable entity but to regard it as a node within a network, in exchange with other cultural products such as newspaper discussions about the role of women or sentimental romances.

It might be more useful, however, to narrow down the topic of your research: You could invest in the question of how the text (visually and verbally) *represents* categories of difference such as gender and/or class. What I find interesting, for instance, is that there seems to be a paradox operating in Brinkley's graphic serial in which ideologies of female agency are often coupled with expositions of female dependency (Meyer 1548). In this regard, you may also want to have a look at how a category such as class ties into the representation of the serial's protagonist named Golden Eyes. This would be what you might call an intersectional approach to the text, which means you look at how categories of difference relate to one another and how they are negotiated in the serial.

There is still more to explore: For a larger project, you may also consider the traditions of representations of women in the magazine culture of the turn of the century (for instance from the so-called Gibson Girls to the Brinkley Girls). You could explore the diverse forms and ways of "staging" specific "types" or images of women and their role in society, identity politics, and gender ideologies (see Kitch; Banta; Sturken and Cartwright). In this regard, you may also situate your analysis of the graphic serial in what you might call "middle-brow" literary modernisms with special emphasis on the target audiences and their active participation in the construction and proliferation of meaning (e.g., Audience and Fan Studies; reception theories; see Keyser; Jenkins).

Finally, you may also focus on the Brinkley Girl figure and look at its proliferations outside of the newspaper serial. It is interesting to note that Golden Eyes and other Brinkley Girls also appeared as illustrations in all kinds of poster ads, in other cartoons, and in advertising campaigns for cosmetic products in particular. Drawings were furthermore printed in magazines such as *Cosmopolitan* or *Good Housekeeping*, and the Brinkley Girls were celebrated in a number of songs in such shows as the *Ziegfeld Follies* (see Robbins, *Nell Brinkley*). A possible theoretical framing for such an endeavor could draw on ideas, categories, concepts, and methods from Transmedia Studies and Seriality Studies (e.g., Denson and Mayer).

To be cont'd ...

One thing should be obvious: Depending on the questions you pose, and depending on the epistemological insights you pursue, your findings may differ. But why would we select Brinkley's cartoons in the first place?[5] How can it be justified that "a choice of topic is a contribution to one's field" (Cohen and Higonnet 15)?

So, here is my explanation: I consider the *Golden Eyes* serial instructive and representative as a visual–verbal, popular, widespread, and widely consumed response to, and participation in, debates and discourses at a specific historical time. An analysis of Brinkley's newspaper serials and "serial queen heroines" (Lambert 6) will shed new light on how sentimental themes, commercial success, the aesthetic dynamics of serialization, and the economic context of capitalist consumer culture in the early decades of the twentieth century interconnect.

I also believe that historically situated close readings will bring about a better understanding of the negotiations of topical (political, social) issues, the comics pages' participation in the war effort and the ways in which they advanced a specific discourse. Looking at these and other syndicated newspaper comics and graphic serials about World War I not only opens new approaches to questions of the cultural significance of popular, serial texts in the early twentieth century. It also allows for new insights into the representations of women's roles in times of crisis as well as negotiations of masculinity and patriotism in the mass newspapers.

Notes

1 There are many insightful studies on visual culture and popular culture out there: *Practices of Looking* by Marita Sturken and Lisa Cartwright (2001), Vanessa Schwartz and Jeannene Przyblyski's *Nineteenth-Century Visual Culture Reader* (2004), *The Introduction to Visual Culture* edited by Nicholas Mirzoeff (2007), Margaret Dikovitskaya's *Visual Culture* (2005), the textbook *The World Is a Text* by Jonathan Silverman and Dean Rader (2009), John Storey's *Cultural Theory and Popular Culture* (2006), and *Popular Culture Theory and Methodology*, co-edited by Harold Hinds, Marilyn Motz, and Angela Nelson (2006).
2 See, for instance, Elkins' *Visual Studies*. With the "transnational turn" in American Studies, a paradigm shift occurred, bringing attention to the interconnections of cultural phenomena and objects across national boundaries. Here see, for example, Wilson and Dissanayake, *Global/Local*. See also Denson, Meyer, and Stein, *Transnational Perspectives*.
3 The episodes of this newspaper serial are available online at the Billy Ireland Cartoon Library and Museum: <http://cartoons.osu.edu/digital_albums/nell-brinkley/1.php>. See also Robbins, *Brinkley Girls*.
4 The following paragraphs draw on ideas I have formulated in an essay published in slightly different form in my article "Patriotic Laughter?," esp. 1538–48.
5 For this question, see Decker's demand to "make [the] criteria for selecting aesthetic objects more explicit" (122).

Works cited

Banta, Martha. *Imaging American Women: Idea and Ideals in Cultural History.* New York: Columbia UP, 1987. Print.

Barker, Chris. *Cultural Studies: Theory and Practice.* Third ed. Los Angeles: SAGE, 2008. Print.

Brinkley, Nell. *"Golden Eyes" and Her Hero, Bill.* 31 Mar. 1918–23 Feb. 1919. *The American Weekly* supplement. New York: The Star Company (subsidiary to King Features Syndicate), 1918–1919. Newspaper Serial.

Cohen, Margaret, and Anne Higonnet. "Complex Culture." *The Nineteenth-Century Visual Culture Reader.* Ed. Vanessa R. Schwartz and Jeannene M. Przyblyski. New York: Routledge, 2004. 15–26. Print.

Decker, Christof. "American Studies as Media and Visual Culture Studies: Observations on a Revitalized Research Tradition." *American Studies/Amerikastudien* 57.1 (2012): 115–28. Print.

Denson, Shane, and Ruth Mayer. "Grenzgänger: Serielle Figuren im Medienwechsel." *Populäre Serialität: Narration – Evolution – Distinktion. Zum seriellen Erzählen seit dem 19. Jahrhundert.* Ed. Frank Kelleter. Bielefeld: transcript, 2012. 185–203. Print.

Denson, Shane, Christina Meyer, and Daniel Stein, eds. *Transnational Perspectives on Graphic Narratives: Comics at the Crossroads.* London: Bloomsbury, 2013. Print.

Dikovitskaya, Margaret. *Visual Culture: The Study of the Visual after the Cultural Turn.* Cambridge, MA: MIT P, 2005. Print.

Edgar, Andrew, and Peter Sedgwick, eds. *Key Concepts in Cultural Theory.* New York: Routledge, 1999. Print.

Elkins, James. *Visual Studies: A Skeptical Introduction.* New York: Routledge, 2003. Print.

Greenblatt, Stephen. "Culture." *Contexts for Criticism.* Ed. Donald Keesey. New York: McGraw Hill, 1997. 446–50. Print.

Hall, Stuart. "Encoding/Decoding." *The Cultural Studies Reader.* Ed. Simon During. Second ed. London: Routledge, 1999. 507–17. Print.

Haselstein, Ulla, Berndt Ostendorf, and Peter Schneck. "Popular Culture: Introduction." *Popular Culture.* Ed. Ulla Haselstein, Berndt Ostendorf, and Peter Schneck. Special Issue. *American Studies/Amerikastudien* 46.3 (2001): 331–8. Print.

Hinds, Harold E., Jr., Marilyn F. Motz, and Angela M.S. Nelson, eds. *Popular Culture Theory and Methodology: A Basic Introduction.* Madison: U of Wisconsin P, 2006. Print.

Jenkins, Henry. *Textual Poachers: Television Fans and Participatory Culture.* New York: Routledge, 1992. Print.

Kelleter, Frank, "Populäre Serialität: Eine Einführung." *Populäre Serialität: Narration – Evolution – Distinktion. Zum seriellen Erzählen seit dem 19. Jahrhundert.* Ed. Frank Kelleter. Bielefeld: transcript, 2012. 11–46. Print.

Keyser, Catherine. *Playing Smart: New York Women Writers and Modern Magazine Culture.* Piscataway, NJ: Rutgers UP, 2011. Print.

Kitch, Carolyn. *The Girl on the Magazine Cover: The Origins of Visual Stereotypes in American Mass Media.* Chapel Hill: U of North Carolina P, 2001. Print.

Lambert, Josh. "'Wait for the Next Pictures': Intertextuality and Cliffhanger Continuity in Early Cinema and Comic Strips." *Cinema Journal* 48.2 (2009): 3–25. Print.

Mayer, Ruth. "Populärkultur." *Metzler Lexikon Literatur- und Kulturtheorie: Ansätze – Personen – Grundbegriffe.* Ed. Ansgar Nünning. Third ed. Stuttgart: Metzler, 2004. 535–6. Print.

---. *Serial Fu Manchu: The Chinese Supervillain and the Spread of Yellow Peril Ideology.* Philadelphia, PA: Temple UP, 2014. Print.

Meyer, Christina. "Patriotic Laughter? World War I in British and American Newspaper and Magazine Comics." *Heroisches Elend/Misères de l'héroïsme/Heroic Memory: Der Erste Weltkrieg im intellektuellen, literarischen und bildnerischen Gedächtnis der europäischen Kulturen/La Première Guerre mondiale dans la mémoire intellectuelle, littéraire et artistique des cultures européennes/The First World War in the Intellectual, Literary and Artistic Memory of the European Cultures.* 2 vols. Part 2. Ed. Thomas Stauder and Gislinde Seybert. Frankfurt am Main: Lang, 2013. 1525–52. Print.

Mirzoeff, Nicholas. "The Subject of Visual Culture." *The Visual Culture Reader.* Ed. Nicholas Mirzoeff. London: Routledge, 2007. 3–23. Print.

---. *An Introduction to Visual Culture.* 2nd ed. London: Routledge, 2009.

Mitchell, W.J.T. *Cloning Terror: The War of Images, 9/11 to the Present.* Chicago, IL: U of Chicago P, 2011. Print.

---. *Iconology: Image, Text, Ideology.* Chicago, IL: U of Chicago P, 1986. Print.

---. *Picture Theory: Essays on Verbal and Visual Representation*. Chicago, IL: U of Chicago P, 1994. Print.

---. "Showing Seeing: A Critique of Visual Culture." *Journal of Visual Culture* 1.2 (2002): 165–81. Print.

---. *What Do Pictures Want? The Lives and Loves of Images*. Chicago, IL: U of Chicago P, 2004. Print.

Parker, Holt N. "Toward a Definition of Popular Culture." *History and Theory* 50.2 (2011): 147–70. JSTOR. Web. 12 May 2014.

Research Unit Popular Seriality – Aesthetics and Practice. "Central Project." http:// www.popularseriality.de/en/projekte/aesthetik/index.html. 2014. Web. 10 May 2014.

Robbins, Trina. *Nell Brinkley and the New Woman in the Early Twentieth Century*. Jefferson, NC: McFarland, 2001. Print.

Robbins, Trina, ed. *The Brinkley Girls: The Best of Nell Brinkley's Cartoons from 1913–1940*. Seattle, WA: Fantagraphics, 2009. Print.

Rogoff, Irit. "Studying Visual Culture." *The Visual Culture Reader*. Ed. Nicholas Mirzoeff. Second ed. London: Routledge, 2007. 24–36. Print.

Schwartz, Vanessa R., and Jeannene M. Przyblyski. "Visual Culture's History: Twenty-First Century Interdisciplinarity and Its Nineteenth-Century Objects." *The Nineteenth-Century Visual Culture Reader*. Ed. Vanessa R. Schwartz and Jeannene M. Przyblyski. New York: Routledge, 2004. 3–14. Print.

Schwartz, Vanessa R., and Jeannene M. Przyblyski, eds. *The Nineteenth-Century Visual Culture Reader*. New York: Routledge, 2004. Print.

Shohat, Ella, and Robert Stam. "Narrativizing Visual Culture – Towards a Polycentric Aesthetics." *The Visual Culture Reader*. Ed. Nicholas Mirzoeff. Second ed. London: Routledge, 2007. 37–59. Print.

Silverman, Jonathan, and Dean Rader. *The World Is a Text: Writing, Reading, and Thinking about Visual and Popular Culture*. Third ed. Upper Saddle River, NJ: Pearson, 2009. Print.

Sontag, Susan. *Regarding the Pain of Others*. New York: Farrar, Straus and Giroux, 2003. Print.

Storey, John. *Cultural Theory and Popular Culture: An Introduction*. Fourth ed. Athens: U of Georgia P, 2006. Print.

Sturken, Marita, and Lisa Cartwright. *Practices of Looking: An Introduction to Visual Culture*. Oxford: Oxford UP, 2001. Print.

Traube, Elizabeth G. "'The Popular' in American Culture." *Annual Review of Anthropology* 25 (1996): 127–51. JSTOR. Web. 16 Apr. 2014.

Wilson, Michael. "Visual Culture: A Useful Category of Historical Analysis?" *The Nineteenth-Century Visual Culture Reader*. Ed. Vanessa R. Schwartz and Jeannene M. Przyblyski. New York: Routledge, 2004. 26–33. Print.

Wilson, Rob, and Wimal Dissanayake, eds. *Global/Local: Cultural Production and the Transnational Imaginary*. Durham, NC: Duke UP, 1996. Print.

5 American Studies and/as Cultural Studies

Detectives, dancers, dolls

Martin Klepper

Have you ever heard of the Savoy Ballroom? Of Bud Billiken? Or of Nancy Drew? Perhaps you have: If you love swing dance, you may know that the Savoy was a legendary dance club in Harlem that opened its doors in 1926 – the same year in which the famous US Route 66 was established. If you ever resided in Chicago, you may have been in town in August when the annual Bud Billiken Parade (the second largest parade in the United States) is held. And you may have heard that Robert S. Abbott, the founder of the *Chicago Defender*, one of the largest and most venerable African American newspapers in the States, invented the parade in 1929, three years after the opening of the Savoy – incidentally also the year of the "Black Tuesday." By that time, Bud Billiken had been the mascot (a doll, actually) of the paper's junior section for a few years. One year later, in 1930, the year in which the Depression really started hitting (ironically also the year in which the first American supermarket, King Kullen in Queens, NYC, opened), Nancy Drew, the first serial girl detective, started solving cases (she carried on until 2004).

What did the Savoy, Bud Billiken, and Nancy Drew (and, perhaps, the other events) have in common, apart from their occurrence in a few consecutive years? Obviously, all of them were a part of what we call popular culture – albeit different formations within popular culture. All of them addressed children, adolescents, and young adults and indicated a serious transformation in the ways Americans (Black and white) imagine coming-of-age. All of them involved questions of social, racial, and gender roles: Should girls be detectives? Should African American children take possession of Chicago's streets and their futures? Should young adults engage in wild contortions (as *Life Magazine* wrote about swing dancing in the Savoy – before swing became "white") and, *horribile dictum*, in a desegregated environment? All of them dealt with mobility: Nancy Drew solved her cases with the help of her sleek roadster and even used aircraft support if needed. The Bud Billiken Clubs marched through the city. The Savoy provided the space for an explosion of body energy: The Lindy Hop was named after Charles Lindbergh's celebrated first transatlantic flight. Physical mobility was supposed to translate into social mobility. Nancy defends the values of the aspiring white middle class; Bud Billiken fortifies African American kids on their thorny paths through white territory; and even music and dancing were widely understood as possibilities to head out of the misery of the Depression. All of them indicated a new stage in American culture, and I will use these examples to discuss American Studies as a specific version of Cultural Studies. In order to understand this connection it is vital to consider the relation between cultures and the institution of the nation.

Culture and nation

In the late eighteenth and throughout the nineteenth century, the Global West began reflecting the idea of culture. Culture is one of the terms (like "history" or "the nation") that sprang up in the course of a complex self-reflective turn in Western history, which was the effect of the industrialization, of colonialism and empire-building, of the rise of capitalism, the rationalization of political processes, and of what the German sociologist Niklas Luhmann called "functional differentiation" (707–76, my trans.). Western societies began to practice large-scale division of labor. Individuals and groups specialized and learned to speak specialized languages: the jargon of law or of religion, the jargon of the education system or of the economy, the jargon of politics, or of arts and letters.

Functional differentiation (or *modernization*, to use a contested term) had advantages over earlier forms of organizing societies (formations of center-and-periphery such as the ancient city-states or the medieval palatine systems; stratified societies such as feudal states). Appropriating a term from Karl Marx, one could say functional differentiation "unfettered" the forces of the specialized subsystems so that each field developed rapidly, fostering innovation and economic growth. Nevertheless, Luhmann speaks of the "catastrophe of modernity" because differentiation also brought vast, new problems (683, my trans.).

One of these problems was a general sense of discontinuity. Times were felt to be changing – not in the earlier sense of cyclical changes (e.g., of seasons), but in the sense of a linear movement into an unknown future. "History" was the term given to this general transformation. Earlier societies in the West would speak of the history of calligraphy or of military history, but never of "history" as such (Koselleck 93). "History" as a term on its own implies uncertainty and instability: Where is the arrow of time heading? Another problem was a heightened sense of disunity. If everybody speaks a different language or jargon and if, in times of revolutions, even the political system may change overnight, what keeps a society together?

A third problem, related to the second, was a sense of fragmentation and displacement: Functional differentiation went along with urbanization and the disintegration of traditional communities. In addition, the European states, through conquest and colonialism, had spread out over distant territories – a major event in the history of globalization (Reichardt 31–34), exporting a part of their elites, which became Creole ruling classes. What was their allegiance?

A partial answer to these questions was the idea of the "nation." Societies increasingly began to define themselves internally through a sense of belonging to a national whole and externally through the difference to other nations and the exclusion of those who did not "belong." In the light of discontinuity, disunity, and displacement (hallmarks of a distinctly modern sensibility), what could establish the cohesiveness of the "nation," especially if it was spread out across continents? The American political scientist Benedict Anderson and the British historian Eric Hobsbawm have explored the origins of national feelings and traditions. In *The Invention of Tradition* (1983), Hobsbawm suggests that national traditions function to create consensual collective identities even though traditions are more often than not constructed or invented and projected into the past (13–14). In *Imagined Communities* (1983/91), Anderson argues that "the nation" is a collective imagination, stabilized by purported traditions, narratives, songs, images, symbols, etc.[1] His book explores how the idea of the nation emerged in the context of the rise of a printing culture, of capitalism, and of what he calls Creole elites in the European colonies (47–65).[2] Anderson identifies the rise of nationalism exactly here: in the American colonies, from where it spilled back to Europe.

The idea of "culture" complemented "the nation" as an answer to the problems of modernity. In analogy to the usage of "history," Europeans and Americans, before the eighteenth century, would have known terms such as agriculture or horticulture, but not the term "culture" as such. Now, the concept of "culture" compensated for a lost sense of rootedness. In 1871 the British anthropologist Sir Edward Burnett Tylor defined culture as "that complex whole which includes knowledge, belief, art, morals, law, customs, and other capabilities and habits acquired by man as a member of society" (1). According to this definition, "culture" refers to the symbolic and material practices in society, coherent beyond discontinuities, disunity, and displacement. "Culture" rather than territory, kinship, or political allegiance could then be the stuff that keeps a society together. Could it also mark the difference in and between societies?

The politics of culture

"Culture" and "the nation" evolved as complementary terms. Anderson's imagined community ("the nation") is founded on a sense of shared symbolic and material practices. Tylor's complex whole ("culture") is the essence of what evolves into the idea of the nation. Tylor, like the vast majority of thinkers at the end of the nineteenth century, was an evolutionist; but he was also a universalist, who stipulated different stages of culture – savage, barbarian, and civilized (in this order) – while simultaneously rejecting any essential differences between societies (all went through the same stages).

Tylor used the terms "culture," "civilization," and "society" almost synonymously in the uncountable singular and in a descriptive mode. The English poet and critic Matthew Arnold used the term in a normative sense. In his periodical essays published under the suggestive title *Culture and Anarchy* (1867–69), he argues that "culture" should become the means to overcome the civil fractures of a divided British society. The American novelist and critic William Dean Howells, using the term "civilization," made similar arguments in his editor's column in the *Atlantic Monthly* (1871–81).

In Arnold's (but also in Howells's) vision, culture was a standard of refinement rather than a description of symbolic and material practices. It was a part of education, "the study of perfection" (Arnold xvi), and the dissemination of "the best which has been thought and said" (Arnold viii). Arnold (and Howells) called for a new valuation of arts and literature, the pinnacles of civilization, as a remedy against anarchy and barbarism. Both saw culture as a means to reconcile society – for them cultural education would "do away with classes" (Arnold 49). Yet, at the same time, their normative definition of culture lent itself to defining and justifying differences.

Thus, culture became an additional source of difference within and between nations. Within nations, these differences could morph into a question of "distinction," or of "cultural capital," a term the French sociologist Pierre Bourdieu coined in order to explain differences in access to power and prosperity that could not be attributed to ability. Howells, who considered himself one of the "literary elect," described what he called the "unthinking multitude" as "puerile, primitive, savage" (54) – not coincidentally linking those lacking formal education to children and "savages."

Between nations, as Anthony Appiah shows, literature and art could be seen as "a key to the national spirit" (88). For Arnold, the national spirit crystallized in Shakespeare; for Howells, the US "national spirit" was expressed through a familiarity with European (and some European American) "masters." Arnold and Howells thus identified "culture" as a white and Western standard of human development, an accomplishment that needed to be passed on to the less fortunate, the children, the "unthinking multitude," and the "primitive." Quoting French philosopher Jacques Derrida, German sociologist Dirk Baecker notes that "all culture is originally colonial" and explains: "[A]ll terms, which we employ to describe a culture, a different culture or our own culture, are terms contaminated by violence" (28).

Entrepreneurs and motivational teachers

On 12 March 1926 the Savoy Ballroom was opened by white entrepreneur Jay Faggen, Jewish businessman Moe Gale, and African American manager Charles Buchanon. Incredibly successful, it was located in the heart of Harlem on Lenox Avenue and, unlike most ballrooms, had a no-discrimination policy. Night by night, the Savoy opened its doors to dancers and musicians, who developed new dances to jazz and swing music. One of the most famous was the Lindy Hop, performed by the Savoy Lindy Hoppers or Whitey's Lindy Hoppers (Herbert "Whitey" White was a former African American boxer who had started as a bouncer at the Savoy). The latter came to perform on

Broadway and in successful movie productions such as the Marx Brothers' *A Day at the Races* (1937). The Savoy and the Lindy Hop were part and parcel of the "dance craze" during the Great Depression. While the American economy collapsed, the Savoy prospered. Even though the Savoy was owned by a white and a Jewish proprietor, the early characterization in *Life* shows the hegemonic gaze with which the new practices on the dancefloor were viewed. And not only the white press saw jazz music and swing dance as a serious menace to American culture (Miller and Jensen).

Abbott's *Chicago Defender* was one of the African American newspapers that initially accepted jazz only as a temporary activity for talented musicians who were waiting for worthier engagements (in classical music). Abbott, a son of former slaves, was in league with many African American intellectuals and leaders such as W.E.B. Du Bois who sought progress toward equality and justice through access to highbrow culture (Schenbeck). The *Defender*, which was a motor of the "Great Migration" of African Americans from the South to the North in the 1910s and '20s, advertised classical music, theaters, and fine restaurants, and featured stories of successful African American citizens in Chicago. Abbott's journal not only included a full entertainment section and featured life style ads on almost every page, it also reared its own future audience with the pages of the *Defender Junior* and the Bud Billiken Clubs, whose members solicited new readers. At the same time, this engagement furthered their personal pride, their education, their involvement in the community, and their advancement toward middle-class respectability (Rutkoff and Scott 318). To adult readers, as well, Abbott preached the gospel of self-reliance: "Eventually your efforts will bring the reward they deserve" (*Chicago Defender*).

Edward Stratemeyer also believed in middle-class respectability, albeit of a distinctly white kind. The creator of countless juvenile book series, including the Nancy Drew adventure stories, had been an avid reader of Horatio Alger books (see Chapter 11). In Alger's texts (usually orphaned) boys acquire middle-class respectability through hard work and benevolent support ("luck and pluck" as it was called). Stratemeyer discovered the market for cheap juvenile fiction ("fifty-centers") and made the Stratemeyer Syndicate into a business venture by providing the story lines and "farming out – in assembly-line style – the writing to hungry professionals" (Kismaric and Heiferman 13–15). He developed a formula for the books: twenty-five chapters per book, connected by cliff-hangers, intense action, no touching or kissing, no excessive violence. It was Mildred Wirt, one of Stratemeyer's professionals, who made Nancy Drew into a success. Wirt wrote twenty-two of the first twenty-five adventures, turning Nancy into an unusually confident, competent, and independent girl-character. Navigating life with her dashing roadster, Nancy became an unlikely (because distinctly emancipated) role model for girls in Depression America.

The success of Nancy Drew, similar to the success of Bud Billiken and the Savoy dancers, has its roots in a combination of social, economic, technological, and cultural conditions. One of them was a long-standing tradition of "American rituals of self-improvement" (Ostendorf 19). If you watch the 1936 musical *Swing Time* starring Ginger Rogers and Fred Astaire, you will detect a plate at the dance school in which the two stars dance for the first time together: "To Know How to Dance is to Know How to Control Yourself." Self-improvement through self-control, self-confidence, and instrumental reason grew into a veritable self-help market in the 1920s and '30s, propelled by authors such as Dale Carnegie (*How To Win Friends and Influence People*, 1936) or Napoleon Hill (*Think and Grow Rich*, 1937). In their own individual ways, Herbert "Whitey" White, Bud Billiken, and Nancy Drew also functioned as motivational trainers who introduced their followers to a culture of mobilization, discipline, pride, and self-realization.

Popular culture/mass culture

The 1920s and '30s mark a moment of radical transformation in American culture, in which popular culture and mass culture became hegemonic within the national cultural matrix. As we have seen, the nineteenth century developed a concept of culture, according to which highbrow arts would function as a corrective to the perceived infantilizing/barbarizing effects of capitalism and immigration (see Levine 171–77). Alan Trachtenberg writes:

> The culture of the Gilded Age, we might then say, contained a particular idea of culture as a privileged domain of refinement, aesthetic sensibility, and higher learning. [...] Culture and refinement, then, conveyed a political message, a vision of a harmonious body politic under the rule of reason, light, and sweet, cheerful emotion. (143)

In the 1920s, the "contortions" at the Savoy, Abbott's tabloid techniques and attacks against white supremacy, and Stratemeyer's "trashy and poorly written" as well as "morally threatening" stories (Hamilton-Honey 93) appeared to undermine this ideal. Emily Hamilton-Honey attributes the attempts of American libraries to remove Stratemeyer books from their shelves to the low cultural capital these books had. White politicians, such as Arkansas governor Charles Brough, attempted to hinder the circulation of the *Defender* because of its alleged incitement of race riots (1919). Anne Shaw Faulkner, writing in the *Ladies Home Journal* in 1921, explained to her readers that jazz "produces an atrophied condition on the brain cells" until "very frequently" the listeners are "actually incapable of distinguishing between good and evil, right and wrong" (16). It seemed as if one could only face mass culture with riot gear.

But such attacks did not prevent the triumph of popular culture. On the one hand, book serials, swing and jazz, Black newspapers, and the Bud Billiken Parade catered to commercial and capitalist interest (white businesses queued up to sponsor the parade). As a result, the affinity between a liberal economy and mass culture is one of the central themes in discussions of popular cultural practices. The German philosophers Theodor W. Adorno and Max Horkheimer reserved the skeptical term "culture industry" for the likes of Stratemeyer, Abbott, and businessmen like Faggen, Gale, and Buchanon (Horkheimer and Adorno 94–136). Horkheimer, Adorno, and the Frankfurt School, who made a normative distinction between high and low culture, noticed the tendency of capitalism to compromise earlier folk or popular traditions by colonizing them (into mass culture) through processes of standardization (uniform structures), pseudo-individualization (make-believe choices), distraction (from the realities of class warfare), investment in instrumental rationality (efficiency thinking) and affirmation (entertainment instead of critique). To be sure, none of these accusations is completely wrong.

On the other hand, popular culture is more than the fifth column of capitalism. Douglas Kellner, who defines culture as a "highly participatory activity" (2), rejects the early Frankfurt School's dichotomy between high culture and low culture: "[O]ne should see critical and ideological moments in the full range of culture, and not limit critical moments to high culture and identify all of low culture as ideological" (29). Similarly, Susie O'Brien and Imre Szeman criticize the elitism of Horkheimer and Adorno (110) and remind their readers that "contemporary cultural production is contradictory" (112). This is very much the position the Birmingham School, aka British Cultural Studies (see Chapter 3), championed. John Fiske, for instance, declared that popular culture is always involved in a struggle between in-corporation (commercialization) and ex-corporation (resistance). It is, as it were, always on the edge: A "site of struggle, but, while accepting the power of the forces of domination, it focuses rather upon the popular tactics by which these forces are coped with, are evaded or are resisted" (17–18). Frank Kelleter has therefore suggested exploring popular culture as a particularly modern, dynamic field of practices offering opportunities for producers, recipients, participants, or users to connect in various ways to earlier or other cultural practices ("Populäre Serialität" 13–17).

As a societal practice, popular culture has a particular relevance in the United States. Cultural scholar Berndt Ostendorf has pointed out that, in contrast to European usage, the term "popular" acquired a positive, "post-revolutionary" *American* meaning and legitimacy early on (4). In other words, popular culture also "rode to its victory on the coattails of republican self-government and popular sovereignty" (3). Because of a tradition of anti-elitism and anti-intellectualism, of common sense as a normative attitude, and of a special valorization of instrumental reason, his argument goes, popular culture was always taken more seriously in North America than in Europe. Stratemeyer, Abbott, and Herbert White became cultural icons; Nancy Drew, Bud Billiken, and the Lindy Hoppers cultural heroes.

American Studies as Cultural Studies

As a consequence, American Studies have always included explorations of popular culture. With an understanding of culture along the lines of Tylor's inclusive idea of "complex knowledge" or British cultural scholar Stuart Hall's overarching definition as "shared conceptual maps" (18), American Studies as Cultural Studies explore the traditions, structures, politics, cleavages, and conflicts negotiated between highbrow and lowbrow culture, between culture as industry and culture as participatory space (Jenkins et al.), between culture as empowering/unifying and as colonial/violent force.

According to Hall, "Cultural Studies has multiple discourses" (qtd. in Storey 1). Chapter 3 of this volume systematizes some of these discourses. As a practitioner of American Studies as Cultural Studies you may find yourself torn between approaches more interested in the unlikely coherences and structural processes at work in the perpetual reproduction of the "imagined community" and approaches more interested in the asymmetries, inequalities, and mechanisms of dominance and coercion that characterize these reproductions.

On the one hand you will find scholarship that strives to understand how symbolic patterns, narrative devices, and material practices evolve to continually redefine what American culture might be. Researchers investigate how literature and mass media operate to sustain a sense of connectedness (Kelleter, "Trust and Sprawl" 43–44) or how "webs of significance" (Geertz 5) connect widely diverse areas of society. Here, Kulturwissenschaft as a German academic subject, Media Studies, and Cultural Anthropology fuel American Studies.

On the other hand, you will find scholarship that insists on the co-relation between culture and power. Oliver Marchart has identified the terms "culture," "power," "identity," and the constitutive links between them as the magic triangle of Cultural Studies (33–36). He explains that social identities (with their parameters of social differentiation such as "race," class, gender, ability, age, etc.) are produced through the medium of culture in a network of very concrete power relations (12–13). Similarly, in his essay "The Work of Representation," Hall explains how the subject is produced through cultural representation (54–61). Here, American Studies are energized by British Cultural Studies (the Birmingham School), by the Frankfurt School, by Queer and Gender Studies as well as Critical Race and Critical Whiteness Studies.

It may look as if working according to the first approach means looking at relatively anonymous or even abstract structures and as if working according to the second means concentrating on agents and concrete actions. But John Storey, referring to the Italian journalist and philosopher Antonio Gramsci, reminds us that structure and agency cannot be neatly separated: "It is the 'Gramscian insistence', before, with and after Gramsci, learned from Marx, that we make culture and we are made by culture; there is agency and there is structure" (5). With this in mind, let us look one last time at the detective, the dancers, and the Bud Billiken doll.

The breakthrough of a commercialized mass culture (whose seeds had been planted in the early nineteenth century) in the age of the radio, mass-circulated newspapers, the vinyl record, and the movies had a lasting effect on American culture. It cemented the gap between highbrow and lowbrow, with intellectual and elite culture often positioning itself against the mass-cultural sphere. It unified the United States through the national reach of its media; and it mobilized an ever-growing part of the American population in the pursuit of an ideology of social advancement, self-reliance, self-realization, and personal ambition. In this sense, it became part and parcel of the cultural imaginary, which the German Americanist Winfried Fluck has characterized as a stage for an accelerating tendency toward individualization: an "unlimited and ever escalating dynamic of imaginary self-empowerment" (*Romance* 263; see also *Das kulturelle Imaginäre*).

This dynamic, accelerated by modernity and capitalism, is more than visible in Nancy Drew's fearless and independent use of pragmatic and instrumental reasoning in her efforts to repair the world. It is palpable in the Lindy Hoppers' efforts to discipline their bodies into vehicles of their will and their hoped-for success. And it is present in Bud Billiken's refusal to see the *Defender* juniors fettered to their inherited stations in life. But on a closer look, the imagined communities and conceptual maps implied by these practices differentiate radically along their social contexts. They reveal different visions of growing-up, of social advancement, of mobility, and of communal life.

Nancy Drew demonstrates time and again that a girl can stand her ground, that nineteenth-century feminine virtues such as domesticity, piety, purity, and submissiveness will not do for the twentieth century. But this is also a privileged, middle-class-centered, and extremely white ground, where poverty appears as villainy and the bad guys are failed social climbers. Here, mobility is a question of merit, and merit is literally visible and genealogically pre-structured. The Bud Billiken Clubs also put much emphasis on merit and individuality, but self-reliance and even mobility have a clear collective touch in the sense of American sociologist Patricia Hill Collins's concept of "situated standpoints." Community work and allegiance are stressed, and this vision includes the knowledge that individual mobility is only possible through group mobility (of African Americans).

Most of Whitey's Lindy Hoppers were drafted into the army in 1943. The Savoy closed in 1958. The Lindy Hop and swing stayed on to be appropriated by white popular culture. The dream of mobility and social advancement became true for some of the original dancers, but in the very same year in which the group was founded, in 1935, the first race riots in Harlem clouded the vision of a desegregated community for another thirty years: an entire generation. With their complex histories, these examples call for an exploration of the conflicts, negotiations, and continuations in the symbolic and material traditions and structures that have sustained the detective, the dancers, and the doll.

Notes

1 For Anderson, national feelings are by no means necessarily negative. He points to various liberation and democracy movements, for which the idea of the nation was instrumental.
2 Anderson has been criticized with the argument that the idea of the nation has also emerged elsewhere.

Works cited

Anderson, Benedict. *Imagined Communities: Reflections on the Origins and Spread of Nationalism*. London: Verso, 2006. Print.
Appiah, Anthony K. "Race, Culture, Identity: Misunderstood Connections." The Tanner Lectures on Human Values. U of California, San Diego. 27 and 28 Oct. 1994. Philpapers.org. Web. 20 Apr. 2015.
Arnold, Matthew. *Culture and Anarchy*. 1869. Bristol: Thoemmes P, 1994. Print.
Baecker, Dirk. *Wozu Kultur?* Berlin: Kulturverlag Kadmos, 2001. Print.
Bourdieu, Pierre. "The Forms of Capital." *Handbook of Theory and Research for the Sociology of Education*. Ed. John G. Richardson. New York: Greenwood, 1986. Print.
Chicago Defender. Part II. (19 Jan. 1929): 2. Print.
Collins, Patricia Hill. "Some Group Matters: Intersectionality, Situated Standpoints, and Black Feminist Thought." *Fighting Words: Black Women and the Search for Justice*. Minneapolis: U of Minnesota P, 1998. 201–28. Print.
Faulkner, Anne Shaw. "Does Jazz Put the Sin in Syncopation?" *Ladies Home Journal* (August 1921): 16–34. Web. 12 May 2015.
Fiske, John. *Understanding Popular Culture*. Second ed. London: Routledge, 2010. Print.
Fluck, Winfried. *Das Kulturelle Imaginäre: Eine Funktionsgeschichte des Amerikanischen Romans 1790–1900*. Frankfurt am Main: Suhrkamp: 1997. Print.
---. *Romance with America? Essays on Culture, Literature, and American Studies*. Ed. Laura Bieger and Johannes Voelz. Heidelberg: Winter, 2009. Print.
Geertz, Clifford. *The Interpretation of Cultures*. New York: Basic Books. 1973. Print.
Hall, Stuart. "The Work of Representation." *Representations: Cultural Representations and Cultural Practices*. Ed. Stuart Hall. London: SAGE, 1997. 13–74. Print.
Hamilton-Honey, Emily. *Turning the Pages of American Girlhood: The Evolution of Girls' Series Fiction, 1865–1930*. Jefferson, NC: McFarland, 2013. Print.
Hobsbawm, Eric. "Introduction: Inventing Traditions." *The Invention of Tradition*. Ed. Eric Hobsbawm and Terence Ranger. Cambridge: Cambridge UP, 1983. 1–14. Print.
Horkheimer, Max, and Theodor W. Adorno. *Dialectics of the Enlightenment*. Trans. Edmund Jephcott. Ed. Gunzelin Schmid Noer. Stanford, CA: Stanford UP, 2002. Print.
Howells, William Dean. *Criticism and Fiction*. 1891. New York: New York UP, 1959. Print.
Jenkins, Henry et al. *Confronting the Challenges of Participatory Culture: Media Education for the 21st Century*. Cambridge, MA: MIT P, 2009. Print.
Kelleter, Frank. "Populäre Serialität: Eine Einführung." *Populäre Serialität: Narration – Evolution – Distinktion. Zum seriellen Erzählen seit dem 19. Jahrhundert*. Ed. Frank Kelleter. Bielefeld: transcript, 2012. 11–46. Print.

---. "Trust and Sprawl: Seriality, Radio, and the First Fireside Chat." *Media Econo-mies: Perspectives on American Cultural Practices*. Ed. Marcel Hartwig, Evelyne Keitel, and Gunter Süß. Trier: WVT, 2014. 43–61. Print.

Kellner, Douglas. *Media Culture*. London: Routledge, 1995. Print.

Kismaric, Carole, and Marvin Heiferman. *The Mysterious Case of Nancy Drew & The Hardy Boys*. New York: Simon & Schuster, 1998. Print.

Koselleck, Reinhard. *Futures Past*. Trans. Keith Tribe. New York: Columbia UP, 2004. Print.

Levine, Lawrence W. *Highbrow/Lowbrow: The Emergence of Cultural Hierarchy in America*. Cambridge, MA: Harvard UP, 1988. Print.

Luhmann, Niklas. *Die Gesellschaft der Gesellschaft*. Vol. 2. Frankfurt am Main: Suhrkamp, 1999. Print.

Marchart, Oliver. *Cultural Studies*. Konstanz: UVK, 2008. Print.

Miller, Norma, and Evette Jensen. *Swingin' at the Savoy: The Memoir of a Jazz Dancer*. Philadelphia, PA: Temple UP, 1996. Print.

O'Brien, Susie, and Imre Szeman. *Popular Culture: A User's Guide*. Ontario: Thomson & Nelson, 2004. Print.

Ostendorf, Bernd. "Why Is American Popular Culture so Popular?" *American Studies in Scandinavia* 34 (2000): 1–46. Print.

Reichardt, Ulfried. *Globalisierung: Literaturen und Kulturen des Globalen*. Berlin: Akademie, 2010. Print.

Rutkoff, Peter M., and William B. Scott. "Pinkster in Chicago: Bud Billiken and the Mayor of Bronzeville, 1930–1945." *The Journal of African American History* 89.4 (2004): 316–30. Print.

Schenbeck, Lawrence. "Music, Gender, and 'Uplift' in the Chicago Defender, 1927–1937." *The Musical Quarterly* 81.3 (Autumn 1997): 344–70. Print.

Storey, John. *Cultural Studies and the Study of Popular Culture*. 2nd ed. Edinburgh: Edinburgh UP, 2003. Print.

Trachtenberg, Alan. *The Incorporation of America: Culture and Society in the Gilded Age*. New York: Hill & Wang, 1982. Print.

Tylor, Edward Burnett. *The Origins of Culture*. Vol. 1. New York: Harper & Brothers, 1958. Print.

Part III

Concepts of nation building in American Studies

6 The myth of the American West, "Manifest Destiny," and the frontier

Michael J. Prince

The mythology of the American West contributes crucial elements in defining the United States historically and ideologically (for myth and mythology, see also Chapters 10 and 11). These elements are derived mainly from discourses that have, with their frequent retellings and progressively broader application, been diluted in their historical-material specificity to a set of stories with correlated icons, used to interpret Anglo-Europeans' historical encounters with American space and peoples and the young nation's territorial expansion.

They often also provide the filters by which contemporary situations in American society are understood. On 17 September 2001, President George W. Bush drew on this myth cluster when he expressed how he thought Osama bin Laden should be brought to justice: "There is an old poster out West that said 'Wanted: Dead or Alive'" (ABC News), thereby characterizing his adversary as an outlaw and suggesting a corresponding response.

These myths may also broadly suggest a *telos*, a predestined goal for American society, of which the nineteenth-century declarations and policies of Manifest Destiny are but one historical example. They justified in terms of a religious predestination the coast-to-coast appropriation of the North American continent by white Anglo-American settlers.

Cultural myth, then, is equipped so as to provide a series of self-reinforcing filters, narratives, and icons with which one can think about past events, present situations and future choices. The most redolent and widespread of the cultural myths in the United States are "progressive myths," i.e., myths that naturalize a constantly expanding economy and an ever greater "integration" of people and resources into the economic matrix. Other cultural myths overlap with and support the myths of the American West, such as the "rags to riches" and "self-made man" narratives, which are discussed in Chapter 11. Since stories cannot be "argued with" in the same way that one can with a historical or scientific discourse, the social and economic order is presented in them as "natural," just the way things are, a part of the assortment of unquestioned truisms that constitute, to borrow Clifford Geertz's term, "common sense as a cultural system" (75; see also Slotkin, "Myth" 70, 77).

Cultural myths gain in their contemporary relevance when a watershed in historical-material circumstances is near. The United States Census of 1890 declared that there was no longer any "Frontier" in the continental United States, and at that point Wisconsin historian Frederick Jackson Turner set about to analyze the role of the Frontier in the formation of American politics and society. His *The Significance of the Frontier in American History* (1893) suggested that the westward moving Frontier, and the "free land" it made available, had provided a constantly increasing region of opportunity for the ambitious and worthy; the Homestead Act of 1862 can be seen as one political manifestation of this theory (Turner 37, 145).

Turner's historical focus was heavily based on ideological presuppositions of Native American "savagery" being displaced by a more complex European civilization, which further served the notion that the Frontier was "free land," a phrase that occurs no fewer than three times in his paper. In line with the Jeffersonian agrarian ideal and the aims of Jacksonian democracy, the Frontier functioned, according to Turner, as a democratizing area, where the nature of the individual was relatively unhampered by the metropolitan constraints and where a more egalitarian society could develop.

Historian–statesman Theodore Roosevelt also constructed the Frontier as a region out of which something uniquely American arose in the 1890s, while his narrative in the four-volume *The Winning of the West* was more focused on the conflict with the denizens of the Frontier territories. "[The] rifle-bearing freemen who founded their little republics on the western waters gradually solved the question of combining personal liberty with national union" (xviii). Turner's and Roosevelt's influential texts described and uncritically endorsed the settler colonialism that would ultimately come to displace the Native American population.

The cultural force of these historical texts has been increased by their privileged position in further scholarly queries concerning American identity and "American Exceptionalism." Henry Nash Smith's ground-breaking *Virgin Land* (1950) introduced the notions of myth and symbol as useful tools for discussing historical occurrences in the light of the myth of the West, launching what has been termed the Myth and Symbol School (see Chapters 1 and 3). Leo Marx's *The Machine in the Garden* (1964) characterized the American Frontier as harboring a constitutive tension between the pastoral and the march of technology. Annette Kolodny's *The Lay of the Land* (1975) brought Freudian and feminist analysis to bear on the colonists', and later the Anglo-Americans', experience of the wilderness and Frontier. Richard Slotkin's *Regeneration through Violence* (1973) kicked off a trilogy that traced the Roosevelt strain of the mythological West through almost four centuries of North American history. Jane Tompkins's *West of Everything* (1992) discussed the distinctive elements of the Western film and novel, casting this genre as highlighting violent release as a discursive answer to women's domestic literature, an influential genre in nineteenth-century America. The analytical models themselves, however, are tinged with myth-based presuppositions that are extremely difficult to exorcise.[1]

Myths of the "West": from the Western to outer space

The Western, it has often been suggested, is "the most American of all genres" (see, for instance, Birgel; Cantor 114; or Quay 191). As straightforward as it sounds, however, this definition is problematic since it codifies an "American Experience" and determines what is "American" and, implicitly, who is an "American." Like the central myths of the American West, which have been outlined above, the notion of the Western as a quintessentially American genre is based on and perpetuates exclusive ideas of a national identity centered around the categories of "race," ethnicity, religion, and gender. In this sense, if the Western is still perceived as particularly American this also bespeaks the enduring significance and allure of an efficacious mythology of predestined white, male, Anglo-American dominance and mastery over a continent that is imagined as uncultivated and uncivilized.

Yet as a genre, the Western is everything but monolithic. It can be traced back to eighteenth-century captivity narratives and to the Frontier romances by James Fenimore Cooper, whose enormously popular Leatherstocking tales started in 1823 and were soon appropriated in diverse popular forms, from dime novels to popular theater (see Cawelti, "Masculine Myths" 84). Providing a formula for the "field of action that centers on an encounter between civilization and wilderness" (Cawelti, *Adventure* 193) and placing questions of good versus evil center stage, the Western is related to the quintessentially modern genre of crime fiction: Influential critic John G. Cawelti, in fact, argues that the particularly American branch of crime writing, hard-boiled detective fiction, constitutes a hybrid form between detective fiction and the Western (*Adventure* 80). Not so surprising, then, the first American narrative film – Edwin S. Porter's *The Great Train Robbery* (1903) – is, arguably, both a crime film and ... a Western (see Moody 228). From the nineteenth century to this day, American (popular) culture is replete with Western references, from classical comics to graphic novels and from Hollywood movies to more recent so-called quality TV (for another reading of a Western, see also Chapter 23). Science fiction – just think of *Star Wars* and the *Star Trek* franchise – can often be categorized in terms of the Western, as I will argue (using another example) in my case study.

"Though we need to understand the Western in terms of its expression of American myths, it was first and foremost a kind of story," Cawelti writes in the revised introduction to his classical *The Six-Gun Mystique Sequel*. "Thus, to begin to understand its power and significance, we must first define the narrative patterns that gave Westerns their recognizable and distinctive shape" (3). A story of eventual mastery of good over evil, the Western as genre is also vitalized by its distinctive motifs and characters: barbed wire and the American bison, the Lone Ranger or the trapper. It is substantiated by references to American myths presented as realities, as Frontier life and Manifest Destiny, and to (real) history presented as myth, for instance in references to people such as Daniel Boone or to Deadwood, the historical place that has recently become the setting of a neo-Western re-negotiation of Frontier life (see Cantor).

The Western, furthermore, is also ambivalent in its ideological agenda. It might well be accused of perpetuating the very myths that normalize a hegemonic white male subject position. At the same time, it can also be argued that it may function as a counter-narrative to repressive normative ideologies, as Jane Tompkins points out in her discussion of the "Western as answer to the domestic novel" (39). The following section, in fact, will employ the myths of the American West and the notion of the Frontier as a regenerative space in a reading of a popular culture text from 1956, Philip K. Dick's early "pulp" science fiction novel *The World Jones Made*. Science fiction is generically positioned to perform societal critique by positing alternative futures and setting them in opposition to the contemporary situation for comparison or contrast (James 96–97, 113). In my reading, I will contrast the original ideological context and political motivations for the concept of Manifest Destiny with the naturalized expansionist activities depicted and endorsed in the novel. The characters embrace the spatiality and ethos derived from the historical and imaginative experience of the American Frontier, and actions and settings from an imaginary West are integrated into the novel.

Dick is known for writing at prodigious speed for a market that was not particularly fussy about literary aesthetics. His style of production, his renown for idiosyncratic thematic vantages, and the openness of the science fiction genre make a discourse possible that, on the one hand, sometimes interrogates and challenges cultural myths while, on the other hand, sometimes uncritically absorbs and endorses them.

Dick's 1956 novel, which is set in a post-apocalyptic 2002 world, is oddly prescient in contrasting naturalized certainties, which the myths of the West can support, with provisional secular sensibilities with regard to gender, "race," and tolerance more in tune with a more contemporary world, which goes by the name of "Hoff's Relativism" in Dick's novel.[2] The novel, in fact, depicts a crisis caused when this institutionally sanctioned cultural relativism and an attendant loss of future goals meet with certainties of cultural myth in a post-nuclear-war America, which are justified within the narrative world.

The World Jones Made opens with a small group of specially bred human mutants attempting to escape an environmentally controlled enclosure; their ultimate emigration from Earth and resettlement on Venus is the parallel plot to the rise and fall of the charismatic prophet, Floyd Jones. The link between the two plot lines is a secret police agent, Doug Cussicks, who is charged with protecting the mutants from the racialist, mutant-hating followers of Jones until they are safely off Earth.

Dick employs assumptions and prescriptions from two myth clusters that both involve the Frontier as a generative and defining space for American identity. Broadly speaking, these two versions are based upon, on the one hand, an agrarian ideal and, on the other, a growing conflict with the indigenous population, typifying the Frontier as a marker between productive agriculture (and *civilization*), on the inside, and the *wilderness* of savage war-fare with the "Indians" (a conflict termed "regeneration through violence" by Slotkin) on the outside. The agrarian sub-myth features yeoman farmers, represented in Dick's novel by the aspirations and actions of the Venus-bound mutants; the regeneration-through-violence sub-myth involves warriors dedi-cated to an "ethnogenesis" agenda of race improvement through warfare, here led by the figure of Floyd Jones. Both of these versions of the Frontier myth co-exist and overlap on many points, in historical texts as in Dick's novel. In *The World Jones Made*, they occur as two distinct ecologies and, eventually, as two different worlds.

One prevalent form of the regeneration-through-violence Frontier dynamic is derived from Roosevelt's account of the progress of the "Anglo-Saxon race" (Slotkin, *Gunfighter* 42–44). Here, a select group flees a decadent metropolis for the challenges of a Frontier outpost, eventually coming into conflict with the indigenous population. For Roosevelt, this process is one of "race conflict" in which savage means are not only necessary, but justified. It results in a successful colony, which serves as a center for another round of the cycle.

Floyd Jones, a precognitive mutant who can predict one year of the future with absolute certainty, represents the regeneration-through-violence dynamic. Even though he himself is the product of a family farm, the agrarian impulse holds little charm for him; after the war he could not return to "the monotony of farm chores [and] the aimless activity of the farm" (Dick 52).

Jones is an interesting figure in a discourse so heavily charged with cultural myth, as he himself is tragically doomed to relive his known "future history," without the power to change it. His factual precognition, furthermore, is proble-matic for the authorities and their ideology of tolerance, so-called "Hoff's Rela-tivism." This officially sanctioned ideology is intended to curb the excesses that triggered the nuclear war; it allows one to say whatever one wants, as long as it can be proven. Any matter of opinion, however, is strictly against the law; and thus, the potential force of religions or other totalizing belief systems seems to be disabled.

Jones is revealed as a carnival side-show act, obsessed with a pronounced dislike for the visitation of Earth by interstellar migrants known as "drifters." Though the drifters are unthreatening gelatinous blobs, and in spite of the heavy protection the newly founded Federal Government, "Fedgov," for short, enjoys, Jones's rhetoric and mission and the attendant interaction between Jones's followers and the interstellar migrants play out the regeneration-through-violence sub-myth.[3]

First, the Earth is positioned as the invaded Frontier, demanding a strong defensive gesture to prevent drifter colonization of the home planet of *Homo sapiens*: "Why do you think the drifters are here? It's obvious they're settling. They're doing what we should be doing: they're out searching for habitable planets" (Dick 41). This explanation is based upon Jones's application of the template of the myth to new circumstances: In this case, it is the drifters who undergo a separation that will lead to their "regeneration" and the humans are cast in the role of Native Americans.

With relentless energy and vision, Jones's characterization of the drifters initiates a groundswell movement that slakes humanity's thirst for purpose, meaning, and hope. His myth-ideology enables him to garner support by mandating "savage war" on the invaders at home (61) and by sending out scouting ships to exterminate them while searching for inhabitable worlds for humankind (73), turning the tables on the invaders by savage warfare as a legitimate part of territorial expansion endorsed by the Frontier myth. In line with the mythic presuppositions of the character of Frontier spaces, Earth, the civilized center, is "overpopulated [and] undernourished," corrupted beyond repair, but the universe could supply "[e]ndless resources" and a refuge for those fed up with Fedgov's restrictions and longing to exercise their initiative (41). For those who accept Jones's mythically corroborated premises, there is only one possible answer: "ON TO THE STARS" (103).

The hatred for the drifters and the violence depicted against them are clearly criticized by Dick. Yet ambiguity is present: The fact that Jones does indeed motivate people to actions they find meaningful is not lost on the police agent Cussicks, his wife, and his boss, who observes: "[W]ithout the spur, the hatred, the sense of fighting an enemy, we just sit around" (84). However, the second narrative of Venus-bound mutants gives the lie to this, for this program, under the aegis of Fedgov, has no other purpose than successful interplanetary colonization, writing the imperial ambitions of the historical assumptions of Manifest Destiny larger upon the solar system.

Jones and his movement have incorporated the meta-narratives endorsed by the regeneration-through-violence mythology; when the mutants arrive on Venus, the agrarian sub-myth variant of the mythologies of the American West is unequivocally recognizable. Ironically, this small group of mutants are themselves the product of a form of genetic manipulation, with the express intent of acclimatizing them to the environment they will come to colonize.

Unlike the ethnogenesis subtext of the regeneration-through-violence sub-myth, essentially presupposing the old Darwinian saw of the "survival of the fittest," the Venus mutants are the product of a scientist-cum-patriarch, Doctor Rafferty. Having removed "embryos [from his] wife's womb and placed [them] in an artificial membrane," Rafferty proudly informs agent Cussicks: "I sired each one of them; my wife and I are the parents of the whole group" (112). The "natural" method of sending shiploads of humans to Venus in the hopes that a handful would adapt to the environment is deemed too costly and too slow (116). Rather, taking a cue from Aldous Huxley's *Brave New World* (1931), the embryos are exposed to the stresses of Venus to help them adjust to their future habitat.

> If this works, if the mutants survive, we can go and perfect our techniques. Develop mutant colonies for various other planets, for more radical environments. Eventually, we can populate the universe – survive anywhere. If we succeed, we'll have conquered totally. The human species will be indestructible. (116)

While the method is smoothed with scientific efficiency, Fedgov's aims and those of Floyd Jones and his followers are not so different. Both are intending actions that will spread humankind to the interstellar Frontier, able to "survive anywhere" and "[conquer] totally" (116).

Lest Doctor Rafferty's sanguine hopes strike the reader as exaggerated, an 1846 letter written by explorer, politician, and land speculator William Gilpin provides some historical perspective on Manifest Destiny. Gilpin would become a major figure in the Republican Party under Lincoln, and as a young man he strongly advocated a transcontinental railway to transform North America into an American empire, settled and developed by the efforts of stout pioneer farmers. He writes:

> The *untransacted* destiny of the American people is to subdue the continent – to rush over this vast field to the Pacific Ocean [...] – to regenerate superannuated nations [...] – to confirm the destiny of the human race – to carry the career of mankind to its culminating point. (Gilpin qtd. in Smith, *Virgin Land* 37)

As is apparent, the inventors of Manifest Destiny in the early and middle part of the nineteenth century were content with "only" one continent. The technological possibilities inherent in the *zeitgeist* of the postwar years have merged in Dick's novel with these myth-justified aspirations, legitimating ambitions that go beyond continents. And, once the colony is established on Venus, it is clear that the agrarian strain of the mythology of the American West may not be free of some of the presuppositions of its more aggressive myth partner.

Only two of the twenty chapters of *The World Jones Made* take place on planet Venus. While they require some point of reference to make sense of the new landscape, they uncritically adopt the agrarian myth. Feature after feature is spun out that corresponds to a Frontier freeholder farm. Dieter, a settler, has domesticated a "dobbin," which pulls a homemade wagon (148). As the wagon rolls through the countryside to Dieter's homestead, the topography of the yeoman farm is superimposed on the Venusian geography.

> Behind them, Louis' cabin dwindled. He and Irma had single-handedly built it. [...] The cabin [...] was surrounded by acres of cultivated land. The so-called *corn* grew in dense clumps; it wasn't really corn, but it functioned as corn. [...] Standing glumly in the shed beyond the cabin were a variety of indigenous herbivores, drowsily munching moist hay. A number of species had been collected; [...] Already, ten types with edible flesh had been catalogued, plus two types secreting drinkable fluids. (149)

Corn, cart, cabin, crops, four seasons of cultivation – the agrarian ideal has made the interplanetary jump with unusual vigor. In spite of the fact that their stated intent was *not* to replicate the civilization they left, that is what they have achieved.

After the rush of relief the mutants experience when the birth of a child verifies the viability of the species (193–94), the agrarian ideal morphs into the savage warfare motif, only without violently exterminating the natives, but rather by turning them into an underclass. When the oldest mutant, Louis, inquires about a herd of bipedal creatures that Dieter has tied up, he is informed:

> "That's my herd of wuzzles. [...] Tests I've conducted show the wuzzle is more intelligent than the Terran horse, pig, dog, cat, and crow put together.
>   They're going to be our helpers," Dieter revealed sleekly. "I'm teaching that particular herd to perform routine chores. So our minds will be free for creative planning." (194–95)

With this promise of freeing time for more august pursuits, the freeholder farm is briefly cast in the light of something akin to a Southern plantation, with the wuzzles in the role of enslaved Native or African Americans. But there are also some strains of the ethnogenetic subtext of the savage warfare mythology when the newborn child is referred to as "the new wuzzle. The replacement wuzzle, a better wuzzle to take the place of the old" (198).

In *The World Jones Made*, the ethnogenesis element inherent in the migration of the drifters and the settler colonization on Venus of the mutants casts humans first as victims and then as benefactors in this myth dynamic. While criticizing some particulars – the mob action against the drifters, for instance – this novel still uncritically embraces the mythologies of the Frontier. Even though the race-hatred of Jones is criticized, the assumption that enslaving and replacing the former dominant species of Venus is natural, and indeed propitious, demonstrates the power of myth to disguise a culture's fundamental – naturalized – assumptions, which thus become invisible to critique, exacerbating an evaluation of the character of historical events or finding solutions to future challenges.

Notes

1 In Sacvan Bercovitch and Myra Jehlen's *Ideology and Classic American Literature*, most of the section entitled "Reassessments" features essays by Nash Smith, Marx, and Slotkin wherein they each requalify their views in light of a revision of the ideological presuppositions that have been uncritically absorbed into their critique. Smith is aware that an assumption of North America as "empty" has worked its way into his analysis: "[When] I imagined I was operating without hypotheses, I was sometimes unwittingly using those of Turner" ("Symbol and Idea" 27). Marx

relents in his argument for insulating myth critique from the political, connecting "political pastoralism [with] the mentality figured forth by 'classic' American literature" ("Pastoralism" 36). And Slotkin's cultural myth perspective is transformed from the naturalness of "archetype" to an analytical tool that is anthropologically supported and culturally contingent ("Myth" 75–78).

2 The accompanying volume, bound *dos-à-dos*, was Margaret St. Claire's *Agent of the Unknown*. The Ace Double as publisher is practically a guarantee of its novels' "pulp" credentials, though this form of publication was not reserved for science fiction. William S. Burroughs's first book, *Junky* (1953), was also published this way.

3 The reader will be struck by Dick's use of Nazi Germany as a reference point in this novel, a characteristic of a significant portion of his early work (Sutin 46, 113–14).

Works cited

ABC News. "Bush Says Bin Laden Wanted Dead or Alive." 17 Sept. 2001. http://abcnews.go.com/Politics/story?id=121319 Web. 22 May 2014.

Bercovitch, Sacvan, and Myra Jehlen, eds. *Ideology and Classic American Literature.* Cambridge: Cambridge UP, 1987. Print.

Birgel, Franz A. "The Only Good Indian is a DEFA Indian: East German Variations on the Most American of all Genres." *International Westerns: Relocating the Frontier.* Ed. Cynthia J. Miller and Bowdoin Van Riper. Plymouth: Scarecrow P, 2014. 37–62. Print.

Cantor, Paul A. "'Order out of the Mud': *Deadwood* and the State of Nature." *The Philosophy of the Western.* Ed. Jennifer L. McMahon and B. Steve Csaki. Lexington: UP of Kentucky, 2010. 113–38. Print.

Cawelti, John G. *Adventure, Mystery, and Romance: Formula Stories as Art and Popular Culture.* Chicago, IL: U of Chicago P, 1976. Print.

---. "Masculine Myths and Feminist Revisions: Some Thoughts on the Future of Popular Genres." *Mystery, Violence, and Popular Culture: Essays.* Madison: U of Wisconsin P, 2004. 79–94. Print.

---. *The Six-Gun Mystique Sequel.* Madison: U of Wisconsin P, 1999. Print.

Dick, Philip K. *The World Jones Made.* 1956. New York: Vintage, 1993. Print.

Geertz, Clifford. *Local Knowledge: Further Essays in Interpretive Anthropology.* New York: Basic Books, 1983. Print.

James, Edward. *Science Fiction in the Twentieth Century.* Oxford: Oxford UP, 1994. Print.

Kolodny, Annette. *The Lay of the Land: Metaphor as Experience and History in American Life and Letters.* Chapel Hill: U of North Carolina P, 1975. Print.

Marx, Leo. *The Machine in the Garden.* Oxford: Oxford UP, 1964. Print.

---. "Pastoralism in America." *Ideology and Classic American Literature.* Ed. Sacvan Bercovitch and Myra Jehlen. Cambridge: Cambridge UP, 1987. 36–69. Print.

Moody, Nickianne. "Crime in Film and on TV." *The Cambridge Companion to Crime Fiction.* Ed. Martin Priestman. Cambridge: Cambridge UP, 227–44. Print.

Quay, Sara E. *Westward Expansion.* Westport, CT: Greenwood P, 2002. Print.

Roosevelt, Theodore. *The Winning of the West.* Vol. 3. *The Founding of the Trans-Alleghany Commonwealths 1784–1790.* 1889. Lincoln: U of Nebraska P, 1995. Print.

Slotkin, Richard. *Gunfighter Nation: The Myth of the Frontier in Twentieth-Century America.* New York: Atheneum, 1992. Print.

---. "Myth and the Production of History." *Ideology and Classic American Literature.* Ed. Sacvan Bercovitch and Myra Jehlen. Cambridge: Cambridge UP, 1987. 70–90. Print.

---. *Regeneration through Violence: The Mythology of the American Frontier, 1600–1860.* Middletown, CT: Wesleyan UP, 1973. Print.

Smith, Henry Nash. "Symbol and Idea in *Virgin Land.*" *Ideology and Classic American Literature.* Ed. Sacvan Bercovitch and Myra Jehlen. Cambridge: Cambridge UP, 1987. 21–35. Print.

---. *Virgin Land: The American West as Symbol and Myth.* Cambridge, MA: Harvard UP, 1970. Print.

Sutin, Lawrence. *Divine Invasion: A Life of Philip K. Dick.* London: Harper Collins, 1989. Print.

Tompkins, Jane. *West of Everything: The Inner Life of Westerns.* Oxford: Oxford UP, 1992. Print.

Turner, Frederick Jackson. *The Frontier in American History.* 1893. New York: Holt, 1953. Print.

7 The city and the country

Complicated places in Toni Morrison's *Jazz*

Dorothea Löbbermann

Introduction

In this chapter, I want to pursue a simple argument: that in American culture, the city and the country are complicated places. I am using Toni Morrison's novel *Jazz* to exemplify this. Published in 1992 – one year before the author was awarded the Nobel Prize in Literature – its story takes place in 1920s New York, with flashbacks leading into the rural South of the nineteenth century. This timeframe allows us to consider a long historical stretch, from the era of American urbanization to late twentieth century's concepts of urbanity. A complex literary text, *Jazz* plays with and helps us analyze cultural and literary traditions, themes, and representational strategies. Focusing on Black American history, and written by an African American woman, it lets us understand better how city texts, which are predominantly written from a white perspective, are raced and gendered. Furthermore, a self-reflexive narrative situation allows us to analyze the problems of urban representation. Last but not least, Morrison's novel helps us reflect on the mystification not only of the city, but also the country. I will begin this chapter with an overview of the relationship between city and country in American culture in order to establish the parameters within which *Jazz* can be understood as a cultural text.

The city and the country are important social, economic, and symbolic spaces in American culture that enjoy a rich historical relationship. This relationship is characterized by a structure of opposition that pits city and country against each other. In the colonial period, for instance, European settlers understood the city as a bulwark of white homogeneity and moral control ("civilization") against the alleged wilderness of the Natives (see Danbom). In the twentieth century, in contrast, urban space was often depicted as a wilderness in itself, an uncontrollable "concrete jungle" inhabited no longer by a white elite, but by immigrants of diverse classes and "races."

Examples of the oppositional structure between country and city abound. They find a source in the 1790s debate between Thomas Jefferson and Alexander Hamilton, who envisioned the future of the nation as either decentralized and agrarian or federalized and urban. Congress voted for Hamilton's proposal, which set off the gigantic process of the United States' urbanization at the same time as it made the country a symbol of freedom (i.e., freedom from state control). This debate has had many repercussions in American culture and explains how central the concepts of city and country are for American national identity. And it is still alive, even if processes of suburbanization, digital media, and the New Urbanism have somewhat detached this conflict from topography.

The cultural work of fiction and representation

The city and the country, then, are concepts as much as they are topographical places and social spaces. Cultural artifacts – paintings, photographs, movies, and novels of urban and rural spaces – give expression to these concepts, creating ever-new materializations. They can perpetuate and reinforce myths, and they can alter and modify them. They can also deconstruct them and discuss the myth's usefulness; they can make places complicated.

And complicated is what these places are. The simple opposition of country (with the connotations of either "free" or "backward") and city ("oppressive" or "liberal") occludes the fact that both cities and rural spaces are complex, multidimensional, and internally contested places. The rural South in the nineteenth century is a site of white gentility (*and* poverty) as well as of African American slavery (*and* resistance). Plantation novels and slave narratives are cultural expressions of these different concepts.

Likewise, the city of the twentieth century is an immoral jungle (Martin Scorsese's *Taxi Driver*, 1976), a site of middle-class desire and sophistication (Woody Allen's *Manhattan*, 1979), a semiotic labyrinth (Paul Auster's *City of Glass*, 1985), a battle-ground of African American masculinities (Gordon Parks's *Shaft*, 1971), and so on. All of these concepts unfold in the same space (New York City) and roughly at the same time. But they are not only different *interpretations* of the place; in their sum they also make us see how many concepts of it coexist.

The city and the country in American Studies: "America" as "country"

When American Studies were founded in the 1930s, the common understanding of the United States was rural rather than urban. This idea of "American" culture as a product of the country, of the land, of nature – country is a slippery notion, really – stems, in part, from the history of American colonization and late urbanization, and in part from the American desire to distinguish itself from Europe. Early American Studies thus stressed the significance of nature and landscape in American literature and painting of the 1850s (see Matthiessen) or the myth of the West as "virgin land" (see Henry Nash Smith). As early as 1964, Leo Marx identified an "urge to idealize a simple, rural environment" in American popular and literary culture, which he traces back to Jean de Crèvecoeur's idealization of the rustic American in his 1782 *Letters from an American Farmer* (Marx 5). This is the ideal against which conflicts between fictional characters and their environment unfold.

Both in literature and painting, American culture of the eighteenth and nineteenth centuries was mainly dedicated to the representation of rural spaces (see, e.g., the stories of Washington Irving, the novels of James Fenimore Cooper, the paintings of Frederick Church). In the later nineteenth century the genre of local color fiction explored the varieties of American cultures in their regional specificities from the consciousness of an urbanizing nation (e.g., Kate Chopin, Willa Cather, Sarah Orne Jewett). Indeed, the rural aspects of America continue to be significant for US cultural production: see literary texts in which white male characters fight with or within (post-)nature (e.g., Ernest Hemingway, Annie Proulx, Cormack McCarthy) or Native American writers' redefinitions of the relationship between humans and land (Sherman Alexie, Leslie M. Silko) or films that explore the "Big Country" as a visual and social space, most importantly Western movies (e.g., William Wyler's *The Big Country*, 1958).[1]

The city and (post-)modernity

Within an ideology shaped by agrarianism, the city became the "other" space. Considered the first American city novel, George Lippard's sensationalist and best-selling *The Quaker City: A Romance of Philadelphia Life, Mystery, and Crime* (1845), with gusto demonizes the city where innocent girls melo-dramatically end in captivity and prostitution and innocent men are drawn into an abysmal underworld. The detective plots that Edgar Allan Poe intro-duced stem, at least partially, from this gothic tradition. With the establishment of realism in American literature, the city became a "contact zone"[2] that represented the nation in a nutshell. In William Dean Howells's *A Hazard of New Fortunes*, for instance, New York is the place where Northerners and Southerners, European immigrants, radicals and conservatives, ambitious men and women meet in the founding of a new magazine and negotiate post-Civil-War democracy. When regionalism focused on diverse (but internally coherent) rural cultures that were spread across the nation, city novels explored dynamic urban places of heterogeneous diversity where people of many classes, "races," and ethnicities shared a relatively small space, creating new urban cultures. Urban heterogeneity became a cornerstone in the city's cultural treatment, both on a social level, where questions have been directed at diversity of class, ethnicity, "race," gender, sexuality, etc., and on an aesthetic level, where questions have been directed at a multiplicity of motifs, symbols, voices, perspectives, etc. Whether romanticized or demonized, the city was a place of difference.

At the beginning of the twentieth century, modernism celebrated this city in a new, intermedial fashion. (Toni Morrison's *Jazz*, as we will see, alludes to this literature, painting, and music). For instance, many artists turned Brooklyn Bridge into a multidimensional symbol – Hart Crane in his poem

"The Bridge," Joseph Stella in numerous paintings, Alfred Stieglitz in photography. John Dos Passos applied cinematic techniques and the principle of collage to his novel *Manhattan Transfer*; and in their film *Manhatta*, Paul Strand and Charles Sheeler combined lyrical, painterly, and cinematographic expressions. And urban jazz had a tremendous influence on modern poetry (by African American as well as white American poets). The Harlem Renaissance of the 1920s and '30s, the setting of Morrison's *Jazz*, was the first distinctly urban movement of African American literature, art, music, and politics.

If modernism was the moment in which artists sought to find the heterogeneous city's "synthetic totality" (Balshaw and Kennedy 2), postmodernism – the period within which Morrison writes – is the moment in which fragmentation is no longer forced into a conceptual or aesthetic whole. Stories become increasingly disjointed, increasingly local, and increasingly partial. According to Günter H. Lenz, students of American Studies today need to "explore metropolitan culture(s) as a palimpsest of multiple and different layers and contending meanings." In this setting, urban texts become "intertextual and intermedial force-fields of competing fictions" (12). These texts may identify the city as a labyrinthine text in itself, as Auster's *New York Trilogy* (1987) or David Lynch's film *Mulholland Drive* (2001) perform it (in both, protagonists get lost in a maze of literary and cinematographic allusions to New York and Los Angeles, respectively). Or they may explore race struggles and new urban ethnicities: e.g., Paul Haggis's film *Crash* (2004), Paul Beatty's novel *Tuff* (2000). Or they may explore gender relations, as Siri Hustvedt does when she identifies the urban flâneur as a masculine figure into which her female character slips (*The Blindfold*, 1992) or as Sarah Schulman does in exploring LGBT communities (*Rat Bohemia*, 1995).

As these topics suggest, the city is no longer America's "other" place, but has become a metaphor for (post)modern society (see Balshaw and Kennedy 5–6). It is now the country that has become "other" – as a place for alternative community projects (from 1960s' hippies to contemporary organic farmers). However, if we look closely, this otherness has softened. There is a great continuity between country and city today. A "New Urbanism" has reclaimed the inner cities as commercial and creative centers of an allegedly "post-racial" affluent middle class, creating small town values in the metropolis (see Katz; Neil Smith). At the same time the country – where agriculture is completely industrialized – has become a site for recreation and tourism, i.e., for institutions that reinforce the myth of the country as wholesome, yet stand within the economy of the city. It is this cultural situation within which Toni Morrison's *Jazz* has to be read.

Toni Morrison's *Jazz*

Jazz tells the story of Joe and Violet Trace, an African American couple, who in 1906 leave the racist South for Harlem, New York. The main story takes place in 1926: Joe has fallen in love with a young girl, Dorcas, whom he kills when he realizes that he cannot possess her. At Dorcas's funeral, Violet tries to disfigure the dead girl's face with a knife. Both Violet and Joe have to come to terms with their respective desires and their violent actions, which they do in connecting to the Harlem community and to their respective youth in 1870s rural Virginia. The novel concludes in a spirit of complicated harmony, as Violet and Joe manage to create an almost rural, community-oriented life style in the modern city.

"The City" (as New York is called throughout the novel) is not simply the setting of *Jazz*, but a powerful force, made strong by its inhabitants' needs. Traumatized by their Southern past, the characters desire so much from it that it – or rather, their concept of it – guides their actions. On the train ride to New York in 1906, Violet and Joe imagine the City as a lover/mother:

> They weren't even there yet and already the City was speaking to them. They were dancing. And like a million others, chests pounding, tracks controlling their feet, they stared out the windows for first sight of the City that danced with them, proving already how much it loved them. (32)

It is this love story between the City and its inhabitants that the novel tries to explore. I want to highlight two elements through which Morrison approaches the representation of urban space – genre and narration – that I will discuss in the following.

Genre: detective novel

The center of the plot is Joe's murder of Dorcas. Crime and violence are strong tropes in urban representations. For the genteel middle-class consciousness, the modern, industrialized cities, which attracted an uncontrollable mass of migrants, were prone to vice, crime, violence. City life was thought to be characterized by isolation, and it was murder rather than friendship that connected urbanites. This is why detective fiction has become such a strong urban genre: The power that the detective holds over the imagination stems from the desire to understand the city. Both in literature and film, the detective's work of solving a murder mystery has the larger meaning of explaining the mysteries of the city (see Trachtenberg).

However, Morrison's use of the crime motif varies from traditional genre conventions (see Tally 31–58). In *Jazz*, the search is not for the killer, who is known from the beginning of the text, but for his motives and, even more so, for ways of understanding, reconciliation, responsibility. And instead of a detective who solves the case, we have several characters employed in the reading of signs, the following of traces, the observation of people. One of them is Joe who, once the apprentice of a hunter, is looking for Dorcas as if for prey; another one is Violet, who needs to find out everything about Dorcas and her husband's attraction to her. Most of all, however, the novel's narrator is reading clues and predicting consequences. The desire to detect, the desire to spy, to stalk, is as inherent in these acts as is the desire to find the truth. It is this *desire* to piece together the city that is inherently urban and that is expressed not only in the genre allusion, but also in the figure of the narrator.

Narration

In *Jazz*, Morrison dramatizes the "how" of the telling of the city. Her reference point is the modernist representation of the city, which I sketched out above. Morrison is interested in how modernist writers created almost heroic narrators and in the parts of the city these writers ignore in the process of creating urban totality. The following excerpt shows how the first-person narrative voice is seduced by the city, as it seduces the reader:

> I'm crazy about this City.
>   Daylight slants like a razor cutting the buildings in half. [...] A city like this one makes me dream tall and feel in on things. Hep. It's the bright steel rocking above the shadow below that does it. When I look over strips of green grass lining the river [...] and into the cream-and-copper halls of apartment buildings, I'm strong. Alone, yes, but top-notch and indestructible – like the City in 1926 when all the wars are over and there will never be another one. (7)

The lyricism of this passage – its syncopated rhythm, its bifurcated imagery – has the same power over the reader as the city has over the narrator. Indeed, the narrator charms the reader as the city charms the narrator (see Balshaw 93). Echoing paintings of American modernism in which high-rises and elevated tracks create abstract areas of light and shadow, this passage illustrates how the description of the modernist city empowers the narrator, who imparts this feeling of strength to the reader.

But the reader is also made aware of the deception that the city enacts. The double meaning of "crazy" in the first line is the first indicator for this; besides, every reader of *Jazz* knows that "all the wars" were not "over" in 1926. Morrison here undermines the narrator's credibility. There are limits to the narrator's knowledge and power.

Cities, in the words of Hana Wirth-Nesher, "promise plentitude, but deliver inaccessibility" (8). The city that "loves" Joe and Violet, the city that the narrator is "crazy about," is the fantasy of a total entity – "the City." This city will always remain a fantasy because cities can never be grasped in their entirety, neither in representation nor in life. The city is "rendered legible [...] by multiple acts of imagination" (Wirth-Nesher 9) – both in real life (I imagine the urban spaces I have no access to because I am too Black/white, too female/male, too rich/poor) and, in intensified form, in representation (see Wirth-Nesher 10).

We can observe this in Morrison's *Jazz* through the narrator's wish to control the story. "Sth, I know that woman," is the first sentence in the novel (3), pulling the reader into the gossipy situation of neighbors talking, in this case, about Violet. But this narrative voice, which in the beginning of the text is so sure of its knowledge – it even predicts another murder to happen in the end (6) – eventually realizes that it drew the wrong conclusions: "So I missed it altogether" (220). The narrator therefore dramatizes the impossibility to know what happens in the city and to represent it truthfully and in its entirety.

The narrator's partial blindness is one way in which the narrative expresses its urbanity. Another way is its multivoicedness. The narrator's voice alternates with the voices of individual characters who become first-person narrators (e.g., Joe, 121–35) or with extended passages told from a character's perspective (e.g., Violet's, in passages throughout the text). Characters come into focus with individual narrative perspectives – the dead girl's best friend, the dead girl's aunt – throwing a new light on the protagonists whom the readers thought they knew and enlarging the mosaic of voices and perspectives. This overlapping of voices, this fragmented narration, this unfulfilled desire to know more about the others, recreates the city's heterogeneity.

This multiperspectival technique is not essentially urban (William Faulkner has prominently used it in his rural fiction), but it has become understood as a means to capture the city. A contemporary popular example of this is the multiplot film. These movies that do not center on one protagonist and their story, but create a web of intersecting stories with multiple protagonists – like *Short Cuts* (1993), *Crash*, or *Magnolia* (1999) – use this technique to dramatize the racial tensions within cities, the discrepancies between the rich and the poor, the missed chances between characters.

De/mystifying city and country

What the narrator of *Jazz* "misses altogether" is the characters' ability to transform the city into a home. "It was loving the city that distracted me," the narrator confesses, while the characters were "putting their lives together in ways I never dreamed of" (220–21). This love for the city, I claim, is Morrison's translation of the fascination with the city as it was expressed in modernism; its failure is an expression of her skepticism toward this fascination. The city, Morrison says, promises freedom, equality, and justice to the disenfranchised African American population of the beginning of the twentieth century, but it cannot keep these promises. At the end of the twentieth century, when the novel was written, it is clear that American cities are still segregated and divided by "race" and income (see Neil Smith; Keith and Cross). However, demystifying the city is not the original work of *Jazz* (this is a topos in urban representation): It is demystifying the cultural work of modernist representation that makes this novel such an important piece of writing.

And it is not only the city that is demystified here, but so is the country. The African American perspective of *Jazz* enables us to see through the ideological constructions of the rural myth. From an African American perspective, the country does not connote freedom but slavery and its equally violent aftermath. It does not connote whiteness or racial purity, but a complicated racial history of oppression, violence, and miscegenation. But neither does the country connote naivety and ignorance: African Americans and other oppressed groups were always in the position to deconstruct the myths; they were always already modern subjects. "I've been a New Negro all my life," muses Joe in *Jazz* (129), alluding to a term that expressed the Harlem Renaissance concept of a new Black modernity (see Locke).

In contrast to the urban passages of *Jazz*, however, the country is not described in detail, as landscape. *Jazz* is told from a historical perspective in which the city is the "other." Where the city is an object of fascination that is invoked in many powerful descriptions of the dazzling cityscape, the country is just there. It is not an object of the gaze but an environment in which characters act and react.

The country is the place of the ancestors, but not all of them are supportive. Violet's grandmother feeds her granddaughter dangerous stories about a beautiful white-looking boy, her mother commits suicide, Joe's mother is a madwoman living in the wilderness. Slavery is in every family's recent past, and the county is characterized by racial violence, dispossession, and poverty. It is this experience that creates Violet's and Joe's desire for the city; it is this experience with their ancestors that makes it hard for them to become old.

The novel ends with a glimpse of happiness that is urban and rural at the same time. In their attempt to understand the murder, the girl who died, and her attractiveness to Joe, Violet reaches out to other characters, and eventually creates a network that brings herself and Joe back into the community. Their life now has the sereneness of country life: On evening walks, "if they get tired they sit down and rest on any stoop they want to and talk weather and youthful misbehavior to the woman leaning on the sill of the first-floor window" (223). Morrison here transforms the urban cityscape into a community space with country values (see Morrison, "City Limits").[3] This country, however, is not a sentimental projection but a complicated place.

Conclusion

The complicated character of the city in *Jazz* finds a guiding metaphor in the motif of music that runs through the whole text. Within an arguably "jazzy" structure,[4] references to dancing (see the first quotation, above), musicians, and jazz parties abound. Equally important are references to music's material culture: to records, record players, and the music industry. Morrison captures the historical moment when rural blues enters the urban scene, which creates new styles (urban blues, jazz) and subjugates these to a system of commercial profit. The Jazz Age was founded on this proliferation of Black music, which was distributed mainly by a white industry and was soon taken over by white performers. A novel like F. Scott Fitzgerald's *The Great Gatsby* (1925) can describe 1920s New York with almost no references to Black culture. It is the Blackness of the Jazz Age – "the click of dark and snapping fingers" (227) – that Morrison restores to the cultural imagination. In writing Blackness into the modern American city, *Jazz* challenges its readers to rethink (white and Black) representations of urban space as *raced*. At the same time, Morrison uses the complex structure and potentially open form of jazz as a foil on which her complex narration of city and country unfolds.

Notes

1 Of course many more genres beside the Western focus on rural spaces. Influential TV shows like *Little House on the Prairie* and *The Waltons* have glorified the country; the recent television serial *True Detective* demonizes post-Katrina Louisiana.
2 Mary Louise Pratt's concept of the "contact zone" is useful to explore the city as a site of difference, see Lenz.
3 In her analysis of urban representation in *Jazz*, Balshaw convincingly distrusts this transformation (94–99).
4 The reception of *Jazz* has seen many attempts to compare the novel's narrative structure with a jazz composition, see Alain Munton's "Misreading Morrison" as a critique of this approach.

Works cited

Balshaw, Maria. "Elegies to Harlem: Looking For Langston and Jazz." *Urban Space and Representation*. Ed. Maria Balshaw and Liam Kennedy. London: Pluto, 1999. 118–40. Print.

Balshaw, Maria, and Liam Kennedy. "Introduction: Urban Space and Representation." *Urban Space and Representation*. Ed. Maria Balshaw and Liam Kennedy. London: Pluto, 1999. 1–24. Print.

Danbom, David B. "Why Americans Value Rural Life." *Rural Development Perspectives* 12.1 (1997): 15–8. Print.

Katz, Peter. *The New Urbanism: Towards an Architecture of Community.* New York: McGraw-Hill, 1993. Print.

Keith, Michael, and Malcolm Cross. "Racism and the Postmodern City." *Racism, the City and the State*. Ed. Michael Keith and Malcolm Cross. New York: Routledge, 1993. 1–30. Print.

Lenz, Günter H. "Mapping Postmodern New York City: Reconfiguring Urban Space, Metropolitan Culture, and Urban Fiction." *Postmodern New York City: Transfiguring Spaces – Raum-Transformationen*. Ed. Günter H. Lenz and Utz Riese. Heidelberg: Winter, 2003. 11–42. Print.

Locke, Alain, ed. *The New Negro*. 1925. New York: Atheneum, 1986. Print.

Marx, Leo. *The Machine in the Garden: Technology and the Pastoral Ideal in America.* New York: Oxford UP, 1964. Print.

Matthiessen, F.O. *American Renaissance: Art and Expression in the Age of Emerson and Whitman*. New York: Oxford UP, 1941. Print.

Morrison, Toni. "City Limits, Village Values: Concepts of Neighborhood in Black Fiction." *Literature and the Urban Experience*. Ed. Michael C. Jaye and Ann Chalmers Watts. New Brunswick: Rutgers UP, 1981. 35–43. Print.

---. *Jazz*. London: Picador, 1992. Print.

Munton, Alan. "Misreading Morrison, Mishearing Jazz: A Response to Toni Morrison's Jazz Critics." *Journal of American Studies* 31.2 (1997): 235–51. Print.

Pratt, Mary Louise. *Imperial Eyes: Travel Writing and Transculturation*. London: Routledge, 1992. Print.

Smith, Henry Nash. *Virgin Land: The American West as Symbol and Mythology*. 1950. Cambridge, MA: Harvard UP, 1976. Print.

Smith, Neil. *The New Urban Frontier: Gentrification and the Revanchist City*. London: Routledge, 1996. Print.

Tally, Justine. *The Story of Jazz: Toni Morrison's Dialogic Imagination*. Münster: LIT, 2001. Print.

Trachtenberg, Alan. "Mysteries of the Great City." *The Incorporation of America: Culture and Society in the Gilded Age*. New York: Hill and Wang, 1982. 101–39. Print.

Wirth-Nesher, Hana. *City Codes: Reading the Modern Urban Novel*. Cambridge: Cambridge UP, 1996. Print.

8   Religion and the American difference

Jan Stievermann

On 6 December 2007, the former governor of Massachusetts and then first-time contender for the presidential nomination, Mitt Romney, gave a speech at the George Bush Presidential Library in College Station, Texas. The immediate purpose of the speech was to alleviate concerns about Romney's controversial Mormon identity, but the speech also moved the audience from that fraught topic to more general reflections on "Faith in America," in both senses suggested by its chosen title. Throughout his oration Romney evoked the outstanding vitality and pluralism of religion in the United States, which he set in sharp contrast to other parts of the world. In Europe, the Christian churches "seem to be withering away," and its "magnificent cathedrals" now frequently stand empty. At the same time, the Middle East and other regions are plagued by the terrorism of "radical Islamists," who "do their preaching not by reason or example, but in the coercion of minds and the shedding of blood." Not so in America, where disestablishment created a bustling market-place of religion based on tolerance and competition through persuasion. "We do not insist on a single strain of religion," Romney emphatically asserted, "rather, we welcome our nation's symphony of faith."

The speech points to some verifiable distinguishing features of the religious situation in the United States. More importantly, however, the words of the Republican candidate reveal much about America's national ideology and the role of religion therein. Americans tend to think of their country as exceptionally religious, which, in turn, is seen as an important dimension of America's exceptionality more generally. This "religious difference" is at the same time real and imagined, not least because of the ways in which the notion of this difference shape or reinforce forms of cultural expression and behavior. While a minority of Americans, often joined by skeptical observers from abroad, is overwhelmingly critical of the (perceived) importance of religion in the nation's life, the great majority welcomes it. For them, the American "religious differ-ence" is an essential part of what holds the nation together and gives it moral purpose. It is sometimes seen as a positive sign of the United States' divine election. Many Americans, whether or not they identify with Romney's poli-tics, would join him in asserting that their religiosity is crucial to what makes America "America" and what makes Americans good citizens. They would also follow him in saying that they "do not insist on a single strain of religion."

Following a long tradition, Romney's remarks ultimately imply two separate but interconnected kinds of "faith in America." One is specific and rooted in a particular historical faith tradition or denomination at home in America; the other is theologically unspecific, without formal organization or central authority, and its primary focus is the nation itself. Following a highly influential 1967 essay by Robert Bellah, scholars generally refer to this second kind of "faith in America" as civil religion, even though Bellah's specific understanding of civil religion has received substantial criticism. The two kinds of faith in America are connected, as most religious communities in the United States have incorporated elements of the discourse of civil religion, both for affirmative and critical purposes, and developed their own version of the national vision of America as a "nation under God." There is a widely held assumption that faith in America as a nation is sustained by the particular faith traditions in America. In the following, a brief survey of religion in America will be provided, followed by a more detailed discussion of the "American religion" and its quite different renditions by Romney and Barack Obama.

Religion in America

Europe's cathedrals may not be quite as empty and America's churches, synagogues, and temples may not be quite as full as Romney pictures them. Still, there can be no question that religious vitality is stronger in the United States than in other Western nations. America has not been excluded from the processes of modernization and secularization, but, for a variety of reasons, these have played out in a different manner. American religiosity has remained robust, although it has become ever more diverse and its nature has changed quite dramatically over time, as, for instance, traditional forms of churchliness and modes of denominational organization and loyalty have eroded under the forces of individualization, pluralization, commercialization, and the socio-political polarization of US society. Yet even as they register these changes, polls and studies consistently show the continuing strength of religious beliefs, participation, and activities. According to a recent survey by the widely respected, nonpartisan Pew Research Center, more than 75 percent of all Americans today claim a religious affiliation for themselves, whether in a formal sense (probably half of all Americans are active members of a denomination), or in the sense that they strongly identify with a religious tradition or organization.[1] Even higher are the numbers of Americans who affirm more or less generic religious beliefs (Chaves 33–42), such as the existence of God or a higher power (93 percent) or of heaven (86 percent) and hell (73 percent). Around 40 percent of all Americans self-report participating in corporate worship on a regular basis; 69 percent say they pray at least several times a week. Although studies that have closely monitored the actual activities suggest that in reality their level might be significantly lower and that, for instance, probably only around 25 percent go to worship regularly (Chaves 42–54), this is still very high when compared to Western Europe. Also the very fact that 40 percent want to represent themselves as regular worshippers speaks loudly about national culture.

Overall, the United States is still a predominantly Christian country by a wide margin. About 71 percent of its citizens self-identify with some form of Christianity, and about six percent are currently affiliated with a non-Christian religious tradition. However, these six percent represent an important and persistent trend toward pluralization that has made the United States one of the world's most religiously diverse nations (see Eck). By the early twentieth century the United States was already harboring a substantial Jewish minority and small Muslim, Buddhist, Hindu, and Sikh communities, among others. The number of non-Christian Americans has increased steadily since the Hart–Celler Act of 1965 abolished national quotas on immigration. Immigrants now come predominantly from Asia, and South and Middle America, but also from the Middle East and Africa. Especially significant is the growth among the diverse Buddhist and Muslim groups: the latter might be in the process of overtaking American Jews as the largest non-Christian minority at 1.9 percent.[2]

The same developments in immigration have also spurred the further diversification of Christianity. The United States is now home to virtually all branches of both Eastern and Western Christianity that exist around the globe as well as to a few uniquely American ones. Most of these denominations are fairly small. The single largest one is the Roman Catholic Church at 20.8 percent, while American Protestant denominations collectively comprise 46.5 percent. Pluralization means, among other things, that America is on the brink of losing its traditional Protestant majority.

While the United States began as an overwhelmingly Protestant nation, even the Protestantism of the Founding Era was divided into a great multiplicity of churches and movements that had been transplanted from Great Britain (such as Anglicanism or Episcopalianism, Congregationalism, and Presbyterianism) but also from Continental Europe (such as German Lutheranism).[3] Since then Protestantism continued to proliferate by leaps and bounds, as existing traditions evolved and split, native varieties of Protestantism arose, and more and different groups were founded by European and then also non-European immigrants who kept pouring into the country and organized new ethnic churches, such as the Scandinavian Lutheran churches during the nineteenth century or the Korean Presbyterian churches of the more recent past. There are currently more than 220 Protestant churches and a host of smaller groups. Disestablishment (the separation of state and church) and free religious exercise, as guaranteed under the First Amendment of the Constitution, created an ecclesial environment (associated with the term denominationalism) in which churches are independent voluntary associations that all enjoy the same liberty to follow their beliefs and practices and to employ their own ministers, but also face the necessity of supporting themselves financially. Importantly, this means they compete with each other for adherents. In the early years of the United States, one important way some groups sought to generate large numbers of followers was through popular revivals. These aimed to produce a highly emotional conversion to a Christ- and Scripture-centered life of religious activism – the hallmarks of a new "evangelical" style of Protestantism, at once intensely experiential and practical.

This style came to dominate American Protestantism, while the more formalist but theologically liberal traditions (associated with the term mainline Protestantism) have dramatically declined in recent years and now together represent less than 15 percent. In the nineteenth century evangelical churches from two denominational families proved most adept at riding the waves of revivalism: Methodism and Baptism. Their descendants still represent the largest groups among Protestants, even as non-denominational forms of Protestantism are on the rise. A number of homegrown religious movements have also sprouted from the soil of Protestant revivalism, including Mormonism, Seventh-day Adventism, and Jehovah's Witnesses, whose particular teachings break from historic Christian dogma, but have nevertheless proven highly attractive. For instance, Mormonism is now embraced by 1.6 percent of all Americans.

In the twentieth century, evangelicals were joined by a new and rapidly growing denominational family, the Holiness and Pentecostal churches, which give even more intense expression to conversionist spirituality through enthusiastic forms of worship involving diverse gifts of the spirit. Today a quarter of the American population belong to evangelical churches, which have become more and more closely wedded to political and cultural conservatism over the past four decades. The traditional African American churches (representing 6.5 percent of the total population) are an exception to this rule; most of them are in the Baptist tradition and conjoin a specifically African American form of evangelical theology and worship with progressivist politics.

American Catholicism owes both its numerical strength and enormous heterogeneity to the shifting patterns of migration. During the nineteenth and early twentieth centuries millions of Catholics from Western and Eastern Europe arrived in the United States. But since 1965 the largest group of immigrants have been Latino Catholics, who not only have a different tradition of theology and charismatic worship but also different political interests than their co-religionists of Irish or Italian descent. This is one example of how in the United States religious and ethnic or racial identities are inseparably intertwined, which is one reason for the persistent strength of religion but also a continuous cause of conflict, internal differentiation, schisms, and denominational proliferation.

Despite or because of the constitutional separation of church and state, religion in America has also always been highly politicized – another reason for its persistent vitality but also polarizing power. Throughout US history ordinary partisan politics but also major reform causes and protest movements across the political spectrum – ranging from abolitionism, the women's rights movement, and Prohibition to the Civil Rights Movement, anti-war protests, and the campaigns of the Christian Right against legalized abortion – were driven by religious organizations and informed by theological ideas. In the current "culture wars" one also finds religious groups on both sides of the frontline, with liberal Protestants and Latino Catholics mostly supporting Democrats and white evangelicals and conservative Catholics mostly supporting Republicans.

The United States is therefore not simply more religious than most Western nations but it is also religious in a unique way: Next to pluralism and denominationalism, distinguishing features include the persistent robustness of evangelical Protestantism as a voting bloc and the way in which religion, empowered by a tradition of voluntarism and lay participation, has remained very much public and political. Indeed, religion is interwoven with every strand in the fabric of American civic and cultural life, past and present.

The American religion

In 1967 Bellah argued for the existence of a civil religion that flourished alongside the historic faith traditions in the United States and had been overwhelmingly shared by Americans, but was now in danger of collapsing in the face of the socio-cultural and racial conflicts of the 1960s. Since then scholars have pointed out the danger of giving too much credit to the mythic images and language of this civil religion and of naively accepting its inclusivist promise.[4]

Rather, American civil religion is to be understood as a symbolic discourse, a set of ritualistic practices, and as a cultural memory that seeks to create social cohesion by sacralizing a specific understanding of the nation, its institutions, founding ideals, and values. However, from the beginning, the elite of white Anglo-American Protestant men who not only ruled the nation but also dominated its public culture excluded large groups of Americans from this imagined community on grounds of their "race" or religious affiliation, even as these would also invoke their version of the founding ideals to push for a more inclusivist understanding of the nation. Well into the twentieth century the prevalent way in which American civil religion was interpreted and enacted was not only unabashedly Protestant-centered and frequently anti-Semitic as well as anti-Catholic but also had no room for African Americans or other racial minorities.

At the heart of American civil religion is the belief that the national community has, from the very beginning, stood in a special relation to the Divine (however defined) and that the revolutionary ideals of political and religious liberty, inalienable rights, and the free pursuit of happiness enshrined in the founding documents as well as the political organization of the United States are essentially an expression of divine will for man. The historic mission or destiny of the United States is to answer the divine will by realizing these ideals. Thus, the whole of American history appears as providential, as guided by a higher purpose, of which the nation might be falling short, but which is still leading it onward toward an imagined fulfillment in the future.

The historical roots of this vision of America can be traced back to the "covenantal theology" of the Puritan settlers, who understood their communities as having entered a special covenant with God and hoped that New England might be God's New Israel, chosen to play a special part in the latter days and subsequent millennium, or thousand-year reign, of Christ on earth. During the Revolutionary Era this theological tradition was amalgamated with political Republicanism as well as other elements of Enlightenment philosophy, such as the notion of natural rights and human perfectionism, and transferred to the newly founded nation as a whole (see Noll).

The resulting sense of national chosenness together with the secularized version of "civic millennialism," in which American democracy figures as the culmination point of historical progress, constitute the core of "American Exceptionalism." From the very beginning it was part of this civil religious belief in the nation's exceptionality that, as Romney would put it in 2007, "our religious liberty" is "fundamental to America's greatness." That there exists, in Romney's words, an "essential connection between the survival of a free land and the protection of religious freedom" was indeed a conviction shared by all Founding Fathers, including those who, like Franklin and Jefferson, had moved far beyond the boundaries of Protestant orthodoxy. The national edifice, in this very traditional view expressed by Romney, is based on a set of "great moral principles" or "American values" allegedly shared by all the very diverse historical religions to which its citizens hold, regardless of the "differences in theology [that] exist between the churches in America." The foundation of this assumed "common creed of moral convictions" would erode if Americans became less religious. Following a long tradition, which reaches back to Puritan Dissent, Romney thus asserts: "Freedom requires religion just as religion requires freedom."

The Puritans also bequeathed to the developing American civil religion a highly flexible mode of (rhetorical) representation. Derived from the sermon form of the Jeremiad, this mode has a basic structure of "critical affirmation," in which a chastisement of collective sins against the founding ideals goes hand-in-hand with their affirmation. In this mode, the nation's divine mission is evoked for the purposes of criticizing the nation's failure to carry it out, while even the harshest criticism ultimately asserts what is imagined to be the original promise of America. Expanding upon the work of Sacvan Bercovitch, Catherine L. Albanese has argued that this biblically based rhetoric constitutes the very foundation of the "American religion" or what she refers to as "public Protestantism" (399–400).

Ever since the Early Republic, official oratory has been a main medium of civil religion. From the days of Washington and Jefferson, inauguration ceremonies have represented a high point of such oratory, when the newly or re-elected President acts out his role as high priest of the American creed. This role is largely independent of the President's party affiliation, even though his rendition of the American creed will bear different political emphases. This is well illustrated by Barack Obama's Second Inaugural Address, delivered on 20 January 2013, which also shows how seamlessly such an enactment can move between affirmation and prophetic criticism.

Obama begins with the formulaic invocation of the "founding creed," "the enduring strength of our Constitution," and "the promise of our democracy":

> We recall that what binds this nation together is not the colors of our skin or the tenets of our faith or the origins of our names. What makes us exceptional – what makes us American – is our allegiance to an idea articulated in a declaration made more than two centuries ago.

This refers, of course, to, the Declaration of Independence, whose opening Obama then cites. After this "scripture reading" follows the exegesis and application. Obama emphasizes that "while these truths may be self-evident, they have never been self-executing," and that the past two hundred years of American history have been a continuous struggle to realize the true meaning of the freedom that America received as "a gift from God." This struggle, as articulated by Obama, has involved many things, from the fight against slavery to the programs of the New Deal, but was always carried forward by the conviction "that fidelity to our founding principles requires new responses to new challenges; that preserving our individual freedoms ultimately requires collective action." From this premise, he is then able to move on to advocate both a variety of reform agendas to address persisting national ills (the necessity of comprehensive healthcare, true racial equality, programs to improve education and advance sustainable energy sources, etc.) and an expanded understanding of national inclusiveness that would also encompass gays. This Jeremiad-like part about the unfinished task of "our generation" "to make these words, these rights, these values of life and liberty and the pursuit of happiness real for every American," is finally brought full circle with the concluding liturgical formula of all civil religious speeches: "God bless you, and may He forever bless these United States of America."

In addition to oratory, other media of civil religion are performative (parades, the national anthem, and other patriotic music), pictorial (famous paintings), or monumental (national sites or memorials). The National Mall, with its visual axes to Capitol Hill and the White House and its accumulation of war memorials, statues, and museums, is certainly the most sacred site of civil religion.

Already during the first hundred years of nationhood, as Linder puts it, there emerged a distinct and fairly stable "system of worship" that, besides the inauguration, comprised

> special ceremonies, holidays and symbols which fused piety and patriotism and melded God and country. For example, the most prominent of

the civil religion holidays have come to be Memorial Day, the Fourth of July, Thanksgiving Day, and more recently, Martin Luther King, Jr. Day, each designed to promote public expressions of faith in the chosen nation. (281)

During the same period, a stock of textual references and mythic stories of iconic heroes and martyrs developed, which to this day constitute the main repertoire of American civil religion. This repertoire, however, allows for much interpretive flexibility, and occasionally new material is also added to the unofficial canon.

Quite typically, both Romney and Obama, in addition to invoking the indispensable founding documents and Fathers, pay tribute to the sacrifices made for liberty in the Civil War (Obama also cites Lincoln's "House Divided" speech of 1858, another classic of civil religion), and America's wars abroad, undertaken, in Obama's words, to "defend our people and uphold our values." That America's foreign wars are ultimately fought so that the world might be "made safe for democracy," as Woodrow Wilson said in 1917, has been a fixture in the rhetoric of Exceptionalism since the United States, over the course of the twentieth century, became first a world power and then the world's sole superpower, which required a reconfiguration of the idea of national chosenness into that of a global "redeemer nation." Both men also allude to the 1963 March on Washington and Martin Luther King's "I Have a Dream" speech on the steps of the Lincoln Memorial, which famously pushed to expand the discourse of civil religion to include African Americans and make their struggle an expression of America's founding values. The references to King demonstrate the fairly recent, but now consensual, inclusion of King and the Civil Rights Movement (or rather of a deradicalized inter-pretation of them) into the mythic narratives of upward social mobility and the progressive advance of liberty and equality.

At the same time, each speaker puts his own political spin on these topoi and attempts to make small but significant revisionist interventions. Following his bow to the oft-cited "greatest generation," who undertook "first to defeat Fascism and then to vanquish the Soviet Union," Romney speaks about how

America faces a new generation of challenges. Radical violent Islam seeks to destroy us. An emerging China endeavors to surpass our economic leadership. And we are troubled at home by government overspending, overuse of foreign oil, and the breakdown of the family.

Romney here at least indirectly asserts the necessity and righteousness of the "War on Terror," begun by George W. Bush after 9/11, by suggesting a line of continuity between the contemporary conflicts and World War II. He likewise legitimizes a strategy of "being tough on China" by suggesting an analogy to the clash of systems with the Soviet Union during the Cold War. This dis-tinctly Republican slant on foreign policy issues is matched by an equally conservative perspective on domestic policy, where "big government" programs of the kind advocated by Obama are represented as an assault on American liberty, and the post-1960s overthrow of traditional sexual mores and family values as a threat to the nation's moral foundation. Significantly, Romney in this context implies a direct connection between "the cause of abolition, or civil rights" and the cause for "the right to life itself," thereby seeking to represent the anti-abortion movement as an expression of quintessentially American religious convictions.

Obama, on the other hand, uses the same kind of rhetorical genealogies to advocate a foreign policy built on the conviction "that enduring security and lasting peace do not require perpetual war," even as military action is necessary at times. America's greatest generation, he tells the nation, also managed to turn "sworn enemies into the surest of friends – and we must carry those lessons into this time as well." Diplomacy and international cooperation must once more become the main means through which the United States fulfills its historic mission, supporting "democracy from Asia to Africa, from the Americas to the Middle East" and acting "on behalf of those who long for freedom." For Obama, the advancement of liberty and equal rights from the Founders to Martin Luther King today finds its continuation in the fight against persistent forms of discrimination on account of gender, "race," or sexual orientation, and in the fight against growing economic injustice. Thus, Obama puts "Selma," a central site in the collective memory of the Civil Rights Movement, next to "Seneca Falls," the place of the first American women's rights convention in 1848, and "Stonewall," the bar in Greenwich Village where gay men clashed with police in 1969, catalyzing the movement for gay rights.

It is important to emphasize that civil religion not only comes to the fore on special occasions but also permeates many aspects of everyday life in America. During the Cold War, "In God We Trust" was put as a national motto on all paper currency, and the phrase "One Nation under God" was added to the Pledge of Allegiance that children in public schools recite every morning. The rituals, symbols, and values of civil religion are more or less obviously present at ordinary sport events as well as in popular films and music. Here, too, the discourse can be employed with prophetic-critical intentions. But ultimately even such usages work to strengthen a sacred sense of solidarity and loyalty to the nation as a higher spiritual unity. This cohesive function becomes especially prominent during times of crisis, such as wars, or in response to national disasters. The days and months after 9/11 saw a virtual outburst of civil religion on the official as well as on the popular level.

The defamation of Muslims as un-American after 9/11 served as a reminder that the boundaries of the civil religious discourse have always been as contested as the precise meaning of its symbols and stories. Any expansion of the original WASP self-definition of Americanness has met and continues to meet with much resistance. But as a general tendency, the American creed, which originally served to consolidate a nation dominated by white evangelical Protestantism, has been broadened to accommodate racial minorities and the country's growing ethno-religious pluralism. First, the massive immigration of Roman Catholic Christians and then "the growing importance in national life of adherents to Judaism" made it necessary in the mid-twentieth century "by definition, to enlarge the spiritual canopy of American civil religion" (Linder 282). A decisive moment for the integration of Catholics was the election of President John F. Kennedy at the height of the Cold War. Before his nomination Kennedy had to publicly confront the still-widespread anti-Roman fears and prejudices on several occasions, most famously his appearance before the Greater Houston Ministerial Association in September 1960.

Romney references this iconic moment to bolster his own candidacy in the face of deeply ingrained anti-Mormon sentiments among parts of the American population. Following Kennedy's strategy, Romney assures his audience that "no authorities of my church [...] will ever exert influence on presidential decisions," nor would he "confuse the particular teachings of my church with the obligations of the office and of the Constitution." From here Romney moves on to say how he appreciates "features in every faith I have come to know" in America (explicitly including Muslims), and how the diversification beyond the old understanding of the Judeo-Christian tradition should not be seen as a threat to the nation but a source of its moral strength, as all of these faiths are different cultural expressions of the same divine "source of life's blessings."

While still resisted in many quarters, this pluralistic vision of American religion put forth by a Mormon candidate reflects how over the course of the twentieth century, driven by forces of demographic and social change, the "American civic faith has grown conceptually from evangelical Protestantism-in-general, to Christianity-in-general, to theism-in-general" (Linder 282). It remains to be seen whether and when this discourse might also be able to incorporate members of non-theistic or polytheistic religious traditions, as in the case of Hindu and Buddhist communities. More doubtful still is how America will be able to harmonize its self-image as an exceptionally religious nation with the rapidly growing minority of "nones" (that is people who either have no specific religious affiliation or are programmatic atheists), and how this group, which currently stands at 22.8 percent, can develop and sustain civil religious commitments to the nation without the underpinnings of a historic religion.

Notes

1 Unless otherwise noted, all numbers here and in the following are from the 2014 US Religious Landscape Survey by the Pew Research Center – Pew Forum on Religion and Public Life.
2 According to the Pew survey, around 0.3 percent of the overall population today identifies with a Native American religion. For a helpful guide to the rich diversity

of traditions and groups encompassed by this category, see the *Encyclopedia of Native American Religions*, edited by Arlene Hirschfelder and Paulette Molin.

3 For a short narrative introduction to American religious history, see Gaustad and Schmidt; more comprehensive treatments are offered by Ahlstrom and in the volume edited by Stein, which also provide extensive bibliographies on a great variety of themes and subjects. An indispensable reference work is the *Encyclopedia of American Religious History*, edited by Queen, Prothero, and Shattuck.

4 For a critique of Bellah and a survey of the scholarly debate on the concept of civil religion, see Lippy.

Works cited

Ahlstrom, Sidney A. *A Religious History of the American People.* New Haven, CT: Yale UP, 1972. Print.

Albanese, Catherine L. *America, Religions and Religion.* Third ed. Belmont, CA: Wadsworth, 1999. Print.

Bellah, Robert N. "Civil Religion." *Daedalus* 96.1 (1967): 1–21. Print.

Bercovitch, Sacvan. *The American Jeremiad.* Madison: U of Wisconsin P, 1978. Print.

Chaves, Mark. *American Religion: Contemporary Trends.* Princeton, NJ: Princeton UP, 2001. Print.

Eck, Diana L. *A New Religious America: How a "Christian Country" Has Become the World's Most Religiously Diverse Nation.* New York: HarperOne, 2001. Print.

Gaustad, Edwin Scott, and Leigh Schmidt. *The Religious History of America: The Heart of the American Story from Colonial Times to Today.* Rev. ed. New York: HarperOne, 2002. Print.

Hirschfelder, Arlene B., and Paulette Molin, eds. *Encyclopedia of Native American Religions.* New York: Facts on File, 2001. Print.

Linder, Robert D. "Civil Religion." *Dictionary of Christianity in America.* Ed. Daniel G. Reid et al. Downers Grove, IL: InterVarsity P, 1990. 281–3. Print.

Lippy, Charles H. "American Civil Religion: Myth, Reality, and Challenges." *Faith in America: Changes, Challenges, New Directions.* Ed. Charles H. Lippy. Vol. 2. Westport, CT: Praeger, 2006. 19–36. Print.

Noll, Mark A. *America's God: From Jonathan Edwards to Abraham Lincoln.* New York: Oxford UP, 2002. Print.

Obama, Barack. "Second Inaugural Address." 20 Jan. 2013. Transcript at American-Rhetoric.com. Web. 11 May 2014.

Pew Forum on Religion and Public Life. *US Religious Landscape Survey.* 2014. Web. 11 Oct. 2015.

Queen, Edward L. II, Stephen R. Prothero, and Gardiner H. Shattuck, Jr., eds. *Encyclopedia of American Religious History.* Third ed. New York: Facts on File, 2009. Print.

Romney, Mitt. "Faith in America." 6 Dec. 2007. Transcript at AmericanRhetoric.com. Web. 11 May 2014.

Stein, Stephen J., ed. *The Cambridge History of Religions in America.* Cambridge: Cambridge UP, 2012. Print.

9 Politics and political institutions

Reading the American presidency in *White House Down*

Marcel Hartwig

In a nation thriving on stories, what the Founding Fathers once regarded as the "structural characteristics of the Presidency – unity, secrecy, decision, dispatch, superior source of information" (Schlesinger 18) – has, over the 240 years since the Declaration of Independence was signed, translated into the individual characteristics of a chosen "charismatic leader" (see Weber). The political institution once drafted at the 1787 Constitutional Convention was turned into an individual character sketch saturated with symbolic markers that make the American president a single-handed protector of national unity (see Shell 227). The historicity and contingency of this image of the symbolic father of the nation, however, has been concealed by a long tradition of representing the American president as a national icon in popular culture and political discourse. National achievements, historical turning points, and the memory of particular presidential characters have become the building blocks of any representation of a historical or fictional president.

Meanwhile, the cultural image of the presidency as institution, traditionally created through mythical representations of select versions of incumbents, has been naturalized into the idea of the American president as an individual and thus also fallible character that as such cannot harm the structural institution of the American presidency. Thus, the media image of the president conceals the bureaucratic apparatus that makes the American presidency. Aesthetic and narrative formulas form the notion of the American president in place of its structural characteristics. For example, it is a common tradition to represent incumbents as individual American citizens until they are elevated at the very moment they are chosen to lead.

To be sure, such a common narrative setup is directly linked to the structural idea of civilian control in the American presidency. At the Constitutional Convention of 1787 there was a firm belief in sparing America the trials and tribulations of aristocratic despotism "by making the Commander in Chief a civilian who would be subject to recall after four years" (Schlesinger 17). In the presidential narrative, then, the incumbent at the denotative level is rendered as an American citizen. At a connotative level this individual is associated with qualities such as patriotism, charisma, and virtue. At a mythic level the presidency as sign triggers an ideological notion: the political institution that produces leadership as both an individual citizen's service to the country and a result of an individual's participation in cultural mythemes such as those of self-reliance, rugged individualism, and love for the country. In that sense, media images are about "more than simple historical recreation, more than the narrative re-enactment of a public life and times" (Scott 166).

But how are these media images to be read and why are they readable at all? This seemingly naive question requires a more elaborate analysis than is apparent at first sight. After all, each media product must rely on both the political education and the cultural knowledge of its audience to be comprehensible. In order to make meaning of these images, then, one has to have a certain knowledge about a national historical continuum that constitutes the American president as a significant political institution. On its own such a continuum is indifferent to any individual at any given time. What constitutes the power of this continuum, however, is that audiences understand both the institution of the US president and its relevance to the idea of the American nation (see Chapter 8).

This further depends on the population's access to education as well as its level of media literacy. A president's relevance is made comprehensible by the media image of an individual in this position. Media images thus, at the same time, render the memory of a certain president, commemorate select activities, and function as data carriers of a collective memory. Eventually, it is the media image of the president that turns the individual incumbent into an "emotional institution" (Crawley 9). Accordingly, viewing media images of any American president, be they fictional or biographical, is a vital part of the socialization process of individual members of a larger community. Thus, by watching and comprehending presidential media images, audiences can create and indeed reaffirm a cultural knowledge about the American presidency (see Crawley 13). In this way, the assumed need for a president is naturalized. With media images comes a structure the majority of American citizens participate in that includes going to the polls, following presidential debates and announcements, obeying national laws, organizing in political groups, campaigning against a political decision, etc. A whole set of cultural experiences thus is arranged around an assumed truth of a political institution.

From this vantage point, this chapter aims at showing how the myth of the American presidency comes to life in popular culture. The film *White House Down* will serve as a case study to get to the bottom of the mythemes inherent in the political institution of the American presidency. Thus, the following argument will address origins and notions of the institution's mythology and analyze media aesthetics – that is the visual elements (i.e., lighting and picture composition), their interaction in media formats, and their perception (see Zettl 3–16) – used to render the "American" in this institution visible.

Representing the president in film

American film has focused on establishing and maintaining the American presidency as an emotional institution ever since the American Mutoscope and Biograph Company released the first presidential short film, *William McKinley at Home, Canton, Ohio* (1896). D.W. Griffith, who became Biograph's principal director, was to devote himself to capturing the emotional image of Abraham Lincoln in *Birth of the Nation* (1915)[1] and in the biopic *Abraham Lincoln* (1930). Lincoln, in fact, remained a "saint-like figure" (Mausbach, Schloss, and Thunert 16) in most of Hollywood's pre-studio and studio era productions, such as *The Dramatic Life of Abraham Lincoln* (1924), *Young Mr. Lincoln* (1939), or *Abe Lincoln in Illinois* (1940).[2]

Hollywood, in fact, seems to have a penchant for capturing the life and quality of past presidents. In *The Presidents on Film* (2007), Sarah Miles Bolam and Thomas J. Bolam list more than 400 commercial films that portray 40 out of 43 presidents. In an accompanying study, *Fictional Presidential Films*, they list about 230 films released between 1930 and 2011 showcasing fictional presidents. This tremendous stock has often staged the president as predestined leader (e.g., *Sunrise at Campobello*, 1960), as romantic widower (e.g., *The American President*, 1995), as action hero (e.g., *Air Force One*, 1997), yet occasionally also as crooked potentate who eventually turns to the better (e.g., *Gabriel over the White House*, 1933), or even as unscrupulous and unprincipled enough to allow his staff to put a blanket over murder (e.g., *Absolute Power*, 1997). In film, the president is depicted to inspire a plethora of emotions ranging from worship to ridicule to, rarely, abhorrence. Yet, by maintaining the presidency as an emotional institution, none of these films actually harms the structural characteristics of the political institution. On the whole, their focus is always on the president as an individual and thus also a potentially fallible character (see for example *Nixon*, 1995; *Frost/Nixon*, 2008; and *W.*, 2008).[3]

However, this is not to say that the medium necessarily tries to elevate into office an individual candidate, rather it is about creating an awareness of the social, political, and historical importance of the American president through the narrative of an individual, be this a fictional or historical character. In this sense then, presidential films have both a civic function and an ideological one: They inform and continue (re-)writing "history with lightning," as Woodrow Wilson once said (Benbow). Then again, they perpetuate dominant American values and myths, a belief in the necessity of the constitutional framework, and they reassure the electorate in keeping up the system. In short, they naturalize the status quo of American representative democracy.

In order to understand how media reinforce mythic messages, Roland Barthes's seminal *Mythologies* studies photography's "power to convert" (105). While promoting easy-to-remember slogans and a candidate's portrait, electoral appeal works on a level that addresses the familiar, i.e., it elicits an emotional response. In this respect, existing leaders or candidates running for an office are relieved from any markers of the truly political in their representation. Instead, photography works as an "anti-intellectual weapon [that ...] spirits away politics" (Barthes 105). Apparently, the aim of electoral photography is to satisfy the mainstream conservative need to affirm the candidate's integrity, health, and likeability (see Barthes 106). Taken together with markers of party affiliation and respective slogans, these are signs within a more complex campaign vocabulary that represents character traits as innate to a specific candidate and thus merges candidate and office as ideal image – even before the voting public would go to the polls. In other words, it addresses notions of a candidate's charisma. Hence, photographic representations of aspirants and office-holders render them as individual representatives of an emotionally charged and sanctified national institution. The faces of candidates allow filling the abstract office and institution with the charisma and personality of the indi- vidual candidate, even if this means to allow for a degree of moral uncertainty, since charismatic structures are "characteristically *unstable*" (Weber 18).

Thus, when trying to grasp the myth of the presidency, any analysis must target representations of charismatic authority that encode the strength of character hoped-for in the holder of this symbolically elevated office. As media images "parade politics [...] as part of a structure that informs the movie audience's pervasive world-view" (Scott 10), the actual decline of charismatic structures has to remain invisible in such representations.[4]

Besides film, television series elaborate a more complex media image of the presidency. This is due to the format of serial narration, which allows a vaster narrative capacity, a greater cast, several subplots, and thus the aesthetic of narrative complexity. In the twenty-first century, several television series have addressed the presidency without equating the individual president with the presidency. Accordingly, administrative positions such as the chief of staff, the communications director, and the press secretary here gain greater impor- tance. Among these, the president again appears as an individual at the center of this governmental enterprise and is rendered as an emotional institution: an idealist and scholar (*The West Wing*, 1999–2006), a disgraceful character (*Scandal*, 2012–), a principled team player (*Commander in Chief*, 2005–2006), a historical hero (*John Adams*, 2008), or a woman and representative of the African American community (*State of Affairs*, 2014–).

In genres such as electoral photography, movies, or television series, media images prove to be the furnace that is forging the notion of the "presidential." However, the Constitution of the United States does not prescribe a president's personal background. Section 1 of Article II only details the prerequisite conditions for an individual candidate to run for office, i.e., he/she should be a natural born citizen as well as a resident of the United States for at least fourteen years and should not be younger than thirty-five. Other than that, Article II settles the electoral process, the duties of the president as commander in chief of the Army and Navy of the United States, the arrangements of the annual State of the Union Address, and grounds for the removal of the incumbent. There are no prescriptions for a candidate's social status, values, denomination, ethnicity, or gender.

Peter Lösche (14–15) proposes that a candidate's presidential quality is based on his/her self-confidence, political experience, charisma, and his/her communicational skills. While political experience is a qualitative category measured by an individual's achievements, none of the other categories are self-explanatory. Rather, they address concepts that can only be grasped by the quality of emotional response a candidate can inspire in his/her electorate. As Barthes holds, in electoral photography each candidate must inspire the idea of a "physical climate" (e.g., facial features, clothes, haircut) through his/her "photogenic" qualities (106).

Added to this is the quality of the "known" characteristics of past candidates. Taking into consideration all of the forty-four American presidents,[5] the following demographics apply: "43 of the 44 American presidents have been white male" (Moore 286), "a large majority of Presidents (34 out of 41 [now 37 out of 44]) have been college graduates, [...] most (26 out of 41 [now 28 out of 44]) have been lawyers" (Gilbert 2), and forty-two of the forty-three are claimed to have King John of England as their common ancestor (see Farberov). Although these demographics help to understand the average appearance and interests of individual presidents, they are not helpful in understanding the character of the American president as an iconic figure. In order to assess the charismatic qualities of this president, it may be helpful to follow Weber and Barthes and ask how media representations of the American president render the familiar and the known visible. How do they naturalize ideology? How do these images exert their "power to convert" the voting public to maintaining the institution? How, in these representations, is the president's charismatic authority evoked? To work on these questions, this chapter will turn to a recent film representation of the American president in Roland Emmerich's *White House Down* (2013).

White House Down

In 2013, mainstream cinema saw the White House under attack no fewer than three times. Roland Emmerich's *White House Down*, Antoine Fuqua's *Olympus Has Fallen*, and Jon M. Chu's *G.I. Joe: Retaliation* all detail how terrorist groups take over the building, which is both the American president's official residence and, symbolically, the control center of American political power. What should these narrative frames tell us about the current state of American politics or even the perception of the American president?

Michael G. Krukones (143) recommends "[r]eview[ing] the movies produced in the United States during any era [... to] discover a cinematic canvas of the nation's history on which is presented the attitudes and beliefs of the people toward its leaders and political institutions." If we are to follow this instruction, the three films at hand contribute to dominant discourses of national security, foreign relations, and the strength of the executive power. Only two of these – *White House Down* and *Olympus Has Fallen* – have the president as protagonist and focus on the "redeeming hero" narrative of a member of the president's security detail. Whereas the first film features a liberal and diplomatic African American president who has to learn to raise arms instead of his voice against domestic terrorist forces, the latter shows a Caucasian widower who, after the loss of his wife, has grown too weak to make decisions beyond family concerns; he and his son are both in dire need of protection from North Korean forces during the takeover. It is only in *White House Down* that the president is allowed to show courage and become a hero himself.

Directed by a German director and screenwriter, this film merits a closer reading, not least because, to an extent, it subverts both conservative gender roles and notions about generational competence. Also, the film's fictional President James Sawyer is a film version of the sitting forty-fourth president: "Sawyer is the big-screen version of Obama, down to the Nicorette habit, professorial bent and his smart, strong First Lady," Mary Pols argues.

White House Down centers its story on the political education of a young adult flag-twirler, Emily Cale (Joey King). It illustrates how the knowledge of political institutions also impacts the social bonds with her father, a capitol policeman. As *White House Down* progresses, the relationship between Emily and her father John (Channing Tatum) who, since his divorce from Emily's mother tries to take on more responsibility for his only child, is first characterized by separation and, later, consolidation. In the film's narrative, Emily is taken as a hostage by terrorists seizing the White House. This, eventually, strengthens the bond between Emily and John.

John served in the war in Afghanistan and his absence from home has caused a split both in his marriage and in his relationship with Emily. In the film narrative, John is the living emblem of the American myth of upward mobility, of initial failure, and eventual success. Over the course of the film, the capitol policeman repeatedly has to decide whether to save the president or his own child. Eventually he learns that he can only save his daughter by saving the president. In other words, saving political institutions is saving the lives of the families that live in the sociopolitical sphere these institutions are creating. Symbolically speaking, then, saving the president and saving Emily is the same, as it means saving the national as well as the individual family.

The division in the Cale family is mirrored in the initial plot of the "national family." This is represented in the Senate's and Congress's vote on President Sawyer's "Middle East Peace Plan." At the beginning of the film, it is announced that both Democrats and Republicans will vote along their party lines, causing a tie that is reminiscent of the GOP's obstructionist stance particularly during Obama's second term in office.[6] The tie is a visible rift in domestic politics that by the same turn causes a divide in the invisible politics of national security. As soon as the vote for the Peace Plan is delayed, the terrorist attack happens. Again there is a symbolic link between the national and an individual family as the head of this attack is none other than Martin Walker, the head of the presidential security detail, who has lost his son during a military mission in the Middle East. Ultimately, this foreign policy issue has caused the division in both Cale's and in President Sawyer's families. In both the national and individual families, patriarchal characters are mediators of this breach: John with his military training and President Sawyer with his power as the nation's commander in chief who was proposing his Peace Plan at a G8 summit meeting in Geneva – symbolically a meeting of further national families.

The film revises visions of masculinity by mirroring John and President Sawyer on further levels of the narrative. Initially, John unsuccessfully seeks employment in the White House security detail and President Sawyer is unpopular due to the peace negotiations and his missing military background. Perhaps due to their early representation as "weak" men and fathers, the two protagonists are rendered as outsiders in their socio-political environments: John is taking his daughter to see the White House as compensation for a flag-twirl performance he missed at Emily's school, a symbolic reminder of his absence during the war in Afghanistan. He seems to be highly aware of his inadequacies and attempts to make up for these.

In more traditional action films, John's daughter Emily would function as the moral center. However, she is upstaged in this role by both a father who seizes moral responsibility and a president who gives family advice to John. Emily is subverting conservative gender concepts by being in a traditionally male position as a place holder for receiving and processing political information. Her character is depicted as a highly motivated schoolgirl deeply interested in national political culture. Also she is tech savvy enough to keep and operate a vlog on current government news on YouTube from any geographical location. When the American presidency, as symbolized by the White House, comes under attack by the rogue mercenary unit, this also initiates John's and President Sawyer's repositioning as symbolic father figures.

What follows is a game of replacements. John is replacing the totalitarian angry white man Walker, who wages a personal vendetta against Sawyer because of a covert military operation that cost the life of his son Kevin. John as a counter-Walker character and military hero, who has successfully returned from his combat mission, rises to be a more idealized member of staff of the presidential detail by the end of the film. By killing Walker's mercenaries, Cale is virtually erasing the followers of the corrupted father figure and restores himself as patriarchal hero for his daughter. In contrast, wrongly considered killed in action, President Sawyer is first replaced via the 25th Amendment by Vice President Hammond who has fled on Air Force One. After the terrorists shoot down the aircraft, the next to take office is Eli Raphelson, the Speaker of the House.[7]

As Raphelson and Walker eventually are discovered to have plotted the terrorist takeover as a favor to the military industrial complex, both the killing of Walker by the president and the joint dismantling of Raphelson connect the antagonists with the film's title: Cale and Sawyer literally take down the White House as run by these war-prone and rogue public servants. Both Raphelson and Walker are domestic, ultraconservative, white American paramilitary terrorists. This concept becomes readable due to their casting as old or aging white men in old-fashioned business suits, and also through the setup of their team that consists solely of white and even right-wing-activist soldiers. Visually, this conservative appearance is countered by the *mise-en-scène* of President Sawyer, who changes into Air Jordans and Cale, whose appearance is basically reduced to a muscle shirt and business trousers during the takeover.

In such clothes, they sport guns, ignore the damage they bring to the White House, and decide to risk their lives for the hostages, including Cale's daughter Emily. As a result, they both appear as nonchalant, free-minded, noble, and reckless – in short, as rugged individualists countering right-wing conservatism. Interestingly, both characters at this point of the narrative balance their revised gender performance toward a more conservative stance as well: The rugged individualist has been the quintessential male role model since the nineteenth century. In addition, in Sawyer's reckless measures, gun-slinging actions, and his casual dress, *White House Down* sustains the myth of the American president as a national hero as well as the quintessential American, who is not necessarily tied to institutional structures and has a sense of both family values (he eventually risks his life for Emily's), military duty, and honor. In the end, Cale and Sawyer not only take down corrupted government representatives, but they also foil their plans favoring the interests of the defense industry, and thus diminish the very possibility of successful lobbyism. Defeating these ideas in turn makes President James Sawyer an ideal demo-cratic leader whose Peace Plan stands for notions of (re)conciliation and progressivism.

In representing the American president, *White House Down* also takes demographic conventions into consideration. While resembling the sitting President Barack Obama, James William Sawyer's first two forenames allude to a British heritage. In the film, a news anchor refers to him as a scholarly conscientious objector and thus mocks Sawyer's higher education. The pre-sident's lack of practical experience in making political decisions on security is put to debate and visually refuted when he is shown sporting a gun, a rocket launcher, and when he eventually single-handedly kills Walker. Furthermore, Sawyer is experiencing his very private pursuit of happiness: In a telecast speech on poverty, he reveals he was raised in poor circumstances, which did not prevent him from succeeding in a steep political career. Here, he again serves as a mirror to John's story of upward mobility.

More problematic, however, is the racialized rendering of this fictional president. Not only do the film's two-shots repeatedly legitimate Sawyer's existence as being due to Cale, his white male savior who only once leaves his side and thus initiates Sawyer's reckless heroism.[8] But also Sawyer has to sport basketball shoes and at the same time has to drop his glasses before he can become the rugged action hero. Symbolically, in this vision of an ideal African American president then has to lose his brains for brawn, steal a weapon, and become trigger-happy.

Even though labeled "presidential hyper-pulp" (Rabin), *White House Down* underlines the merits of political education and informs about the American presidency not only with regard to the president's diplomatic mission, but also to his role as commander in chief. Moreover, the film manages to reformulate what Althusser and Balibar would call "the structure of the social formation" (209).[9] In addition, if Baudrillard's claim that "even outside the movie theatres the whole country [the US] is cinematic" (56) holds true, mainstream films such as *White House Down* have to be taken very seriously in their function to reconsolidate both hegemonic and resistant forces. They repeat and reinforce national myths and recreate the charismatic authority of the American president by turning the political institution into an individual character who is both successful and potentially fallible, yet who in the end saves both the domestic and the global, the private and the public, the national and the individual family/families.

In conclusion, the analysis of films dealing with the American presidency exposes the institution of cinema as an intersection of ideological myth-making and political education, as was exemplified on the basis of *White House Down* in this chapter. Hence, the cinematic fashioning of politics merges the fictional with the socio-political and subtly indoctrinates both national symbols and the myth of the American presidency.

Notes

1 By 1947, more than 200 million people had seen the film in the United States alone, see Bolam and Bolam, *The Presidents on Film* 115.
2 The "studio era," referring to a time when the American movie industry was controlled by five big production companies, ended in 1954.
3 Crawley (40) describes the various film presidents as "men of action, righteousness, moral fortitude and in the last decade, men capable of moral deceit. [...] It is only when the president shows courage that the audience is able to connect with him emotionally, thereby protecting the presidency despite the man."
4 Weber (17–24) sees the decline of individual charisma as resulting from the ongoing development of institutional structures (e.g., a party's bureaucratic apparatus).
5 This number refers to presidential terms. As Grover Cleveland is the only president to have had two divided terms (1885–1889 and 1893–1897), a total of forty-three men have held the office.
6 During a fundraiser in La Jolla, CA in May 2014, President Obama attacked the Republicans by commenting on "[t]heir willingness to say no to everything"; he concludes that because of them "nothing works" (Curl).
7 Other popular examples that narratively imagine situations of presidential succession, and thus discuss the 25th Amendment to the United States Constitution and the Presidential Succession Act, are *The Man* (1972), *My Fellow Americans* (1996), the season four finale of *The West Wing* (2003), and *Olympus Has Fallen* (2013).
8 John Cale's initials (J.C. for Jesus Christ) literally render him as a mythic white Christian savior.
9 Althusser and Balibar define social formation as the "totality of instances articulated on the basis of a determinate mode of production" (207). This is the interplay of everyday social practices and relations that are here maintained through the ideological structure of film: *White House Down* maintains the presidency as an institution of authority and tradition and reaffirms the social practice of, e.g., going to the polls to keep the political structures of domination in place.

Works cited

Althusser, Louis, and Étienne Balibar. *Reading Capital.* Trans. Ben Brewster. London: New Left, 1970. Print.

Barthes, Roland. *Mythologies.* 1957. Trans. Annette Lavers. London: Vintage, 2000. Print.

Baudrillard, Jean. *America.* 1986. Trans. Chris Turner. New York: Verso, 1988. Print.

Benbow, Mark E. "Birth of a Quotation: Woodrow Wilson and 'Like Writing History with Lightning.'" *The Journal of the Gilded Age and Progressive Era* 9.4: no page. Web. 28 Sep. 2014.

Bolam, Sarah Miles, and Thomas J. Bolam. *Fictional Presidential Films: A Comprehensive Filmography of Portrayals from 1930 to 2011.* Bloomington, IN: Xlibris, 2011. Print.

Bolam, Sarah Miles, and Thomas J. Bolam. *The Presidents on Film: A Comprehensive Filmography of Portrayals from George Washington to George W. Bush.* Jefferson, NC: McFarland, 2006. Print.

Crawley, Melissa. *Mr. Sorkin Goes to Washington: Shaping the President on Television's The West Wing.* Jefferson, NC: McFarland, 2006. Print.

Curl, Joseph. "A Desperate President Spews Bitterness, Pessimism." *The Washington Times* (28 May 2014): no page. Web. 30 Jun. 2014.

Farberov, Snejana. "Is Ruling in the Genes? All Presidents Bar One Are Directly Descended from a Medieval English King." *Daily Mail* (5 Aug. 2012): no page. Web. 6 Feb. 2015.

Gilbert, Robert. E. *The Mortal Presidency: Illness and Anguish in the White House.* New York: Fordham UP, 1998. Print.

Krukones, Michael G. "Motion Picture Presidents of the 1930s: Factual and Fictional Leaders for a Time of Crisis." *Hollywood's White House: The American Presidency in Film and History.* Ed. Peter C. Rollins and John E. O'Connor. Lexington: U of Kentucky P, 2003. 143–58. Print.

Lösche, Peter. Einleitung. *Die Ära Obama: Erste Amtszeit.* Ed. Peter Lösche and Anja Ostermann. Bonn: BPB, 2012. 12–30. Print.

Mausbach, Wilfried, Dietmar Schloss, and Martin Thunert. "The American Presidency: History, Politics, Culture." *The American Presidency: Multidisciplinary Perspectives.* Ed. Wilfried Mausbach, Dietmar Schloss, and Martin Thunert. Heidelberg: Winter, 2012. 1–53. Print.

Moore, Jerry D. *Visions of Culture: An Introduction to Anthropological Theories and Theorists.* 3rd ed. Lanham, MD: AltaMira P, 2012. Print.

Pols, Mary. "*White House Down*: DC Meets *Die Hard.*" *Time* (26 Jun. 2013): no page. Web. 10 Jun. 2014.

Rabin, Nathan. "*White House Down.*" *The Dissolve* (10 Jul. 2013): no page. Web. 22 Jun. 2014.

Schlesinger, Arthur M. *The Imperial Presidency.* Boston, MA: Houghton Mifflin, 1973. Print.

Scott, Ian. *American Politics in Hollywood Film.* Edinburgh: Edinburgh UP, 2011. Print.

Shell, Kurt L. "Kongress und Präsident." *Länderbericht USA.* Ed. Peter Lösche and Hans Dietrich von Loeffelholz. Bonn: BPB, 2004. 202–45. Print.

Weber, Max. "The Nature of Charismatic Domination." *Stardom and Celebrity: A Reader*. Ed. Sean Redmond and Su Holmes. London: SAGE, 2007. 17–24. Print.

White House Down. Dir. Roland Emmerich. Perf. Jamie Foxx and Channing Tatum. Sony Pictures, 2013. DVD.

Zettl, Herbert. *Sight, Sound, Motion: Applied Media Aesthetics*. Boston, MA: Wadsworth, 2014. Print.

10 The myth of the American

Intersectionality, the nation, and the family ideal

Antje Dallmann

Dressed in a police uniform, a middle-aged man lingers in the vestibule of a vast house that is decorated for Christmas, trying to get the attention of one of the many children who race past without taking notice of him. Eventually, a well-dressed Mr. McCallister, apparently the "man of the house," makes his appearance. The professed policeman enquires about security measures taken in this family's home, and Mr. McCallister expounds that automatic lights and locks have been installed. Mrs. McCallister eventually pays for the food, ten pizzas, which had been delivered earlier, and informs the visitor that she and her family will be going on holiday to France the next day. At least for this day, the McCallisters share their home with extended family, creating what seems like a huge "patchwork family."

This scene is from *Home Alone* (1990), one of the most popular so-called "family films" ever made. Thanks to countless re-runs on TV, we are well aware that the middle-aged man who so intensely tries to gain someone's attention is not a circumspect policeman, but Harry, half of a burglar duo who call themselves the Wet Bandits and who are reconnoitering an apparently wealthy neighborhood. The narrative's hero is eight-year-old Kevin, the youngest McCallister offspring, who is accidentally left behind the next morning, in the confusion that ensues when the rest of the family leave the house in a rush to catch their flight to Paris.

True to the title, Kevin then finds himself "home alone," for once not tormented by his siblings or unfairly treated by his parents. The day before, he had in fact wished for a future on his own. Yet while alone in this huge house, Kevin, to his own surprise, understands that he really *loves* his family. By the time Mrs. McCallister returns home on Christmas Day, her son has not only survived, but has defended their home against vicious but somewhat simple-minded intruders, and he has realized the importance of this home, of his family, and of family values.

Home Alone: a symptomatic reading

Home Alone was a blockbuster for twelve consecutive weeks; a Christmas movie that stayed in the cinemas well into the Easter season, to become the ghest grossing rental movie of all times. Its excessive popularity rates Chris Columbus's comedy a fitting point of departure to discuss the native myth of the American family, to contrast it with the infinite and volatile realities of real-life families, and to critically think about the functions and consequences of naturalizing and normalizing specific notions of "the American family" and particular representations of family life.

In the following, I propose a symptomatic reading of *Home Alone* to lay open the film's ideological content or what French Marxist critic Louis Althusser called its "problematic." Introduced as a concept by Althusser in *Reading Capital* (Althusser and Balibar 1970), a symptomatic reading attempts to uncover a cultural text's problematic, its underlying assumptions and ideas, by studying closely what is present and what is absent, what is represented and what is not. The main question of my symptomatic reading is how *Home Alone* evokes and constructs the American family as an exclusive, highly ideologized and idealized construct: as a "myth" with broad metaphorical connotations.

To start, let us take a closer look at the McCallister family and at their home, the main setting of Kevin's two-day adventures. From the inside, the house looks spacious and expensive in its costly decoration; establishing shots from the outside reveal a huge three-story building with seventeen windows on the front alone. Located in Winnetka, IL, a village in Cook County sixteen miles north of downtown Chicago, the McCallisters' home is located in one of the most exclusive American suburbs. Even though we never learn Mr. McCallister's profession, and we never find out whether Mrs. McCallister pursues a professional career of her own, we are safe to assume that basic financial worries are not part of their everyday concerns. The open reluctance they exhibit when it comes to paying the pizza man, in fact, could be read as a narrative device that closes the gap with the average spectator, who would never own a house that (in real life) was to sell for more than 1.5 million dollars in 2012 yet for whom to pay 122.50 dollars for a family dinner might easily qualify as a luxury. Thus, the McCallister family, and their downplayed wealth, work as an anchor of identification for a broader audience. As a sign, the McCallisters indicate the viability of what is often understood as the quintessential American myth: the American Dream of upward social mobility and of financial success (see Chapter 11).

Thus, the McCallisters are a wealthy upper-middle- to upper-class family presented as middle-class mainstream. In *Home Alone*, class as a category is intricately and persistently linked to connotations of whiteness, "race," and ethnicity. There are hardly any persons of color in the entire film. As census data reveal, the affluent village of Winnetka is nearly exclusively white (United States Census Bureau). Yet likewise in Chicago's O'Hare International Airport, located in a city that is home to a large African American community, there seem to be no Black travelers. The only person of color who is shown in the crowded airport scenes is a young woman who is credited as "airline counter person." Another Black "airline counter person," this time uncredited, is shown at Paris Orly Airport. Toward the film's end, an African American policeman is involved in arresting the gangster duo. Other than these three characters, who only play very small roles, and apart from a number of Chinese tourists in Paris and a Latina woman as a passenger on the plane to France, everybody in *Home Alone* seems to be white. The only substantial reference to African American culture that appears in the film is a life-size cardboard cutout of NBA star Michael Jordan, which Kevin successfully uses to scare away the burglars on his first night alone.

Thus, the "average" American family, as depicted in *Home Alone*, is well-off and white. It is also characterized in ethnic and religious terms as Anglo-Saxon and Protestant, and their white community is presented as being threatened by crime. Kevin's older brother Buzz claims that "old man Marley," a white man who lives on his own in the house next door, had killed his whole family twenty-five years ago. Yet in a saccharine church scene with Marley's grand-daughter singing in the church choir on Christmas Eve, Kevin learns that "old man Marley" had done nothing more than alienate his son in an argument. Kevin, matured over the days of his parents' absence, advises the older man to contact his son, since – he argues – he, Kevin, would always be happy to hear his father's voice, particularly during the Christmas season.

At home, Kevin finds a video tape of *Angels with Dirty Souls*, a low-key black-and-white gangster movie reminiscent of *film noir* – a reference to Chicago's history as a capital of organized crime. The so-called Chicago Outfit of the Italian American Mafia had originated in South Side Chicago, located like Winnetka in Cook County. Yet all-white Winnetka is introduced as a world apart from this. While crime still exists, it is of a far less professional kind; yet its perpetrators are also marked as ethnic others. (Harry, in fact, is played by Italian American actor Joe Pesci who had just earned an Academy Award in 1990 for his performance as a mobster in *Goodfellas*.) While the McCallisters' white Anglo-Saxon Protestant (WASP) community – in itself an extended family united symbolically by Christmas as a common holiday – is vindicated, crime as a threat from the outside is thus acknowledged and resisted.

When Kevin finds out that the Wet Bandits plan to break into his home, he – who is in the absence of his father "the man of the house" – gets ready. He determines to drive the intruders away, transforming his home into an extended torture chamber. In a daunting scene, Kevin stands behind the back door, a toy gun in hand, waiting for the burglars to arrive, who are then promptly shot at by Kevin. The ensuing fifteen minutes consist of a gruesome slapstick marathon that leads the housebreakers from one ingenious trap to the next and ultimately to their arrest by the police, who find the duo (unrealistically) little harmed. Kevin, a hero, has defended his home and thus his family. He has proven that he has understood the importance of family values, and he is subsequently rewarded by his family's return.

How a film could be G-rated that displays violence on a frightening scale, and violence committed by a child, can only be explained by taking a closer look at its underlying motif: the defense of the American family, its home, and of family values in general. Kevin is alone in his fight since most of his neighbors, his potential allies, are away over the holiday while their houses are also broken into, and even "old man Marley" is preoccupied with family problems of his own. Ultimately, however, Marley joins Kevin, thus also earning for himself an eventual happy ending in the form of a reconciliation with his son.

Police officers, however, are portrayed as helplessly incompetent. The police do not function as an effective "thin blue line" between crime and the public in *Home Alone*. Rather, as Harry's initial disguise indicates, the distinction between police and criminals is not always easy to establish, and thus citizens have to take the law in their own hands if necessary, as well as their (toy) guns if need be.

"Race," gender, and the normative concept of the traditional American family

Home Alone illustrates how

> practices concerning actual American families [...] work to naturalize and normalize racial hierarchy. The multiple meanings attached to the concept of home [...] also speak to the significance of family in regulating the property relations that are so central to racial hierarchy. (Collins, "Like One of the Family" 16)

In this sense, the image of the normative American nuclear middle-class family is by definition white, and it suppresses both alternative family structures and excludes families of color. Historically, "any family relationships that deviated from [the] nuclear patriarchal family ideal – of male breadwinning and female domesticity in a middle-class home – [were regarded] as aberrant," Margaret D. Jacobs argues in *White Mother to a Dark Race* (125), a book in which she discusses rhetoric legitimations for the violent displacement of Native Americans from their home lands in the context of settler colonialism and the importance of exclusive white family ideals (see also Coontz, *The Social Origins* 41–72).

In *The Social Origins of Private Life*, family historian Stephanie Coontz shows that this family ideal is a culture-specific nineteenth-century bourgeois invention, which replaced the earlier understanding of family as "all those living under the authority of a household head" (7). The new family ideal, which emerged in nineteenth-century American culture, conceived of the family primarily as a relationship between parents and children, under the father's ultimate legal and economic control, but ordered by the mother according to Christian principles. This family is located within the private realm and is sheltered against the public sphere. Based on notions of "kinship" and "blood," the modern concept of the family is more exclusive than the one preceding it. In Columbus's film, the McCallisters are presented as the embodiment of this ideal American family, and a relation between "house," "home," and "family" is established. The troubles they encounter are created through their (minimal) diversion from the white normative family ideal.

Representations of families and of family life are ubiquitous in American culture, and mainstream culture generally posits families like the McCallisters as the norm. Not only are the depictions of functional families (or, as cautionary tales, also dysfunctional ones) the stuff that innumerous Hollywood comedies, melodramas, and romances are made of – family sitcom and family saga are among the most popular show formats on American television. From *The Adventures of Ozzie and Harriet* (1952–1966), *Leave It to Beaver* (1957–1963), or *Married … with Children* (1987–1997) and *Modern Family* (2009–), to *Little House on the Prairie* (1974–1983) or *Dallas* (1978–1991) to name only a very few, TV families have captured audiences for decades. Such idealized images of traditional "true American families," however, which are assiduously generated in popular culture, are nothing more than nostalgic fantasies (see Coontz, *The Way We Never Were*).

The ideal trope of a nostalgic yearning for seemingly lost extended-kinship networks of a romanticized past, the so-called extended family was allegedly destroyed by the vicissitudes of modern life. Coontz however shows that, while this historicization is mistaken since this model's "high point occurred between 1850 and 1885, during the most intensive period of early industrialization" (Coontz, *The Way We Never Were* 12), extended families were, for the most part, a product of destitution rather than of emotional proximity.

In watching *Home Alone*, the audience is invited to identify with an idealized white and middle-class family. Simultaneously, a subtle criticism of contemporary family models is advanced: The "extended family," in fact, is dismissed as creating what Harry calls "fancy orphanages." Robert C. Allen proposes to read the extended McCallister family as a critique of what he calls the "postmodern family." "The family home as depicted in *Home Alone*," he argues, "is the site of frantic, uncoordinated activity – children and parents circulating in separate orbits, meeting only when they collide" (110). Allen, thus, reads the McCallisters as a symbol of the patchwork family, a dark specter, which social conservatives perceive as haunting the "traditional American family" since the 1980s. A more recent addition to the broad catalogue of apparent dangers threatening the traditional family, the patchwork family together with rising divorce rates, single, working, and welfare mothers, and same-sex marriage and parenting have become tropes within a conservative discourse on family values that, by affirming the nuclear family as a timeless norm, "stigmatize[s] the deviant, those placed beyond the norm by virtue of their race, sexuality, class, or other social identities" (Peterson 114).

Thus, the depiction of family life in *Home Alone* can be read as a plea for the virtues of a smaller, nuclear family. An invention of the 1950s that has remained a conservative normative ideal of family life ever since, however, the "happy, homogeneous [1950s TV] families were […] a result of the media's denial of diversity" (Coontz, *The Way We Never Were* 31), a diversity both in socio-economic, in ethnic, in racial, and in sexual terms.

As in its nineteenth-century version, strictly defined traditional gender roles are attached to this ideal of family life, in which the mother is responsible for the domestic household and the tasks of child-rearing while the father is cast in the role of the family breadwinner. *Home Alone* does not discuss the parents' professional life, and the film is ambivalent about Kate McCallister's career. On the one hand, she is clad in what could be described as business attire. On the other hand, no household help or nannies are shown or mentioned in *Home Alone*, and the care for five children and the maintenance of a big house – even with no family guests present – should constitute a full-time occupation for Mrs. McCallister as housewife. This ambivalence, arguably, is intentional. While not interested in alienating the growing numbers of working mothers and their families as potential audiences, *Home Alone* still manages to send the message that mothers are and remain primarily responsible for their children and that they are to blame if something goes wrong. Consequently, it is Kate McCallister, not her husband, who duly accuses herself of being a bad parent when realization dawns that Kevin has been left behind in Chicago.

Thus, *Home Alone* – while narrating a seemingly innocent, one-dimensional story – is deeply invested in reproducing and perpetuating a conservative idealized image of the American family: a modern myth of a mainstream American cultural imaginary. Feminist sociologist Patricia Hill Collins, in fact, argues that "hierarchies of social class and gender rely on the rhetoric and practices associated with the American family ideal" ("Like One of the Family," 14). Though ostensibly encompassing everybody in its normative embrace, claiming a white, middle-class family as generic substitute for a far more diverse society, this family ideal naturalizes and normalizes whiteness and middle-class status, and reconfirms traditional gender roles, a specific family model, and heteronormativity as a concept that affirms the identity of sex, gender, sexuality, and gender roles.

The myth of the American family and American nation-building

The concept of the American family, as it emerges in *Home Alone*, illustrates what Roland Barthes has famously described in *Mythologies* (1972) as a contemporary myth. Barthes argues that, in the process of signification, signs acquire a secondary level of meaning (a connotation), thus constituting "second-order semiological systems": namely cultural myths. Through repetition, myths naturalize ideology-laden thought as common-sense truth. Taking up anthropologist Claude Lévi-Strauss's understanding of myths, film theorist Thomas Schatz has made the argument that all Hollywood genres work like myths by affirming binary oppositions in order to resolve cultural contradictions not least, as in *Home Alone*, by radically eradicating difference or by reconstituting difference in terms of binary oppositions.

Coontz describes family as, simultaneously, "the concrete expression of a socially sanctioned relationship between social and biological reproduction" and as "an ideological concept through which people express their ideals about how biological and social reproduction ought to be coordinated" (*The Social Origins* 12). Taking the cue from the second part of this definition, it is obvious that the myth of the American family has to be further investigated since this concept, while functioning as a normative ideal of how individuals should organize their familial relationships, also operates in a broader metaphorical sense.

With its emphasis on "kinship" and "blood" as factors that determine family relations, the modern concept of the family has also served as a "metaphor for nation and even humankind. It functions as a site of contestation over who is familiar and who is a stranger, what is normal and what is deviant," literary scholar Carla L. Peterson explains (115). Already in the eighteenth century, Robert S. Levine claims, "race and nation were linked to notions of family lineage, around the idea of the nation as a family" (53), thus not only scripting Americans as a nation apart from Britons, but also defining Americans as white, since "whiteness, in a slave culture, was part of national belonging, and blackness was explicitly excluded" (53). During and after the Civil War, the family again became the symbol of national belonging: first as belonging to the North or the South, and in the postbellum period as a symbol of the reconciliation between North and South that, in popular culture, was often allegorized through a marriage plot that united a Southern (white) wife and a Northern (white) husband.

In one sense, the myth of the American family transfers gendered and racialized social hierarchies to the realm of nation-building. Their gendered character, however, is complicated by class positionalities. More recent feminist scholarship has shown, thus, that the relation between private and public spheres in nineteenth-century American culture was more permeable than imagined by earlier critics. The production of the private sphere of familial care and the construction of a moral superiority of domestic and Christian values created a field of relative dominance for white bourgeois women, which was increasingly extended into the public. Amy Kaplan, in a groundbreaking article entitled "Manifest Domesticity," argues that

> [w]hen we contrast the domestic sphere with the market or political realm, men and women inhabit a divided social terrain, but when we oppose the domestic to the foreign, men and women become national allies against the alien, and the determining division is not gender but racial demarcations of otherness. Thus, another part of the cultural work of domesticity might be to unite men and women in a national domain and to generate notions of the foreign against which the nation can be imagined as home. (582)

It is the image of a "white nation" that is constructed with the help of an ideology of "manifest domesticity," an image that reverberates in a popular movie like *Home Alone*. Conceptualizing, as Collins ("Like One of the Family" 18) argues, "the US nation-state [...] as a large American national family [that is] understood through the rhetoric of the American family ideal," this film excludes the racially, ethnically, and socially marked other from being recognized as belonging to the "American family" on equal terms.

Beyond the "traditional American family"

"[The] analysis of alternative family structures complicates th[e] opposition between norm and deviance by forcing a shift from an either/or to a both/and paradigm, and, in so doing challenges conventional systems of classification and evaluation," Peterson argues (114). The history of the African American family and its representations provides important insights for a re-negotiation of the concept of family. "Defining slaves as property, US law denied them the right to create families [...]. Bent on economic profit, slaveholders refused to acknowledge that slaves could experience familiarity, or feelings of intimacy for one another" (Peterson 114). To this day, conservative discourses that revolve around the characters of the African American "welfare mom" and the Black "absent father" perpetuate this racist image. Yet already before emancipation, slave narratives such as Harriet Jacobs's *Incidents in the Life of a Slave Girl* (1861) had confirmed the central importance of family and kinship networks for African Americans. In postbellum America, Peterson elaborates, Black

> writers followed the normative impulse in reconstituting the family as bourgeois and patriarchal and emphasizing lineage and inheritance. Yet, [...] this family structure may be seen as deviant in its application to African Americans. It diminished differences between whites and blacks and proved a powerful threat to the norms of white supremacy. (115)

The Black family sitcom, a flourishing genre particularly since the 1990s, provides a fitting example. Modelled on the social conservative, commercial genre of the white family sitcom, it manages to subvert some of the latter's central ideals, functioning as an alternative representation of both the African American family and of its relation to and inclusion into the American nation. In *Sag Harbor* (2010), writer Colson Whitehead explains:

> We were a Cosby family [...]. Father a doctor, mother a lawyer. [...] *The Cosby Show* was the Number-One Show in America [...]. Who are these people? We said: People we know. And we watched it. [...] "They're a real Cosby Family," people said, when acquaintances broke the atmosphere to better orbit. A term of affection and admiration. (193)

Thus, even within the field of commercial TV culture, the representation of alternative models of "postmodern" family life have become more frequent, as, to give another set of examples, more complex inclusions of same-sex couples and parenting in shows like *The L-Word* (2004–2009), *Modern Family* (2009–), *Queer as Folk* (2000–2005), or *The Wire* (2002–2008) equally indicate. *Six Feet Under* (2001–2005) goes beyond simple alternatives by projecting a future genealogy of its characters that leaves behind customary notions of familial belonging. Sociologist Judith Stacey introduces the term "brave new families" that allows for a re-conceptualization of relationships, and Americanist Ralph J. Poole describes them as characterized by "a plurality of family arrangements both with and without children" (170). Poole reads such representations as a potentially "subversive or even – to resort to Foucault's terminology [...] – heterotopian move towards a radically different notion of normality" (171).

The trope of the "traditional American family," thus, constitutes a primary example of how categories of difference such as "race," gender, class, and sexuality intersect (for the concept of intersectionality, see Collins, "Some Group Matters"; Crenshaw; Lorde; see also Chapter 18). With its covert and overt perpetuations of a white, heterosexual, middle-class norm as well as its many contestations, discussions of "the American family" will remain central in negotiations of social and cultural identity and of belonging, of kinship, home, and community in American culture.

Works cited

Allen, Robert C. "Home Alone together: Hollywood and the 'Family Film.'" *Identifying Hollywood's Audiences: Cultural Identity and the Movies.* Ed. Melvyn Stokes and Richard Maltby. London: bfi, 1999. 109–31. Print.

Althusser, Louis, and Étienne Balibar. *Reading Capital.* 1970. Trans. Ben Brewster. London: Verso, 1979. Print.

Barthes, Roland. *Mythologies.* 1972. Trans. Annette Lavers. London: Paladin, 1973. Print.

Collins, Patricia Hill. "Like One of the Family: Race, Ethnicity, and the Paradox of US National Identity." *Ethnic and Racial Studies* 24.1 (2001): 3–28. Print.

---. "Some Group Matters: Intersectionality, Situated Standpoints, and Black Feminist Thought." *Fighting Words: Black Women and the Search for Justice.* Minneapolis: U of Minnesota P, 1998. 201–28. Print.

Coontz, Stephanie. *The Social Origins of Private Life: A History of American Families, 1600–1900.* London: Verso, 1988. Print.

---. *The Way We Never Were: American Families and the Nostalgia Trap.* New York: Basic Books, 1992. Print.

Crenshaw, Kimberlé. "Mapping the Margins: Intersectionality, Identity Politics, and Violence against Women of Color." *Standard Law Review* 43.6 (1991): 1241–99. Print.

Home Alone. Dir. Chris Columbus. Perf. Macaulay Culkin, Joe Pesci, and Daniel Stern. Hughes Entertainment/Twentieth Century Fox, 1990. DVD.

Jacobs, Margaret D. *White Mother to a Dark Race: Settler Colonialism, Maternalism, and the Removal of Indigenous Children in the American West and Australia, 1880–1940.* Lincoln: U of Nebraska P, 2011. Print.

Kaplan, Amy. "Manifest Domesticity." *American Literature* 70.3 (1998): 581–606. Print.

Levine, Robert S. "Race and Ethnicity." *A Companion to American Fiction, 1780–1865.* Ed. Shirley Samuels. Malden, MA: Blackwell, 2004. 52–63. Print.

Lorde, Audre. *Sister Outsider: Essays and Speeches.* Trumansburg, NY: Crossing P, 1983. Print.

Peterson, Carla L. "Family." *Keywords of American Cultural Studies: An Introduction.* Ed. Bruce Burgett and Glenn Hendler. New York: New York UP, 2007. 112–16. Print.

Poole, Ralph J. "Forever Young, Beautiful, and Troubled? Hedonism, Youth Cult, and Family Planning in *Dawson's Creek* and *Queer as Folk*." *Screening Gender: Geschlechterszenarien in der gegenwärtigen US-amerikanischen Populärkultur.* Ed. Heike Paul and Alexandra Ganser. Berlin: LIT, 2007. 148–74. Print.

Schatz, Thomas. *Hollywood Genres: Formulas, Filmmaking, and the Studio System.* New York: Random House, 1981. Print.

Stacey, Judith. *Brave New Families: Stories of Domestic Upheaval in Late-Twentieth-Century America.* New York: Basic Books, 1990. Print.

United States Census Bureau. Winnetka (Village) Illinois, 2014. Web. 15 May 2014.

Whitehead, Colson. *Sag Harbor.* New York: Vintage, 2011. Print.

11 "From rags to riches" and the self-made man

Martin Klepper

It is by pure chance that Ragged Dick meets Mr. Whitney and his nephew Frank in front of the Astor House in the streets of Manhattan. The prosperous gentleman is busy and, to his regret, has to leave Frank all alone on this day even though the boy has never been to the city before. Dick, the bootblack who has just set up his box of tools on the sidewalk, overhears the two. Ever an enterprising boy, he offers his services as a guide. The proposition is rather courageous; after all, Dick is in rags and has not had a chance to wash his face in a while: He is a "street urchin," who swears, plays tricks on boys from the country now and then, smokes, and expends his money gambling or visiting shows in the Old Bowery Theatre. Sometimes he spends the night in a box on the street. Luckily, Mr. Whitney discerns that Dick has an open and honest face and decides to trust him.

But, first, Dick has to wash up and is given a new set of clothes (actually: an old suit from Frank) so that the genteel boy will not be too embarrassed. Dick realizes how "new and pleasant" (Alger 24) the cleanliness feels, is reminded of Cinderella changed into a fairy princess, and exclaims with a glance into the mirror: "I wonder if I ain't dreamin'" (25). And indeed: The new suit is the bootblack's ticket to the American Dream.

Modern myth

Horatio Alger's *Ragged Dick; or, Street Life in New York with the Boot Blacks*, first serialized in a juvenile magazine in 1867 and then expanded into a popular book, can be considered the classic tale of rags to riches, and, as such, a significant instance or building block of the American Dream. The American Dream is a complex concept: We can call it an ethos or, in the terms of the Myth and Symbol School in American Studies (see Chapter 1), a modern myth. It includes the idea of freedom as the opportunity for prosperity and success, usually in the form of class mobility through hard work ("luck and pluck"; see Tebbel 3–18; Decker 1–14).

Ragged Dick enacts a prolonged lesson in this belief. Mr. Whitney will lecture Dick a little later:

You know in this free country poverty in early life is no bar to a man's advancement. I haven't risen very high myself [...], but have met with moderate success in life; yet there was a time when I was as poor as you. (77)

A modern myth, then, is a core narrative – "mythos," in its Greek origins, means speech, narration, plot (see *OED*) – situated in a very specific cultural environment that has a normative (ethically compelling, meant to be imitated) character and a function geared toward community building. The core narrative, the emplotment (structure of action), is very simple: A literally or meta-phorically orphaned boy rises through hard work from life in the streets and in poverty to success, prosperity, and respectability.

Apart from this emplotment, which, of course, leaves room for many variations, the almost allegorical content (*everybody* can be Dick, although we shall see that not everybody is *everybody*), the strong symbolic imagery (the rags and the new suit), cross-references to other myths ("in this free country" alludes to American Exceptionalism – see Chapters 1 and 8) and their normative character, far from simply being fictions, contain claims to reality. After all, *Ragged Dick* is set at a specific time (the 1860s) in a specific place (Manhattan, much of it around Astor Place), and its subtitle invites us to read it like a case study or a historical documentation. No wonder, then, that Frank names historical persons in his endeavor to teach his new friend. Let us listen to the text again:

"Did you ever hear of Dick Whittington?"[1]
"Never did. Was he a Ragged Dick?"
"I shouldn't wonder if he was. At any rate he was very poor when he was a boy, but he didn't stay so. Before he died, he became Lord Mayor of London."
"Did he?" asked Dick, looking interested. "How did he do it?"
[...]
"A good many distinguished men have once been poor boys." (41–42)

A little later, Frank tells Dick the story of Alexander Turney Stewart:[2]

"Stewart wasn't always rich, you know."
"Wasn't he?"
"When he first came to New York as a young man he was a teacher, and teachers are not generally very rich. At last he went into business, starting in a small way, and worked his way up by degrees. But there was one thing he determined in the beginning; that he would be strictly honorable in all his dealings, and never overreach any one for the sake of making money. If there was a chance for him, Dick, there is a chance for you." (54)

Marxist critics would explain that, through these stories, Dick is "interpellated" (Althusser 115–20) as a subject. In other words: The ideology that Frank's stories (and, by extension, Horatio Alger's stories) contain forms Dick into the (useful) subject of "this free country." At first, Dick is skeptical about these "very good stories"; he resists, remarking that, first of all, nobody would employ a Ragged Dick, secondly, he cannot go to school because he has to earn his living, and, thirdly, "I don't believe all the cats in New York will ever make me mayor" (42). However, the sheer force of Frank's stories transforms Dick and, using the metaphor of the storybook himself, he declares: "I mean to turn over a new leaf, and try to grow up 'spectable." And Frank seconds: "There've been a great many boys begin as low down as you, Dick, that have grown up respectable and honored. But they had to work pretty hard for it" (55). Frank's stories have a performative quality: That is, they *create* what they describe; which is exactly how a modern myth functions.

Origins

Ragged Dick, as it were, short-circuits historical models, ideology, fiction, and an implicit (indirect) theory of effect on the young reader (Dick standing in for the latter). Mr. Whitney, who supports Frank in his efforts at conversion, tells Dick his life story:

> "I entered a printing-office as an apprentice, and worked for some years. Then my eyes gave out and I was obliged to give that up. Not knowing what else to do, I went into the country, and worked on a farm. After a while I was lucky enough to invent a machine, which has brought me in a great deal of money." (77)

The student of American Studies notices that Whitney's life follows the models of Benjamin Franklin (printer), Thomas Jefferson (planter), and the uncle's namesake Eli Whitney (inventor), who developed the cotton gin and the milling machine (besides mass-producing muskets for the War Department). Mr. Whitney *is* America. Naturally, Dick is properly awed and learns two additional lessons: "Save your money, my lad, buy books, and determine to be somebody, and you may yet fill an honorable position" (78). Frugality belongs to the road from rags to riches; and so does the virtue of self-reliance: "Remember that your future position depends mainly upon yourself, and that it will be high or low as you choose to make it" (79). And, just like frugality, the conviction that one must be the architect of one's own fortune (a pillar among the convictions of liberalism) has a pre-history.

As scholars of culture we experience that, once we decide to trace ideas into the past (no matter what they are), we realize that they have always existed. Nevertheless (or, perhaps, therefore), we have to historicize and contextualize in order to acknowledge that cultural practices are always dynamic processes rather than static facts. Ideas and myths develop, shift, and transform in exchange with other practices in society (political, economic, religious, scientific, etc.). Reading *Ragged Dick* for historical allusions (like the – not-so-subtle – hints at Franklin, Jefferson, and Whitney) and studying the life and letters of its author yields some markers in the emergence of the American Dream as it became popular in the nineteenth century.

Alger was a Unitarian minister (and the son of one) before he embarked on his literary career; and the Puritan origins of Mr. Whitney's ideal of frugality are obvious: Dick's eventual success is attributed to his "self-denial and judicious economy" (147, 163). Self-denial (we will discuss the "judicious economy" in a moment) is a term that the Puritans used to describe the ideal of completely emptying one's self (of egotism, desires, worldly intentions) in favor of the presence of God. The Puritans' dream of establishing "a city upon the hill," God's kingdom on earth in America, by self-restraint and devout work, is sometimes called the "Old American Dream"; "old," because it was transformed, for instance in Ben Franklin's version in his famous *Autobiography* (1771–90). While the Puritans did not believe that human beings can influence God's plans ("Providence") through their own work, Franklin creatively misunderstood the Calvinist faith as a promise of success in exchange for ethical behavior and useful deeds – the covenant of deeds: If you are good, God will reward you. For Franklin, self-denial had become a means for a purpose. Franklin's ideas had an overwhelming influence on American discourse.

Alger, for instance, alludes to the Founding Father when he illustrates Dick's efforts at saving money (after meeting Frank and Mr. Whitney he opens a bank account and takes on the name "Dick Hunter") with a list of expenses (90): Franklin is famous for his lists in the *Autobiography* geared toward ameliorating his life. Franklin's conviction that an individual can shape his own life ("by choice," as Mr. Whitney would say) was a giant step toward the individualism that undergirds the American Dream. But Franklin still understood "useful deeds" in terms of the community: He wanted to be admired as much as to be rich – even though the phrase "pursuit of happiness," which the Founders included in the Declaration of Independence, did traditionally (since John Locke) refer to private property.

One generation before Alger's book, the ideas of self-reliance and amelioration received an additional boost through Ralph Waldo Emerson and the transcendentalists. The transcendentalists were reform-oriented young men and women from the middle class who sought to make America better through gradual improvements. At the top of the list stood self-improvement; and Emerson advocated the idea of self-reliance in an essay with the same title, in which he argued against the tradition of imitating classical models and in favor of a culture of self-invention. But Emerson was not a materialist: He was writing about the cultivation of the mind, not the purse, and in this sense still represents the Old American Dream.

Context

The times of the Puritans, of Franklin, and Emerson were forever gone when industrialization heralded the era of big business: the Gilded Age. The old governing elite, the gentry, declined both in terms of influence and affluence and the new class of entrepreneurs and business leaders supplanted them. Concomitantly, traditional values such as modesty, community-orientation, and self-sufficiency lost their force; instead, ideals like energy and industry, personal ambition, and self-assertion took hold. The cultural semantics – the terms and concepts in which a society thinks and argues – changed: In *Ragged Dick* (good) characters are described as "enterprising," good deeds are "investments," good deals are "surplus earnings," and success is a "dividend."

However, industrialization had its (huge) social costs: Corruption, exploitation, inequality, pauperism, excessive urbanization, sanitary problems, and the like triggered fears among intellectuals that the country might literally break apart. For many people the consequences of unfettered production and consumption meant not only reification and alienation in the work process, but also an unprecedented sense of insecurity and anxiety: modernity's proverbial experience of contingency. As Heinz Ickstadt has argued, much of the literature (and culture) of the late nineteenth century addresses these problems with fantasies or projects of cohesion aimed to reverse the centrifugal forces of society (77).

In this light, Alger's version of the self-made man (Dick) and his success story (at the end, Dick's friend Fosdick refers to him as "a young gentleman on the way to fame and fortune," 185) offers a clever symbolic solution to the problems: Alger reconciles the contemporaneous belief in entrepreneurial ambition, aggressive self-assertion, and the autonomous individual with the nostalgia for piety (Dick learns to go to Sunday School, 101), republican community values (not only does Dick help his friends, he also receives altruistic support from prosperous guardians such as Mr. Whitney), and self-sufficiency. Capitalism is tamed by religion and republicanism; the "new urban wilderness" (Ickstadt 77) can be a fun and morally rewarding adventure if heeding Ragged Dick's "judicious economy."

Exclusion

The idea that wealth might not be such a sinful blessing (which the Puritans would have feared) was supported by American divines. Richard T. Hughes offers many examples of the "gospel of wealth" (128): The Episcopal bishop of Massachusetts's hearty "Godliness is in league with riches" (129) from the year 1901 is a case in point, just as is Henry Ward Beecher's (Harriet Beecher Stowe's brother) exclamation from 1870:

> So then, I am not afraid to rejoice: Get rich, if you can … And when you shall have amassed wealth, it will be God's power, if you are wise to use

it, by which you can make your home happier, the community more refined, and the whole land more civilized.

And, on the whole, the general tendency of wealth is such as to lead me today to thank God for the increasing wealth of America. (qtd. in Hughes 130)

Beecher's last sentence shows that the marriage between capitalism, spirituality, and self-formation had taken on a nation-building dimension: Wealth was the project of America – in fact, Calvin Coolidge, thirtieth president of the United States, would famously say in 1925: "[T]he business of the American people is business." And, for many, this was no pure coincidence: The "Protestant ethic of hard work and investment in the self" (Davies 381) tended to align with a Darwinist belief in the survival of fittest. Protestant clergyman Josiah Strong wrote in 1885:

[T]his race of unequaled energy with all the majesty of numbers and the might of wealth behind it – the representative, let us hope, of the largest liberty, the purest Christianity, the highest civilization – having developed peculiarly aggressive traits calculated to impress its institutions upon mankind will spread itself over the earth. [...] And can anyone doubt that the result of this competition of races will be the "survival of the fittest". [...] Is there room for reasonable doubt that this race, unless devitalized by alcohol and tobacco, is destined to dispossess many weaker races, assimilate others, and mold the remainder, until, in a very true and important sense, it has Anglo-Saxonized mankind? (qtd. in Hughes 133)

For Strong it was clear that America's army of energetic boys, the Ragged Dicks, Mark the Match Boys, Paul the Peddlers in Alger's over one hundred books, was racially quite distinct. Dick literally rises from boot-*black* to *white* collar (and very often this is enough for Alger's boys, as theirs is a white, middle-class vision), and the color terms are not quite as innocent as they may seem to a white scholar like me at first glance. After all, one of Dick's attributes is the high visibility of his honesty and fundamental goodness. To his regret, being a bootblack, Dick's hands "in spite of all he could do, [...] were not so white, as if his business had been of another character" (112). Poverty is racialized, but as a white boy, you can eventually wash it away. Moreover, whiteness (preferably of the Anglo-Saxon kind) also accounted for the cherished qualities of industry, energy, and self-advancement, and, thus, it is not very surprising that there are no Black characters in *Ragged Dick*.

In 1899, D.P. Brown questioned the gospel of wealth before the African Methodist Episcopal Church: "What is it to us if the wages of the factory employees are increased, if over the door of each of them the sign hangs out, 'No Black Man Wanted Here' [...]?" (qtd. in Hughes 145). And, in *The Souls of Black Folk* (1903), W.E.B. Du Bois perspicaciously sensed one of the great structural problems in America in the twentieth (and twenty-first) century: "To be a poor man is hard, but to be a poor race in a land of dollars is the very bottom of hardships" (697).

If the success story did not include men of color (at least not in the nineteenth century), neither did it include women. While boys read *Ragged Dick*, girls would have read Louisa May Alcott's *Little Women* (1868) – a book still very much influenced by the "Cult of True Womanhood." The only girl that Dick meets in the novel (Ida) needs admonishment: "'Little girls should be seen and not heard,' said her mother, gently" (118). In contrast, boys (at this time) are supposed to be like Dick: wild, ambitious, full of energy and never tired, but eventually formed into restrained and respectable men. James V. Catano has argued that "two opposing sets [...] – self-made versus institutionally defined and masculine versus feminine – provide the basic argumentative structure of the myth of the self-made man" (427). Men are autonomous and self-created, women are institutionally molded. The American male hero is very often an orphan (Ishmael, Tom Sawyer, and by disavowal Jay Gatsby).

Alger's is a men's world, "complete with a surrogate marriage of two homeless boys [Dick and his friend Fosdick share rooms]" (Trachtenberg x), and not altogether without latent homoeroticism (Alger himself had left his ministry among charges of "unnatural familiarity with *boys*"; Scharnhorst 67). Ironically, when ideas about femininity had changed (in the 1920s), both the creator (Edward Stratemeyer) and the author (Mildred Wirt, writing under the pseudonym Carolyn Keene) of the first popular girl detective series, Nancy Drew, who is motherless and tough, were ardent admirers of Horatio Alger (see Chapter 5).

Medium

While the preferred medium for the concept of Manifest Destiny (see Chapter 6) may have been the journalistic pamphlet, the sermon, the political speech, or even the painterly illustration, the American Dream in the manifestation of the rags-to-riches formula has an inherently narrative character: It lends itself to storytelling. When Horatio Alger wrote *Ragged Dick*, popular literature in the United States was coming of age. Emerging in the 1830s and 1840s with the penny press and the dime novel (George Lippard and Ned Buntline are important names), cheap, formulaic, and often serial literature became an ever more significant source of leisure and information toward the end of nineteenth century.

Seriality in Alger's books pertains not only to the publication format (*Ragged Dick* was serialized in the journal *Schoolmate*) but also to the series of trials (neatly ordered in chapters) Dick has to go through on his way to success: trials concerning his own desires and habits as well as trials concerning "misers, usurers, confidence men, thieves, spendthrifts, gamblers, and speculators" (Nackenoff 158), who represent the vicissitudes and anxieties of the era of big business. At the beginning of the twentieth century, when a fully fledged mass culture emerged in America, the success story and the exemplary life of the self-made man were among the most salient patterns of formula fiction (see Cawelti).

As a modern myth, the rags-to-riches formula underwent many modifications, transformations, and transmedializations. Mark Twain (who gave the Gilded Age its name) created the first parody of *Ragged Dick* when his hero *Tom Sawyer* (1876), who by Alger's standards does everything wrong (he lies, is lazy, skips Sunday School, and hates education), becomes the most respected citizen of fictional St. Petersburg. Highbrow literature in the wake of Alger and Twain has taken on the theme time and again: F. Scott Fitzgeralds's *The Great Gatsby* (1925) and Arthur Miller's *Death of a Salesman* (1949) perhaps being the most damning renditions of the myth. Hollywood has used and abused the same storyline in films from Orson Welles's *Citizen Kane* (1941) to Matthew Weiner and AMC's serial *Mad Men* (created 2007) with the self-made Don Draper alias "Dick" Whitman (see Chapters 3 and 15).

Michael Makropoulos has suggested that mass culture is a culture of contingency (openness, chance, incertitude) – not because it problematizes contingency, but because it rewrites contingency as opportunity (10). In this sense the mythical success story is the stuff that mass culture is made of: whether it is the contingency connected to the transformations of class and gender roles (take James M. Cain's popular novel *Mildred Pierce*, 1941 or Kevin Wade's movie *Working Girl*, 1988) or the precarious hopes connected to immigration and racial justice (take Abraham Cahan's novel *The Rise of David Levinsky*, 1917 or Will Smith's movie *The Pursuit of Happyness*, 2006). In its best versions, the catchy plots of the rags-to-riches stories with their trials and tribulations keep negotiating the tensions between an ethos of self-formation and self-cultivation, which (after Emerson) American Pragmatism in the tradition of William James and John Dewey has propagated, and the actualities of sexual bias, racial discrimination, and social inequality. In its worst versions, they make these tensions invisible.

In a culture in which a benign reading of contingency is understood to be the exceptional promise of the country ("anything can happen in America") the rags-to-riches story takes on a nation-building function; it becomes, as it were, a medium for nation-building: a message of opportunity for immigrants and a message of individual responsibility for native-born Americans. Nonetheless: It is (again) by pure luck that Dick, at the end of the novel, is able to rescue the son of a wealthy gentleman, Mr. Rockwell, from drowning and that, as a reward, he receives a position as clerk in his counting room. But good luck was never a good argument against modern myth.

Notes

1 Richard Whittington (ca. 1354–1423) was also a merchant and sheriff of London. His story became popular through a folk tale.
2 Alexander Turney Stewart (1803–1876) was an Irish immigrant who opened several stores in New York: the Marble Palace on Broadway (1848) and the Iron Palace on Broadway and Astor Place. Stewart became one of the wealthiest men in America. Stewart did, however, start out with an inheritance from his grandfather.

Works cited

Alger, Jr., Horatio. *Ragged Dick; or, Street Life in New York with the Boot Blacks.* 1867. New York: Signet, 1990. Print.

Althusser, Louis. *Lenin and Philosophy and Other Essays.* 1970. Trans. Ben Brewster. Intr. Fredric Jameson. New York: Monthly Review P, 2001. Print.

Catano, James V. "The Rhetoric of Masculinity: Origins, Institutions, and the Myth of the Self-Made Man." *College English* 52.4 (1990): 421–36. Print.

Cawelti, John. *Apostles of the Self-Made Man.* Chicago, IL: U of Chicago P, 1965. Print.

Davies, Jude. "Dreiser and the City." *The Cambridge History of the American Novel.* Ed. Leonard Cassuto. Cambridge: Cambridge UP, 2011. 380–92. Print.

Decker, Jeffrey Louis. *Made in America: Self-Styled Success from Horatio Alger to Oprah Winfrey.* Minneapolis: U of Minnesota P, 1997. Print.

Du Bois, W.E.B. *The Souls of Black Folk. The Norton Anthology of African American Literature.* Ed. Henry Louis Gates, Jr. and Nellie Y. McKay. New York: Norton, 2004. 692–766. Print.

Hughes, Richard T. *Myths America Lives By.* Urbana: U of Illinois P, 2003. Print.

Ickstadt, Heinz. "Concepts of Society and the Practice of Fiction – Symbolic Responses to the Experience of Change in Late-Nineteenth-Century America." *Impressions of a Gilded Age: The American Fin de Siècle.* Ed. Marc Chenétier and Rob Kroes. Amsterdam: Amerika Instituut, Universiteit van Amsterdam, 1983. 77–95. Print.

Makropoulos, Michael. *Theorie der Massenkultur.* München: Fink, 2008. Print.

Nackenoff, Carol. *The Fictional Republic: Horatio Alger and American Political Discourse.* New York: Oxford UP, 1994. Print.

OED Online. 2013. "Mythos, n." Oxford: Oxford UP. Web. 19 Sep. 2013.

Scharnhorst, Gary. *The Lost Life of Horatio Alger, Jr.* Bloomington: Indiana UP, 1985. Print.

Tebbel, John. *From Rags to Riches: Horatio Alger, Jr., and the American Dream.* New York: Macmillan, 1963. Print.

Trachtenberg, Alan. Introduction. *Ragged Dick.* Horatio Alger. New York: Signet, 1990. v–xx. Print.

Part IV

Theories in American Studies

12 Post-Marxism, American Studies, and post-capitalist futures

Jodi Melamed

Capital. Commodity. Alienation. Revolution. These and other concepts from the writings of Karl Marx continue to energize American Studies scholars, even as they investigate contemporary conditions of capital accumulation (neoliberalism) and kinds of transnational social struggles (anti-racist, queer, environmental, and indigenous) that differ in degree and kind from those that preoccupied Marx in his historical present. Why does Marx's body of work continue to inspire American Studies? We can identify three influential trajectories of Marxist thought that shape contemporary American Studies scholarship in complex ways:

The critique of capital
Materialism
Historical materialism and post-capitalist futures

The critique of capital

For Marx, the basic antagonism of capitalist society is that when the worker sells her labor power to the capitalist, she receives a wage that is less than the value her labor power produces. The extra value that the capitalist extracts from the worker is called surplus-value and comprises profit. Jumping off from his critique of this uneven relation, Marx theorizes the commodity form, the transformation of money into capital, laws and circuits of capital accumulation, and contradictions internal to capitalism's processes (including the tendency for the rate of profit to fall and the inevitability of crises as historical modes of capitalist production reach their limits). Yet even as American Studies scholars rely on concepts from Marx to sharpen their economic critique, American Studies approaches also turn to Marx to critique the category of "the economy" itself as discrete, as divided, or separable from "the social" or "the political." Sometimes this is done through Marx's critique of the fetish character of commodities, in which "the definite social relations between [people]" assume "the fantastic form of a relation between things" (Marx, *Capital*, Vol. 1 165). Other times, the critique of the "economic" as a discrete category arises from

Marx's more general sense of capitalism as just one mode of organizing social forces, which might be organized differently. (Socialism, for example, would re-organize society such that capital, which is always socially produced, would be socially distributed rather than captured by capitalists.) Finally, American Studies have been influenced by the line of thinking in Marx's "On the Jewish Question." In this early essay, Marx describes the political emancipation offered by the capitalist state (one that guarantees private property rights) as instituting a malicious separation between individual and communal being, between an individual's "real" material (economic) life and the "unreal" realm of (political) citizenship. This artificial, structural separation between the economic and the political forces people to be "egoistic" in their real lives and to see in other people "not the *realization* but the *limitation* of [their] own freedom" ("On the Jewish Question" 230).

Materialism

We find a classic statement of Marx's materialism in the Preface to *A Contribution to the Critique of Political Economy*. Here, Marx famously identifies the mode of production in a given society – its economic structure – as the *base*, on which arises a cultural and ideological *superstructure* corresponding to a specific kind of consciousness. This means "the mode and production of material life conditions the general process of social, political and intellectual life. It is not the consciousness of men that determines their existence, but their social existence that determines their consciousness" (*A Contribution*). While most American Studies scholars reject the idea that consciousness is fully determined by the mode of production, many embrace a materialist analysis that recognizes that distinct historical modes of production (i.e., slave agriculture in the eighteenth century, industrialization in the twentieth century, finance capital in the early twenty-first century) strongly condition social differentiation and hierarchies, knowledge production, and political life. At the same time, American Studies scholars value Marx for identifying another very different sense of consciousness in his "Theses on Feuerbach": a consciousness that is a material social process, a sensuous critical–practical activity that is world-making. Using insights from these short theses and other work from Marx's early economic and philosophical manuscripts to radicalize the base/superstructure concept found in his later writings, post-Marxist American Studies scholars investigate how modes of production depend on forms of consciousness in order to reproduce themselves. This means that ways of thinking *are* conditions of production; they do not merely arise from them (Reddy; Ferguson; Melamed).

   Another influential radicalization of base and superstructure thinking is to be found in Fredric Jameson's interrogation of postmodernism as "the cultural dominant of the logic of late capitalism" (45). This complex phrasing itself corresponds to Jameson's observation that a signal characteristic of late or multinational capitalism, the decentered global network of the "third stage of capitalism" we now inhabit, and of postmodernism, is the sense that the referents of the terms "economic" and "cultural" have collapsed together, which is to say that base and superstructure now lack definite distinction. In part, this is because aesthetic and cultural production have become more integrated into commodity production and because the economic system itself is structured more and more by multiplicities of complex codes and repre-sentational systems, from international media to computational codes to financialization. Yet fundamentally, it follows from a shift in the dynamic of culture: The logic of late capitalism dialectically destroys the autonomy of the cultural sphere and leads to "a prodigious expansion of culture throughout the social realm," so that everything from economic value to state power "can be said to have become 'cultural' in some original and yet untheorized sense" (47). For Jameson, this dynamic of postmodernism, and the unrepresentable totality of late capitalism, entail a loss of distance and generate crises for political art. In response, Jameson proposes "an aesthetic of cognitive mapping – a pedagogical political culture which seeks to endow the individual subject with some new heightened sense of its place in the global system," which, for our purposes, represents an important transformation of Marx's articulation of consciousness as material social process and sensuous critical–practical activity (53).

Historical materialism and post-capitalist futures

In classic Marxism, historical materialism refers to Marx's theory that history moves from stage to stage as the material productive forces of a society (its base) come to outstrip that society's relations of production (its super-structure). This foments a period of revolutionary change during which a dominant class is overthrown by a new emerging class, which "liberates" the society's productive forces by bringing about new political and social relations. Thus for Marx, "[t]he history of all hitherto existing society is the history of class struggles" (Marx and Engels 219). The end game, according to Marx, will come when workers, conscious they are the true agents of production, win control over the means of production and distribute surplus-value socially, freeing humankind from "the realm of necessity" (where one must work to meet one's physical needs) and ushering in a "realm of freedom" (where the "development of human powers" and creativity becomes an end in itself) (*Capital*, Vol. 3 959).

Post-Marxist American Studies scholarship is troubled by the way Marx's historical materialism in some of his most well-known volumes is caught within a Eurocentric dynamic, fixed on industrial capitalism, and theorizes labor in ways that marginalize slavery, colonialism, and the exploitation of women and children. Similarly, American Studies reject the dogma, received more from institutionalized Marxist tradition, that history is developmental, driven by the growth of productive forces alone, and progresses through dis-tinct stages toward a proletariat-led revolutionary socialism or communism.

In keeping with their radicalization of Marx's materialism, American Studies scholars write "histories of the present" that analyze distinct arrangements of *hegemony*. Hegemony is an unstable consolidation of cultural, political, economic, ideological, and social force arrangements, "a whole body of practices and expectations," which "constitute [...] a sense of reality for most people" in a given society (Williams 110). It is a kind of dominance that works by naturalizing the power and privileges of some forms of humanity over others. Despite its appearance of totality, however, hegemony "has continually to be renewed, recreated, defended, and modified" (Williams 112). Hegemony "is also continually resisted, limited, altered, challenged" (Williams 112), so that at times authentic breaks bring about an end to a hegemony, as happened during the demise of legal racial segregation in the US South and at the end of the Cold War. For post-Marxist American Studies scholars, who are savvy to the complex power relations of hegemonies, multiple sites of antagonism and contradiction are important, not only the antagonism between capital and labor. These include anti-racist, feminist, subaltern, indigenous, and decolonial struggles, which can constitute contradictions to hegemony in themselves (including the hegemony of capitalist globalization) and, as such, can plant the seeds of new life worlds.

The complex ways American Studies scholars use key concepts from Marx reflect a long, sustained engagement with Marx's texts and those of influential Marxist and post-Marxist theorists, including Rosa Luxemburg, Antonio Gramsci, Raymond Williams, Louis Althusser, Michel Foucault, Stuart Hall, Fredric Jameson, Gayatri Chakravorty Spivak, David Harvey, and Ruth Wilson Gilmore. At the same time, American Studies scholars have been among Marx's harshest critics: for his failure to recognize the world historical importance of "race" as a historical agency and material force of capitalist development (Robinson); for the violence of rationalist and Eurocentric tendencies in some major works (Said); and for underplaying the differential devaluing of racialized and gendered labor (Lowe and Lloyd). Similarly, for some time American Studies scholars have seen Marx's endeavor to provide a total (and totalizing) critique of capital as one that limits the usefulness of his work for understanding how modernity's major systems of oppression – state, colonial, class, cultural, racial, sexual, and heterosexual oppression – interlock and aggregate with one another in complicated ways (Ferguson). Yet as recent scholarship attests, Marx's approach to social change was multi-linear and not solely class-based (Anderson). In his writings about the US Civil War and against slavery, in his support for national independence movements in Ireland and Poland, and in his late studies of non-Western and non-European societies (among them, India, Algeria, Latin America, and indigenous societies), Marx's theory evidences a deepening concern with the intersectionality of "race," anti-colonialism, indigeneity, and class struggles, and replaces the stageism of his earlier works with an openness to the possibility of the emergence of revolutionary change from non-Western societies (Anderson).

Sleep Dealer

In Alex Rivera's near-future cyberpunk science-fiction film *Sleep Dealer* (2008), the border between the United States and Mexico has been permanently closed to migrant laborers, but US corporations, agricultural businesses, and private households are still able to exploit the labor of Mexican workers through means of a dystopic new technology: node labor. Rather than crossing the border, migrants from the Mexican interior travel to border cities such as Tijuana to work in "info-maquilas," massive factories resembling real-world maquiladoras (huge manufacturing and assembly sites) built in Northern Mexico after the passage of the North American Free Trade Agreement (1994). In these futuristic info-maquilas, migrants have "nodes" inserted into their nervous systems, which allow them to plug into a central computer network and remotely operate drones, which work construction jobs, pick fruit, drive taxis, and provide household labor in the United States. As the manager of Cybertek, an info-maquila, says to Memo Cruz, the film's protagonist, on his first day at the factory, node labor is an American dream come true: It provides all the work without the workers.

In Rivera's nightmarish depiction, workers enter lightless metal factories and find their place among rows and rows of other workers. They insert metal plugs into receptor-nodes all over their bodies, put on special contact lenses and oxygen masks, and then move their bodies slowly, like puppets on strings. In this way, they connect to the global economy through drones, to labor in places they will never physically inhabit, use tools they will never physically touch, and "interact" with American employers, who literally see them as robots. One could hardly ask for a better visual representation of Marx's concepts of labor power, abstract labor, and alienation.

For Marx, capitalism produces value by treating all kinds of mental and physical work as labor power, as a commodification of the human capacity to create, which can be measured in expenditures of muscle, nerve, and brain over time. What is important for the capitalist is not concrete labor (the kind of labor that makes particular things such as sawing wood, weaving rugs, assembling computers, writing books), but abstract labor, pure units of labor power. Labor power enriches the capitalist because it produces more value through its use than the value represented in the wages the capitalist pays to the worker. Rivera's film represents labor power as energy sucked from the bodies and minds of workers, depicted as streams of light sucked up into the global economy. With node technology, we see that all labor is actually abstract labor, able to be virtualized into expenditures of energy, before being distributed (through computer network technology) for specific uses. For the worker, according to Marx and Rivera alike, the result is extreme alienation or estrangement from her own creative capacity, from the objects she produces, and from the essence of her humanity. In *Sleep Dealer*, node labor slowly drains the workers of their vital energy, making them blind and eventually killing them. In the process, they are dehumanized; the workers place their lives into the drones, but then those lives no longer belong to them, but to drones. The connection the node establishes goes two ways: The workers become the machines they operate.

It is impossible to comprehend how Rivera uses science fiction to diagnose contemporary global capitalism's structures of domination and sites of possible resistance without recognizing the limitations of Marxism and turning to post-Marxist approaches. (Indeed, Marx's theory cannot account for the social fact of "cheap Mexican labor," that is, for the way immigration and naturalization laws serve the interests of American capital, making it possible to devalue the labor of Mexican migrants in the United States by excluding them in large numbers from citizenship.) Veering from Marx's focus on industrial labor, the central conflict of the film is not in the sleep dealer factories, but in the rural hinterlands of southern Mexico. The film opens in Santa Ana, a small village of peasant farmers, where global capitalism has penetrated in the form of water privatization. Del Rio Inc., a global water company headquartered in San Diego, California, has dammed the river that once provided communal water for the fields of Santa Ana's farmers. It now charges the farmers exorbitant rates for small trickles of water that barely sustain their shrunken *milpas* (small plots where farmers follow the traditional Mesoamerican agricultural practice of interweaving corn, beans, and squash plants with other indigenous crops).

Depicting a fusion of corporate and military power, Del Rio Inc. maintains a monopoly of control over water resources through a paramilitary force, which includes remotely piloted drones that shoot to kill on sight people who resist water privatization, dubbed "aquaterrorists." In depicting such an extreme penetration of global corporate control over a basic component of life (water), the film shows its interest in *biopolitics*, in particular the biopolitics of *neoliberal governmentality*. The term biopolitics comes from Foucault. It identifies the moment in political modernity where life itself is placed at the center of the political order. When this happens, the work of government becomes the "making live" and "letting die" of populations; states protect, maintain, and increase life for some populations and police, abandon, and shrink life for others. Rivera provides a representation of biopolitics in a time of neoliberal governmentality, in which the style of governance follows the precepts of neoliberal social and economic philosophy, including a belief that free markets are the best way to organize social life and the idea that governments should focus on increasing the capital of financial-asset-owning classes, rather than on social welfare goals such as full employment. In fact, there is no "state" present in the world *Sleep Dealer* shows the audience. Corporations like Del Rio Inc. seem to have full impunity to kill Mexican nationals remotely from their headquarters in the United States. Furthermore, by focusing on water privatization and the use of private militaries in the film, Rivera calls attention to "accumulation through dispossession" as the way elites accumulate wealth in neoliberal times. As Harvey explains, "the corporatization, commodification, and privatization of hitherto public assets has been a signal feature of the neoliberal project. Its primary aim has been to open up new fields for capital accumulation in domains hitherto regarded off-limits to the calculus of profitability" (160).

Post-Marxist approaches help us understand how some of the features of advanced global capitalism represented in *Sleep Dealer* grow out of colonial modes of production. In contrast to Marx's belief that the development of capitalism would rationalize and homogenize social formations as it spread across the globe (producing an international proletariat), post-Marxist approaches recognize that capitalist development "has proceeded not through global homogenization but through differentiation" (Lowe and Lloyd, Introduction 13). Uneven development, mixed modes of production, and the direct penetration of capitalist economic relations into indigenous and peasant life worlds are some of the ways colonial modes of capital accumulation operate. Furthermore, as Jodi Byrd reminds us, the history of science and technology cannot be separated from processes of colonization. From the first so-called "journeys of discovery" undertaken by European explorer-colonizers – whose work included kidnapping, land theft, and indigenous conquest as well as map-making, astronomical observation, and classifying flora and fauna – colonial violence has gone hand-in-glove with scientific advancement. In *Sleep Dealer* this is represented by the node technology, which allegorically collapses colonial resource extraction with racial and wage slavery: As the vital energies of human beings are mined and shipped far away, their bodies are left behind to be worked to death.

At the start of the film, the protagonist Memo Cruz is under the sway of the hegemonic ideology, which normalizes the conditions of corporate capitalist exploitation in Santa Ana. Bored and frustrated by his father's stubborn attachment to the family's traditional lands, Memo seeks to escape his surroundings by hacking into a global web of radio communications, where he eavesdrops on conversations that reinforce the idea that the global corporate order represents progress and prosperity. Neoliberal governmentality further penetrates his rural community through television, in particular the show *Drones*, which, in the manner of the current US television programs *Cops* and *Homeland Security USA*, directs viewers to identify with authority figures who enforce hegemonic orders through violence, representing drone pilots as "heroes" battling "evil-doers." The narrative turns on one episode of *Drones* that takes place after Memo has hacked into the Del Rio Inc. computer system and has unknowingly been targeted as an aquaterrorist. Memo and his brother are watching the show, in which we are introduced to Rudy Ramirez, a Chicano drone pilot working for Del Rio Inc., whose first mission is being played out live on *Drones*. On television, Rudy appears handsome, muscular, and humble, yet proud of his job protecting the assets of Del Rio Inc.; he perfectly fits the "type" of conformist hero-soldier the show promotes. In a moment of tragic alienation, Memo and his brother realize Rudy is being sent to bomb their family home, represented on *Drones* as a mission to blowup a terrorist intercept. As the narrative cuts between point-of-view shots of Rudy piloting his mission and the two boys running home in desperation, their house is bombed and their father, gravely injured, crawls out. After a moment of hesitation, Rudy, following repeated orders, incinerates their father.

Memo leaves Santa Ana for Tijuana in search of a job as a node worker in an info-maquila, so that he can support his family. Along the way, the audience is introduced to a third character who performs virtual long-distance labor, Luz Martinez, an indebted recent graduate of the Institute of Bio-Media, who sells her narrated memories as "stories" on an internet memory market called Trunode. One of these memories is her chance encounter with Memo, which she uploads to Trunode as a story entitled "A Migrant from Santa Ana."

The commodification of memory as story-for-sale at first appears to deepen the film's critique of biopower and the privatization of what is most intimately human. Yet the unfolding of the film's plot redeems Luz's vision that using nodes to share memories with others (she plugs into her Trunode machine, just as Memo plugs in at Cybertek) is a powerful technology for bridging the distance between people, for connecting people to one another and letting them see what others see. The buyer for Luz's memories of encounters with Memo turns out to be Rudy, the Del Rio Inc. pilot. Rudy's guilt at having killed a man from hundreds of miles away while looking him in the face (on screen) is compounded by his experience (through Luz's stories) of Memo's loss of his father. He is affected to the degree that he literally and politically crosses to the other side, crossing the US-Mexican border from north to south, to team up with Memo and Luz and take direct action against the water privatization company. Logging in to Del Rio's drone fighter plane system from Tijuana, Rudy pretends to have received an emergency call in order to take control of a plane and use it to destroy the dam in Santa Ana. In a remarkable sequence, Memo's memory of the landscape of Santa Ana guides Rudy's fighter plane through mountains and gulches, until, in a penultimate climax, his memory of his father throwing a rock at the dam collapses in diegetic time with Rudy's blast as it destroys the dam, freeing the river.

Node technology thus turns out to have a dialectical character. As used by global corporations, it dehumanizes people and increases alienation. But as Memo, Luz, and Rudy use it, node technology intensely humanizes people for one another. It connects them from the inside out, letting them join experiences intimately, to connect across political borders and beyond the boundaries of bodies, of individual identities. Node technology in the film makes possible what Marx failed to achieve through using value as a way to identify the collectivity of human social forces; it makes possible a way for people to feel, recognize, and organize their individual powers as social forces, to act and know themselves as social being, as collective.

But it is not just the technology. It is primarily the form of consciousness that the technology transmits and shares that nurtures resistance. While Marx's *Capital* is a kind of consciousness-raising project (to teach workers they are the agents of production), post-Marxist American Studies theorize a much different and greater historical role for consciousness and culture as sites of contradiction and effective opposition to capitalist social relations. This is rooted in an understanding that the rationality of Western liberal capitalist modernity is not universal, but situated. As colonialism and racial capitalism insert capitalist social relations and their supporting concepts (possessive individualism, property rights, ideologies of white supremacy and normativity) into non-European life worlds, they produce resistances that become embedded in the cultures of people subject to racial capitalist and colonial forms of discipline and exploitation. For example, according to Cedric Robinson in *Black Marxism*, the Black radical tradition emerges as "an enduring cultural complex of historical apprehension" (5), rooted in the capacity of enslaved and racially oppressed people of African descent to preserve, or imaginatively recreate, values, ideas, conceptions, and constructions of reality based in an African past and "informed by the historical struggles for liberation and motivated by the shared sense of obligation to preserve the collective being, the ontological totality" (171). Transmitted from generation to generation as culture, these values, ideas, and conceptions give rise to evolving forms of Black revolutionary consciousness and ideologies of struggle. Similarly, in *The Politics of Culture in the Shadow of Capital*, Lisa Lowe and David Lloyd explain that culture in economic globalization has neither been fully commodified nor homogenized, but in many cases constitutes a site of alternative imaginaries from which to contest the reproduction of capitalist social relations. In this way, "culture becomes politically important where a cultural formation comes into contradiction with an economic or political logic that tries to refunction it for exploitation or domination" (24).

In *Sleep Dealer*, this is precisely the case: A global corporate power, Del Rio Inc., attempts to refunction a Mexican peasant culture of small-holders for biopolitical exploitation by commodifying the water that sustains their way of life. Although Memo initially disidentified with the Oaxacan peasant culture, rejecting his father's attachment to the family *milpa*, his name itself, "memo" short for "memory," prefigures how Memo's home culture will eventually inform his antagonism to the alienating global corporate order. Through node technology, Rudy and Luz are able to share Memo's memory of his father's resistance to water privatization and the culture that sustained that resistance. In this way, cultural and personal memory alike are shared socially and activated for anti-capitalist direct action. At the end of the film, after the dam is destroyed, Memo commits himself to creating what he calls a future with a past, a future whose continuity with a pre-neoliberal, peasant past is symbolized by the *milpa* that Memo plants on the outskirts of Tijuana. This future is dependent on another commitment Memo makes, "to connect" and "to fight." The film's focus on connections between people reminds us that, as Marx theorized, capitalism is, at heart, a set of social relations. It directs us, in line with post-Marxist approaches, to recreate, imagine, and invent modes of human relationality, beyond the predatory modes that characterize capital accumulation in neoliberal times.

144 *Jodi Melamed*

Works cited

Anderson, Kevin B. *Marx at the Margins: On Nationalism, Ethnicity, and Non-Western Societies*. Chicago, IL: U of Chicago P, 2010. Print.

Byrd, Jodi. *The Transit of Empire: Indigenous Critiques of Colonialism*. Minneapolis: U of Minnesota P, 2011. Print.

Ferguson, Roderick A. *The Reorder of Things: The U and Its Pedagogies of Minority Difference*. Minneapolis: U of Minnesota P, 2012. Print.

Foucault, Michel. *The Birth of Biopolitics: Lectures at the Collège de France, 1978–1979*. Ed. Michel Senellart. Trans. Graham Burchell. Reprint ed. New York: Picador, 2010. Print.

Harvey, David. *A Brief History of Neoliberalism*. Oxford: Oxford UP, 2007. Print.

Jameson, Fredric. *Postmodernism, or the Cultural Logic of Late Capitalism*. Durham, NC: Duke UP, 1997. Print.

Lowe, Lisa, and David Lloyd. Introduction. *The Politics of Culture in the Shadow of Capital*. Ed. Lisa Lowe and David Lloyd. Durham, NC: Duke UP, 1997. 1–32. Print.

Lowe, Lisa, and David Lloyd, eds. *The Politics of Culture in the Shadow of Capital*. Durham, NC: Duke UP, 1997. Print.

Marx, Karl. *Capital*. 1867. Vol. 1. Intr. Ernest Mandel. Trans. Ben Fowkes. New York: Vintage Books, 1977. Print.

---. *Capital*. 1867. Vol. 3. Intr. Ernest Mandel. Trans. David Fernbach. New York: Vintage Books, 1977. Print.

---. "On the Jewish Question." 1843. *Karl Marx: Early Writings*. Intr. Lucio Colletti. Trans. Rodney Livingstone and Gregor Benton. New York: Penguin Books, 1975. 211–42. Print.

---. Preface. *A Contribution to the Critique of Political Economy*. 1859. *The Marx Archive*. www.marxists.org/archive/marx/works/1859/critique-pol-economy. Web. 4 Jan. 2015.

---. "Theses on Feuerbach." 1845. *Karl Marx: Early Writings*. Intr. Lucio Colletti. Trans. Rodney Livingstone and Gregor Benton. New York: Penguin Books, 1975. 421–3. Print.

Marx, Karl, and Friedrich Engels. *The Communist Manifesto*. 1848. Intr. Gareth Stedman Jones. New York: Penguin Books, 1988. Print.

Melamed, Jodi. *Represent and Destroy: Rationalizing Violence in the New Racial Capitalism*. Minneapolis: U of Minnesota P, 2011. Print.

Reddy, Chandan. *A Freedom with Violence: Race, Sexuality, and the US State*. Durham, NC: Duke UP, 2011. Print.

Robinson, Cedric J. *Black Marxism: The Making of the Black Radical Tradition*. Chapel Hill: U of North Carolina P, 2000. Print.

Said, Edward W. *Orientalism: Western Conceptions of the Orient*. 25th anniversary ed. New York: Knopf Doubleday, 2014. Print.

Sleep Dealer. Dir. Alex Rivera. Perf. Leonor Varela, Jacob Vargas, and Luis Fernando Peña. Maya Entertainment, 2008. DVD.

Williams, Raymond. *Marxism and Literature*. Oxford: Oxford UP, 1977. Print.

13 Structuralism/Deconstruction

Simon Strick

Introduction: movements

By including Deconstruction with what this book calls "approaches," we have already made an assumption and given a definition: Deconstruction is an approach. The term "approach" implies that a given theoretical and methodological construct moves toward something, approaches it, draws to it, navigates the scholar toward what is approached. The object thus approached is an object because we can approach it. It is somewhere, it has delimitations and a location, we can be far from it or near, even if it is an elusive thing like the meaning of a text or even "American Studies." Approaches carry us nearer to the things we want to know something about, and our methods associate nearness, proximity, and closeness with the things we study. We might execute a "close reading," or a "thick description," to discover the intimate meanings of a text. Approaches are interpretative movements toward nearness, and nearness comes to be equated with understanding.

Deconstruction in this way might not be an approach, as it makes things stranger to us, disintegrating them in an intricate undoing of what they are. Interpretations help us to tell one thing from the other, to pose the question of what a particular thing is for itself and to, maybe, advance a definition. Deconstruction however quarrels with definitions. Philosophically speaking, Deconstruction works to upset ontology, the idea that things are what they are. That is, Deconstruction is less about approaching X in order to find out what it is than it is about undoing X.

This might be confusing to you, and Deconstruction – or Post-structuralism, as it is also called – was just as confusing to the academic world when it developed from Structuralism in the 1960s: People decried Deconstruction as "intellectual gibberish" and "obscurantist theory." A brief look into the historical development is useful to clarify why and how Deconstruction impacted confusingly on the university.

Structuralism 101: Saussure and signs

Structuralism (also Semiology: the study of signs) originated as a method of linguistics developed by Ferdinand de Saussure in the early twentieth century.

Saussure posited that language is a differential system in which the meaning of a word ("cat") stems not from a direct relation to the thing ("that furry animal on my lap"), but rather emerges from the word's differential relation to all other words. Saussure argued that language is made up of signifiers (words, or rather, as in the example above, the phonological sequence "kæt"), signifieds (the mental concepts to which these words, or sounds, refer), and the arbitrary relation between these two. "Arbitrary" in this instance means "not natural," but agreed upon by convention. The actual things in the world (Saussure called these "referents") bear no connection to language at all: There is, simply, no real cat in the dictionary, nor is there one in your head when you think of one. As thought is shaped by language, says Structuralism, the meaning of signs is produced within language itself. Meaning is an effect of the structure of language, emerging from the sign's differential relation to other signs. Every sign evokes the whole network of other signs and its differences from them in order to mean something. "Cat" means something because it is different from "dog," "horse" (conceptual difference) and because it differs from "can," "car," "hat" (linguistic difference). The evocation of this structure of differences is what produces a sign's meaning. To analyze how meaning comes about, Structuralism focuses on systems of signification, or simply: structures. It is the relational differences between a structure's elements that are important, not fixed and isolated definitions.

This method resonated with many disciplines in the 1950s and '60s, and the focus on structures of meaning influenced psychoanalysis (Jacques Lacan), political theory and Marxism (Louis Althusser), history of knowledge (Michel Foucault), and studies of literature, culture, and practical meaning-making in societies. The anthropologist Claude Lévi-Strauss, who also introduced Structuralism as a methodological term, held that cultures, like languages, can be viewed as systems of collective signs and symbols. A culture can be analyzed through the structural relations among its elements and especially its central binary oppositions. These oppositional pairs that organize societies are for example male/female, public/private, nature/culture, family relations/social relations, or cooked/raw.

Structuralism 201: mythologies

Roland Barthes, a French literary scholar, used the structuralist idea to develop a theory of *Mythologies* (1957) in popular culture: A myth – a "secondary semiological system" – in his view is constituted by a system of signs that in their totality evoke the notion of a simple truism, a thing taken for granted, or a popular myth (see also Chapters 9, 10, and 11). Barthes analyzed popular texts like advertising, wrestling, cars, or Mankiewicz's film *Julius Caesar* from 1953. In this latter historical drama (or swords and sandals movie), he notes the exaggerated sweatiness, the ondulated hair, and the stilted performances of white American actors Marlon Brando and James Mason. Barthes reads these as signs producing the myth of "Roman-ness," the popular notion of what Ancient Rome was like.

The function of myth for Barthes is to depoliticize and dehistoricize what is presented by mythologizing it as natural and eternally true. The film's signs of "Roman-ness" (sweat, hair, pathos) are artificial and conventional cinematic devices, but they convey Hollywood cinema as a medium of timeless accuracy and true representation: This is what Romans were like, it is readily apparent. Barthes called this evocation of the "true" or "common-sensical" the ideological function of myth.

Barthes's popular mythologies demonstrate a vital feature of the structuralist method: On the one hand, Structuralism shows that meaning is not a property of the sign itself, but that meaning is evoked by the sign's difference to all other signs. On the other, mythologies demonstrate that structures of signification often hide this very emptiness of the sign and the relationality of meaning: Their effect is one of universal truth, of plain and obvious meaning. The popular myth is what Barthes calls a totalized structure, in which many signs work to produce one meaning ("Roman-ness") that appears as simple, unequivocal, natural, universally true, readily apparent. The method of Structuralism tries to expose the structure of differences that is obscured by the meaning-effects of this same structure.

The point of the structuralist critique is not that hair-styles do not have anything to do with Romans and that some other attribute would be more accurate. Its point is that the meaning of representations is evoked by arbitrary significations, which create the notion of obviousness or common sense. In the structuralist approach, we do not look at things themselves, but we decipher the structures and processes of signification through which things become what they seemingly are.

Toward Deconstruction

Deconstruction works, like Structuralism, as a mode of *reading* a particular text, a structure of signification. This reading does not look for a meaning – or even *the* meaning – of the text, but rather traces the terms of how this meaning (or any meaning) is produced within the textual structure. Deconstruction's central presupposition is that there are no things that are not textual – thinking is structured by the differential terms of language.[1] The eminent protagonist of Deconstruction, the French-Algerian philosopher Jacques Derrida, therefore postulated: "[I]l n'y a pas de hors-texte" – there is no outside of the text, since there is no outside to language that we can think. Consequently, there is no end to reading.

Derrida's work in this sense is the extension of reading, of analyzing textual structures not for their meaning, but for the internal processes of meaning-production. Unlike the structuralists however, Derrida read and analyzed influential texts of Western philosophy. To put it simply, Derrida applied the structuralist principle – meaning emerges from systems of difference – to the philosophical tradition of metaphysics: The ongoing project from Plato to (at least) Immanuel Kant to think the basic principles of the world and to think the question of being. Metaphysics is no less than the thinking of what everything is.

Derrida's argument about metaphysics departs rather simply from two thoughts, and we know the first already from Structuralism: The meaning of a philosophical concept like *presence* is not given, but rather is produced by the concept's difference from another concept, *absence*. Absence is necessarily a part of the definition of presence, as – we can hear Structuralism knocking – words and concepts have no meaning on their own, but only within a structure of differences. Philosophy, an operation only possible in language, is such a structure of differences, and it is built on fundamental binary oppositions such as presence and absence, being and not-being, identity and difference. Secondly, Derrida argues, metaphysics is not only made up of these binary oppositions (presence/absence), but privileges one over the other. His case in point is the opposition of *speech* and *writing*, and we will take a closer look here.

Deconstruction 101: logocentrism

In his 1967 book *Of Grammatology*, Derrida traces how philosophical texts have consistently privileged speech over writing: From Plato to Jean-Jacques Rousseau, all philosophy agrees that speech is nearer to truth. This is apparent in the central philosophical concept of *logos*, the Greek word for word, logic, reason, and speech (in theology, *logos* means "word of God"). The spoken word is associated with reason, presence, and identity: The speaker is present, his[2] identity is certain, and he is conscious of his words' meaning. Against *logos*, philosophy downgrades writing, which it defines as merely a representation of speech, a secondary and insufficient substitute for speaking the truth: Unlike speech, the written word lacks presence (the speaker is not there, we cannot verify what he might have meant) and identity (the author is absent from the text and he has to distance himself from himself in order to write thoughts down). We can see how this simple opposition between speech and writing already calls forth a structure of associated differences (presence/absence, identity/difference), and further, how these attendant oppositions are hierarchically organized. One is always original, the other derivative: speech/presence/identity are original, foundational, and associated with truth; writing/absence/difference are secondary, derivative, and only supplementary to the original.[3]

Putting these two observations together, Derrida argues that the hierarchical order of the metaphysical pairings presence/absence, identity/difference, speech/writing is not a natural given, but an effect of the structure of language. Presence carries meaning because it is defined against absence, and the necessary evocation of absence in defining presence is obscured when philosophy posits presence as original and absence as secondary and derivative. Dealing with the binary opposition speech/writing, Derrida's argument develops its full force: While the philosophical tradition of metaphysics necessarily exists as language, writing, and text (hence, difference), Derrida argues, its primary undertaking is to constantly evoke the *logos* – e.g., speech, reason, presence – as its origin. Metaphysics is therefore caught up in a movement against itself: While it always already is and must be a textual undertaking and an operation within a differential structure, it also must incessantly define text, writing, and difference as secondary and derivative to the original *logos*.[4] Derrida argues that this is the paradox of Western metaphysics – to be necessarily divided against its own terms. While it denounces difference and privileges the *logos*, it can do so only within the differential terms of language.

What follows from Derrida's observation of this paradox? Again, thinking back to Barthes's critique of the popular myth, an analysis of how meaning is produced by differences does not result in the conclusion that meaning is wrong or at fault and something else is more accurate – for example that writing is closer to truth. The point of a deconstructive reading is rather to show two things: First, the conditions of meaning-production, the work of differences. And second, how the structure that produces meaning always obscures its own differential work, so that the meaning produced seems natural, original, and unequivocally true. Deconstructive readings therefore destabilize and denaturalize the meanings a particular text or sign-structure produces. Derrida regards metaphysics as a project of logocentrism: a systematic privileging of presence, identity, reason, and speech in order to obscure its reliance on difference and structures of signification.

We can see how Deconstruction is not an approach that brings us nearer to an understanding of metaphysics, but rather a process of reading the paradoxical and privileging structures of its operation: Reason, identity, and presence become stranger and estranged to us – they emerge not as the natural center of thinking, but rather as products of a privileging rhetorical operation that obscures its own reliance on difference. Generally speaking, Deconstruction's work is the critique of "centrism," of these illegitimate and inevitable obscurations of difference in order to produce presence, origin, the universal. As literary scholar Barbara Johnson explains:

> [D]econstruction is a form of what has long been called a critique. A critique of any theoretical system is not an examination of its flaws or imperfections. It is not a set of criticisms designed to make the system better. It is an analysis that focuses on the grounds of that system's possibility. The critique reads backwards from what seems natural, obvious, self-evident, or universal, in order to show that these things have their history, their reasons for being what they are, their effects on what follows from them, and that the starting point is not a (natural) given but a (cultural) construct, usually blind to itself. (xv)

As my following historical contextualization of the impact of Derrida's deconstructive efforts will show, the French philosopher was not the only person interested in reversing the "natural" order of things and pointing out blind spots in dominant systems of thought. Indeed, while Derrida's textual critique of metaphysics is a singularly important and sophisticated project, much of Deconstruction's importance for American Studies stems from the fruitful connections it established with other modes of thinking. These were less interested in the paradoxes of Western philosophy, but in political change.

Deconstruction 201: political uses

Deconstruction made its first arrival in the United States in 1966, when Derrida attended an all-male symposium at Johns Hopkins University, featuring protagonists of what was seen as old (Jean Hyppolite, René Girard) and new French theory (Paul de Man, Barthes, Lacan). His lecture "Structure, Sign, and Play in the Discourse of the Human Sciences" was later published in a book entitled *The Structuralist Controversy* (Macksey and Donato 1970), generally regarded as the publication to bring Structuralism and Deconstruction to American academic audiences. In the following year, Derrida also published three books in France, which were soon translated into English: *Speech and Phenomena* (1973), *Of Grammatology* (1974), and the essay collection *Writing and Difference* (1978). The important book *Dissemination* in English followed in 1981. These books, dealing mostly with texts of the Western philosophical tradition, laid out the tenets of Deconstruction and introduced the term as such to the American academe.

Derrida's terminology and practice of reading texts against themselves initially resonated strongest with a group of literary scholars, including J. Hillis Miller and Geoffrey Hartman at Yale, who were interested in dislodging the then-reigning approach of New Criticism. Known as the Yale School of Deconstruction, these critics argued that literary texts carried multiple, highly ambiguous, and self-contradicting meanings, a view running counter to New Criticism's focus on establishing the single best and most unified interpretation of a text through rigid, formalist reading. Yet while the Yale School was deconstructing and disrupting unified interpretations of literary classics from Milton to Faulkner, American universities were experiencing ruptures of a more far-reaching kind.

It is important to realize that the 1960s and '70s were a period of unprecedented political upheaval in the United States: In 1968, Martin Luther King, Jr. was shot in Memphis, Tennessee; feminists held the first public speakout against abortion laws in New York City; American troops in Vietnam committed the My Lai massacre, killing hundreds of civilians; a year later, the customers of a gay bar in Christopher Street, New York City fought back against homophobic and brutal police methods in the Stonewall Riots. The Civil Rights Movement, the movement of Second Wave Feminism, anti-imperialist and anti-colonial struggles, and the Gay Liberation Movement are acts of civil unrest protesting against the violence and discrimination with which the white, male, middle-class consumerist and heterosexual mainstream marginalized and oppressed people, cultures, and ways of living. These protests equally ruptured and restructured academic culture, largely through the efforts of protesting students and teachers: The first Black Studies program was organized at San Francisco State University in 1968; the first accredited course in Women's Studies was held in 1969 at Cornell University; Chicana/o Studies were borne of the efforts of the Third World Liberation Front (TWLF) student strike at UC Berkeley the same year,[5] which resulted in the establishment of an Ethnic Studies department at that university.

So, as Derrida was providing analytical tools to deconstruct the privileging structures of metaphysical logocentrism in the 1970s, political activists, academic study groups, and social protesters were working to dismantle structural privileges within the academy, the exclusionary practices of capitalist and patriarchal society, and of US (and European) imperialism. Deconstruction's interaction with these political struggles is important to understand what the theory might mean to you as students of American Cultural Studies today.

Imagine the situation: *Here* is Derrida's sophisticated reading taking apart the binary oppositions in Rousseau's *Confessions* (1782), executed in the philosophical high-language of the Sorbonne in Paris – *there* are groups of students being arrested for protesting the discrimination and exclusion of women in the academy, the imperialist politics of the Vietnam War, and the racial prejudice implicit in the absence of African American literature in their curriculum. What do these critical movements have in common?

Simply speaking, these endeavors were moving against a dominant system (of thought, of society, of politics) that rested on and enforced differences but constructed itself as universal and self-evident. Let us take the feminist struggles of the 1960s and '70s as an example: One central demand of feminist politics was crystallized in the slogan "the personal is political." This slogan was phrased in reaction to the dominant patriarchal view that women's concerns over discrimination pertained more to the private realm, meaning that the questions of women's rights affected only individual women, not society or politics as a whole. Domestic violence against women was regarded as a problem of a woman and her husband (and mostly the wife's fault), not as an issue of society at large and of universal concern. Feminism countered this rationale by simply – and deconstructively – stating that the distinction between private (individual, female) and public (general, universal) concerns is an artificial construction of patriarchal, male power: Patriarchy relegates women to the particular and private while it defines itself as self-evidently universal and of public concern, thereby obscuring its own reliance on a politics of difference. The name of this construction is sexism. The slogan "the personal is political" therefore not only reverses the privilege of terms (private is more important than public), but challenges the distinctions private/public or particular/universal as caught up in patriarchal, male-centered, and sexist politics.

A similar example can be given concerning the anti-racist struggles of the Civil Rights Movement – also met with the mainstream attitude that they concerned only the problems of African Americans, not of society in general. African American critics rightly pointed out that the distinction between marginal and universal concerns is in itself an operation of white racism, which privileges being white as the universal position and relegates the "race problem" to African Americans – thereby obscuring how the idea of general society (not concerned by racism) rests on racial difference: It is constructed as consisting of non-African Americans.

Constructive alliances

In as much as the idea of universality should now feel stranger to you, you might also begin to get a feeling of how the deconstructive critique of dominant systems works. It is important to stress that neither the central concerns of feminism nor the Civil Rights Movement were inspired by Derrida. These movements formulated their points of critique much earlier, and markedly with the intent of not only textually deconstructing, but of abolishing the oppressive structures of sexism and racism. However, it seems like Deconstruction's technique of dislodging universality reflected a common goal of these political projects. For the alliance of feminism and Deconstruction, Seyla Benhabib described that both discovered their "affinities in the struggle against the grand narratives of Western Enlightenment and modernity" (27). These affinities led to one important moment of confluence between political activism and deconstructive theory: As the political changes brought about by feminism and the Civil Rights Movement gained traction in the universities with the institution of new programs and departments, Deconstruction offered an analytical language and procedure for these new, activist disciplines to argue and contend with the often hostile high-intellectual climate of the academy. Deconstruction and aligned theories, like Foucault's critique of discursive power, provided an important critical idiom for these new disciplines.[6]

Deconstruction was embraced by important protagonists of these disciplines, such as Henry Louis Gates, Jr., Houston A. Baker, and Hortense Spillers (African American Studies); Edward Said and Homi K. Bhabha (Postcolonial Theory); Barbara Johnson and Joan Scott (feminism and Women's Studies); Eve Kosofsky Sedgwick and Judith Butler (Queer Studies). It also instilled a resurgence of radical theoretical and methodological (self-)reflection in humanities scholarship. Spivak for example, who had translated *Of Grammatology* in 1976, emerged as one of the major theorists of Postcolonial Theory in the 1980s. One of Spivak's radical points of (self-)critique was the fundamental question "Can the Subaltern Speak?" (1988): Given the complicity of Western universities with an imperialist and neo-colonial politics of discourse and knowledge production, Spivak's question reflected on the very possibility of anti-colonial politics from within US-American academic structures.

Concisely, Deconstruction's questioning of the very terms in which thinking and interpretation operates provided vital instruments for these critical disciplines to reflect their own transition from movement to academic discipline, and to critique the implicit binary opposition between activism and scholarship informing this transition. And importantly, the politicization of Deconstruction's theoretical tenets caused the initial protagonist of Deconstruction to rethink the politics of his theory: Derrida in his later work rewrote "logocentrism" as "phallogocentrism," acknowledging the feminist work (for example, of Luce Irigaray and Hélène Cixous) that had worked out the male-centered, phallic implications of Western metaphysics and its exclusion of femininity from the domain of reason. Much of Derrida's work since the 1980s is concerned with eminently political and ethical questions and followed impulses from the many activist uses of Deconstruction.

There are surely different ways to tell this story of intellectual development and exchange, but I think that the many politicized carriers and critics of Deconstruction – working in feminism, Postcolonial Critique, Critical Race Studies, and Queer Theory – put the approach from off its head, on which it was standing, and placed it upon its feet.

Activist conclusion

So, the first move in an article on Deconstruction as an "approach to American Studies" would be to deconstruct what "approach," "American," and "Studies" mean, and that means to think about what things, concepts, and politics are excluded and obscured by the seeming simplicity and self-evidentiality of these terms. As I have tried to show, this work of Deconstruction is not a clear methodology or approach that gets us nearer to things. It is not an explication of a static sense of the world, of culture, or of texts – it is also not a particular politics. Rather, Deconstruction is the work of American Studies as an academic subject to make itself and its objects strange, unstable, and difficult, to undo (and retrace) the very meaning-making structures we operate in.

For these reasons I have refrained from doing what the other methodological chapters of this book do, which is giving an example of Deconstruction as it is used in scholarly work: that is, to either "deconstruct" a particular object of American Studies (a text, a film, an image) or to explicate how a particular text might be "deconstructing" something else (as Cultural Studies scholars might say: Film X deconstructs stereotypes of Y). I have instead pointed to critical instances – feminism's critique of the private/public divide or Critical Race Theory's dislodging of the difference between racial and universal concerns – to show the use-value of deconstructive thinking. These crucial interventions indicate why it is hard to explain Deconstruction through an "example" or exemplary object: The term example itself derives from Latin *eximere*, which literally means to take something out, make an anecdote, to isolate one thing from its context in order to support a larger point. Feminism's deconstructive handling of public vs. private on the other hand would work precisely against this logic of isolating and subsuming, but demands to think and speak about the entanglement of the general/public and the anecdotal/private, and to destabilize the whole structure of difference. Deconstruction in this regard is an activity, a process that is extensive and encompassing. A book or movie might indeed commit to a deconstruction of gender stereotypes (by showing how unnatural the meanings of gender are). Deconstruction in my book however is not happy with simply *having* deconstructed X (and thus being finished with critique), but rather goes on to expose how this "having deconstructed" in itself destabilizes other significations and constructions, which one would have to deconstruct further in order to analyze the "grounds of possibility" (Johnson) of culture *and* critique in itself. A proper example of Deconstruction as method would therefore be an endless example, and endlessness is the opposite of what an example, and this book, can do.

As work, Deconstruction is – like the political critiques of feminism, Queer Theory, Postcolonialism, and Critical Race Theory, to which American Studies owe as a discipline – an activity, an activism. It is what we do in order to avoid perpetrating and naturalizing specific meanings of culture. It is the necessary work to maintain a view of culture and politics as things that are fluid, vital, open, changeable, complicated, historical, diverse, and in need of being worked through again and again. And in as much as there is no end to culture or politics, and no end to their complications and complexities, there is no end to work.

Notes

1 Of course, the world itself (think of the cat) might not be textual. But we have no way of grasping or approaching the world that is not based on language. The concepts with which we grasp what is in the world are tied to systems of differentiation and signification ("cat" is not "dog" or "can").
2 I am using the masculine form here deliberately, since the implied subject of metaphysical philosophy is male.
3 Rousseau, one of the philosophers Derrida reads, compared speaking philosophy to being in the presence of his lover, while writing down thoughts was like masturbation – merely a substitute for "real love." This may indicate how far the alignment of oppositional pairs reaches.
4 In *Of Grammatology*, Derrida finds traces of this paradox in the texts of many philosophers from antiquity to the Enlightenment, such as Rousseau, Plato, or Hegel. They invariably describe writing as the necessary supplement of metaphysics and simultaneously as the undermining of its central project of the *logos*, or reason.
5 The Berkeley TWLF was composed of various student organizations, such as the Mexican American Student Confederation, the Asian American Student Organization, the Native American Students Union, and the African American Students Union.
6 This alliance between activist disciplines and Deconstruction carried problems as well, as many activists felt that Deconstruction presented a hyper-theoretical

method developed in a highly privileged academic institution. Such critique was voiced for example in Barbara Christian's important essay "The Race for Theory" (1988), which criticized Deconstructionism of invoking (while deconstructing) a fundamentally white, European tradition and therefore marginalizing other traditions of theorization in African American scholarship and culture.

Works cited

Althusser, Louis. "Ideology and Ideological State Apparatuses." 1970. *Lenin and Philosophy and Other Essays.* Trans. Ben Brewster. New York: Monthly Review P, 1971. 121–76. Print.

Barthes, Roland. *Mythologies.* 1957. Trans. Annette Lavers. New York: Hill and Wang, 1972. Print.

Benhabib, Seyla. "Feminism and Postmodernism: An Uneasy Alliance." *Feminist Contentions: A Philosophical Exchange.* Ed. Seyla Benhabib. New York: Routledge, 1995. 17–34. Print.

Christian, Barbara. "The Race for Theory." *Feminist Studies* 14.1 (1988): 67–79. Print.

Cixous, Hélène. "The Laugh of the Medusa." Trans. Keith Cohen and Paula Cohen. *Signs* 1.4 (1976): 875–93. Print.

Derrida, Jacques. *Dissemination.* 1972. Trans. Barbara Johnson. Chicago, IL: U of Chicago P, 1981. Print.

---. *Of Grammatology.* 1967. Trans. Gayatri Chakravorty Spivak. Baltimore, MD: Johns Hopkins UP, 1974. Print.

---. *Speech and Phenomena; And Other Essays on Husserl's Theory of Signs.* 1967. Trans. David Allison. Evanston, IL: Northwestern UP, 1973. Print.

---. *Writing and Difference.* 1967. Trans. Alan Bass. Chicago, IL: U of Chicago P, 1978. Print.

Foucault, Michel. *The Order of Things: An Archaeology of the Human Sciences.* 1966. New York: Vintage, 1977. Print.

Irigaray, Luce. *Speculum of the Other Woman.* 1974. Trans. Gillian C. Gill. Ithaca, NY: Cornell UP, 1985. Print.

Johnson, Barbara. "Translator's Introduction." *Dissemination.* 1972. Jacques Derrida. Trans. Barbara Johnson. Chicago, IL: U of Chicago P, 1981. vii–xxxv. Print.

Lacan, Jacques. *Écrits: A Selection.* Trans. Alan Sheridan. New York: Norton, 1977. Print.

Lévi-Strauss, Claude. *The Raw and the Cooked: Introduction to a Science of Mythology.* 1964. Trans. John Weightman and Doreen Weightman. New York: Harper and Row, 1969. Print.

Macksey, Richard, and Eugenio Donato, eds. *The Structuralist Controversy: The Languages of Criticism and the Sciences of Man.* Baltimore, MD: Johns Hopkins UP, 1970. Print.

Saussure, Ferdinand de. *Course in General Linguistics.* 1916. Trans. Roy Harris. Glasgow: Fontana, 1977. Print.

Spivak, Gayatri Chakravorty. "Can the Subaltern Speak?" *Marxism and the Interpretation of Culture.* Ed. Cary Nelson and Larry Grossberg. Chicago, IL: U of Illinois P, 1988. 271–313. Print.

14 Psychoanalysis and beyond

Analyzing Hannibal Lecter

Katja Schmieder

Hannibal Lecter, an American icon of popular culture

In 1981, the novel *Red Dragon* was published, and since then, a cultural icon called Dr. Hannibal Lecter has attracted broad public attention. A psychiatrist and a cannibalistic serial killer in one person, this fictional character tapped right into and even anticipated contemporary anxieties of American culture.

The early 1980s saw the beginning of an apparent serial killer panic in the United States, and this phenomenon not only sparked a rising interest in psychological aberrations that would enable an individual to commit such horrible crimes. The perceived threat of the deranged serial killer also helped restore the prestige of the FBI, which had collapsed in the 1970s together with J. Edgar Hoover's reputation. The FBI suddenly presented itself as the sole administrator of forensic psychiatry, the science that promised to once and for all solve the mystery of the human mind.

While Thomas Harris's *Red Dragon* was followed by book sequels (1988, 1999, 2006), film adaptations, and, since 2013, by a TV series, the author himself has remained largely inconspicuous. With his seminal novels that permeate the generic boundaries of detective fiction, police procedural, and psychological thriller, Harris has contributed to the so-called forensic turn in American popular culture, as "he satirizes forensic psychiatry, the field that is responsible for filtering information for the courts and recommending who is mad, versus who is bad or evil [...]. Harris's character, Dr. Hannibal Lecter, became the best-recognized villain of late-20th-century America," Packer and Pennington conclude (xxi). Philip Simpson even argues that Harris has created the "Harrisverse" (44), a distinct literary universe. Nevertheless, his books have remained largely neglected by scholarship.

While the Lecter movies were arguably conceptualized for the taste of a broader audience, the decidedly different narrative construction of major aspects of the story, such as the Lecter figure, the endings (especially with *Hannibal*, where the movie completely changes the novel's ending), and the general treatment of psychoanalysis as a motif render the novels specifically prone to an examination that utilizes psychoanalysis in order to produce literary and cultural readings. The following paragraphs not only pay due attention to Harris's writings, they will furthermore attempt to read the figure Hannibal Lecter through the lens of psychoanalytical and post-structuralist criticism.

Psychoanalysis and American Studies

Like many popular forensic crime stories of the last thirty years, the story of the to-date four Lecter novels revolves around the sciences of the mind. The approach of psychoanalytical literary criticism, in turn, deals with psychological processes. It thus focalizes the author, the characters, the text, and the readers and the manifold interactions between them a work of fiction engenders.

Originally conceptualized as a counter-movement against mainstream psychiatry and clinical psychology at the end of the nineteenth century, Sigmund Freud introduced psychoanalysis as a therapy and a theory, both of which constituted a new approach to the human being. In the cultural and historical context of Victorian Vienna, he conceived his ideas with the help of literary texts, analyzing for example *Oedipus the King* by Sophocles or *Hamlet* by William Shakespeare. Among his many followers was C.G. Jung, who introduced the theory of the archetypes and the collective unconscious. Since the overwhelming majority of psychoanalytical thinkers were of Jewish background, they had to leave continental Europe in the 1930s and move to the United States, or – as Freud did – to Great Britain. In Nazi Germany, psychoanalysis became the target of harsh ideological attack, resulting in a general ban during National Socialism. Freud's books were burnt in 1933. However, psychoanalysis as theory and practice has survived. Psychoanalysis, in fact, was well received in the United States and in Great Britain, but with different emphases. In North America the branch called ego-psychology became established most quickly, and psychotherapeutic practices started spreading throughout the major cities.

One of Freud's greatest achievements was the emphasis on the human unconscious and the drives along with the model of the tripartite structure of the human psyche, divided into Id, Ego, and Super-Ego. Throughout his life, Freud reviewed and interrelated his theories and concepts.

In the postmodern intellectual climate of the 1970s and early 1980s traditional approaches in the humanities were questioned and reviewed, and the field of American Studies, too, opened up to a host of new theories and movements. This pluralism of approaches also sparked a renewed interest in psychological and especially psychoanalytical interrogations of culture. French Post-structuralism and feminism might rightfully be identified as the major influences in this diversification process: Thinkers like Jacques Lacan, Jacques Derrida, Luce Irigaray, and Julia Kristeva criticized, revised, and further developed psychoanalysis by utilizing the theories of cultural anthropologist Claude Lévi-Strauss and linguist Ferdinand de Saussure (see also Chapter 13). Their emphasis on language and text in psychoanalysis had a huge impact on the work of American scholars and critics.

The American feminist movement of the 1960s and '70s had a particular share in the critique and renewal of traditional psychoanalysis, as Jane Gallop observes (314). The junction of political and intellectual issues constituted an important aspect in feminism's critique of psychoanalysis, as "feminism promises to save psychoanalysis from its ahistorical and apolitical doldrums" (Gallop 315). Moving away from general accusations of misogyny and homophobia, scholars like Nancy Chodorow helped articulate productive commentaries on and revisions of psychoanalytical theory. Since the 1980s, American psychoanalytical feminist criticism has been firmly established, and such works as the essay collection *The (M)other Tongue* (Garner, Kahane, and Sprengnether), which pinpoints the neglect of the mother in the psychosexual development of the child in "Freud's Oedipal scripts" (Gallop 317), gives evidence of the important feminist debate about different aspects in psychoanalysis.

Psychoanalysis and/in the Hannibal Lecter books

Psychoanalysis itself – its theory, method, and practice – constitutes a crucial topic addressed throughout the Hannibal Lecter tetralogy, and reading the books through the psychoanalytical lens is productive and rewarding for different reasons: The character of Dr. Hannibal Lecter is a trained psychiatrist with a medical degree, who not only lectures his audience on psychology, psychiatry, and psychoanalysis, but who also applies the psychoanalytical method to the characters in the story. Being well versed in the study of the human mind, his figure provides the major path to a Literary Studies analysis of the books' structures and motifs. Harris's fiction "practically cries out for it," (38) Philip Simpson argues, as it deconstructs psychoanalysis not only by commenting on but also by dissecting its very concepts, methods, and practitioners. While Lecter is traditionally studied as a film character – as Anthony Hopkins's role of the ultimately evil, cruel, and whimsical villain – my interpretation provides an alternative, even contradictory view of Lecter as hero. Consequently, the following exemplary readings of the quarter-century spanning the Lecter series look at the character who embraces/incorporates psychoanalysis most, and whom the books construct and explore so differently from the films.

Red Dragon (1981), the Lecter novel whose story chronologically succeeds *Hannibal Rising* (2006), assigns him a place as a rather marginal figure. Sentenced to life imprisonment for multiple murders, Lecter does his time in the maximum security unit of the Hospital for the Criminally Insane in Baltimore. Living on memories, the news about recent crimes, committed by a killer the police call "Tooth Fairy," provides a welcome change. The FBI reactivates investigator Will Graham to help find the serial murderer who kills upper-middle-class families in Southern US suburbia, and Graham feels that he needs to see Lecter for a profile. Lecter, even though he had earlier tried to stab Graham in the moment of his exposure, and even though he toys with people and manipulates them, also supports Graham with information about the Tooth Fairy. However, when Lecter finds out he is played, too, he offers the killer Graham's home address.

Yet the sophisticated way in which Lecter reads and analyzes other individuals cannot be applied to himself: Doctors and detectives regularly fail to categorize and study him as a serial killer, cannibal, and sociopath. They cannot read him, and in their hands psychology becomes a useless, even dangerous instrument. So it comes as no surprise that the FBI, and specifically the Behavioral Science Unit (BSU) with its new panacea – psychological profiling – represents the unified effort to first capture and later study Hannibal. As one of the series' spectacular plot twists, psychological profiling and forensic psychiatry, both of which in real-life police work have become immensely popular since the early 1980s,[1] are ultimately proven to have been wrong from the very beginning: In *Red Dragon* one of the detectives voices about Dr. Lecter that "he had the first and worst sign – sadism to animals as a child" (61). To disprove this claim, one only needs to glance at Lecter's fictional "biography" to find that he has always respected and even protected individuals society deems victims: women, children – and animals. While this move might be considered a retcon,[2] one could argue that Harris satirizes the FBI and its serial killer definition, especially with regard to Lecter's unknown childhood. This twist dismantles the FBI and its spectacular profiling unit for the reader, subtly starting the chain of discrediting the FBI throughout the books.

While *Red Dragon* thematizes the fatal attack on the traditional American family complete with kids, pet, and home, *The Silence of the Lambs* (1988) virtually and literally dissects the human skin and its meaning for one's gender identity. In *The Silence of the Lambs*, Lecter claims center stage together with FBI detective fledgling Clarice Starling, and from his basement cell he again orchestrates the events in the world outside. Lecter not only works through Starling's conflicts but also helps her solve the case of "Buffalo Bill," a multiple killer who murders young women to tailor himself a woman suit made from their skins. Indeed, Lecter manipulates Starling and offers her only clues, not conclusions, but he never lies. It is his "talking cure" that enables Starling to rescue Buffalo Bill's last victim, a US senator's daughter, in the nick of time. Harris's novels, like many other popular texts, condemn the FBI and its patriarchal, bureaucratic structures, and Lecter lectures: "In fact, most psychology is puerile, Officer Starling, and that practiced in Behavioral Science is on a level with phrenology" (*The Silence* 408).

In the ensuing story and the series' third book, *Hannibal* (1999), FBI agent Clarice Starling becomes the target of FBI chauvinists. She is blamed for a failed drug raid, and the men who duped and scapegoated her finally enforce her suspension. Again she can rely on the support of the now free Dr. Lecter, who resurfaces in Italy as the art historian Dr. Fell. In the meantime the FBI is not Lecter's only hunter: Mason Verger, wealthy heir of a big slaughterhouse business and a pedophile whom Lecter disfigures during one of his therapy sessions, offers a huge bounty on Lecter's head. Verger's henchmen kidnap Lecter after his return to the United States, Starling saves his life, and both hide from the world in Lecter's seaside home. In the weeks to come Starling undergoes Lecter's Freudian treatment, and the two cure each other's childhood traumata. They finally punish Starling's nemesis at the FBI, Paul Krendler, and move to South America as lovebirds – to live happily ever after.

Only the last novel, *Hannibal Rising* (2006), focuses almost exclusively on Lecter. While *Hannibal* was already torn to pieces by readers and reviewers for the dethroning of national hero Starling, it was *Hannibal Rising* that garnered the most withering critique and was perceived as a betrayal. By depicting Lecter's traumatic childhood and early youth in Lithuania during World War II, where he had to witness his sister's cannibalization, the dark, evil, mysterious Lecter suddenly becomes disenchanted. However, the account of his formative years also explains the development of his intellectual faculties and his tastes. The meanness and cruelty of the looters of his childhood and, later on, of the FBI, as well as Mason Verger and his bounty hunters, put Lecter's crimes in perspective.

Psychoanalytical criticism in the Freudian way

Based on the paradigm of infantile sexuality and the tripartite structure of the human psyche, Freud developed theories about the interpretation of dreams and about the "uncanny," both of which provide keys to an understanding of the human psyche and literary texts alike. In the following these concepts will be applied in exemplary readings (see *Die Traumdeutung*).

The uncanny

Freud published his theory about the uncanny in his 1919 work "Das Unheimliche," where he reflects at length on the etymological origins of the word, deriving from the German "heimelig" (homey) and "heimlich" (secret) (242–74; my trans.). Freud claimed that experiences and thoughts that had been perceived as homey and cozy in childhood would be repressed and might resurface during adulthood, thus creating an "unhomely," uncanny feeling. The uneasiness lies in the contents of such feelings, contents that range from emotions, like being left alone in a dark room, to childhood fantasies, such as the fear of castration. The motifs we would render uncanny as adults range from concrete images like that of the doppelganger or severed body parts to ideas of repetition and animism. These motifs have dominated gothic literature from its beginnings, and Freud's theories were in large part a response to such literary motifs. Contemporary crime and horror fictions regularly make use of the uncanny and other psychoanalytical concepts to develop plots that focus on broader psychological questions.

The Hannibal Lecter tetralogy carries on the tradition of gothic literature and employs the uncanny in many diverse ways. First of all, the books themselves constitute a series, an uncanny repetition if you wish, and all four stories (even though mostly evolving around Lecter) present a similar, almost repetitive pattern of crimes, namely, serial murders.[3] The first two novels, *Red Dragon* and *The Silence of the Lambs*, virtually mirror each other in terms of plot, and we might almost read *The Silence of the Lambs* as some kind of doppelganger of *Red Dragon* because we encounter the same elements and twists of the plot in both books. Each time Lecter is incarcerated in the maximum security ward of the Baltimore Hospital for the Criminally Insane, and each time he helps solve a case of multiple murder while being a serial killer himself.

The interpretation of dreams

In classical psychoanalysis dreams are understood to provide the "royal path to the unconscious." Due to their latent (hidden) and manifest (remembered) content, classical psychoanalysis assumes that they might be interpreted, not unlike literary texts. Furthermore, their manifest content is shaped through dream work, while dream work encodes the latent content into decipherable symbols by means of displacement and condensation.

Two of the most frequently appearing clusters of dream symbols and literary symbols in the Lecter novels are weapons and other long, phallic objects as representations of the male genitalia and houses as manifestations of the human body itself. For Lecter houses very often function as a replacement for human relationships. Not surprisingly, Lecter Castle and the hunting lodge of his childhood, the residence of his stepmother Lady Murasaki when he was a teenager, and, later, the asylum and the palazzo symbolize lacking or missing human bonds. Rooms, corridors, chambers, and doors serve a different symbolic function, namely that of the female genitalia. While readers might identify Lecter's memory palace with the Freudian preconscious – the part of the human mind that, other than the unconscious, Freud deemed accessible without being constantly available – this portrayal might also indicate Lecter's involvement with and incorporation of the feminine in his own psyche.

Even more obvious in terms of Freudian theory is the frequent use of swords, blades, and all sorts of thrusting weapons. Lecter commits his very first murder out of feelings of retribution because his victim, a misogynistic and racist butcher in France, had sexually insulted his beloved stepmother. Read as a phallic symbol, one might easily recognize the meaning of the penetrating sword when young Lecter punishes his rivaling enemy (*Hannibal Rising* 122). Furthermore, the murders with long, pointed objects could be read as stand-in for sexuality, and the fact that Lecter stops killing when he is finally together with Clarice might support this interpretation.

Sublimation

With regard to the above considerations, killing provides an outlet, even catharsis for Lecter. What if – psychoanalytically speaking – he sublimates his sexual drives through murder? Originally conceived as one of the Ego's defense mechanisms, i.e., one of the means by which the Ego mediates between the Id and the Super-Ego, Freud soon conceded that sublimation did not serve to pinpoint neurotic symptoms but was rather a healthy mechanism to channel and divert potentially harmful libidinal or sadistic energy. Sublimation even delivers an explanatory model for artistic creativity. In the character of Dr. Hannibal Lecter this concept is vividly illustrated: By becoming a medical doctor and a connoisseur, a scientist and an artist, he sublimates certain drives that might otherwise have been harmful to him. However, Harris gives this mechanism another twist when actually reversing the idea of sublimation: It seems that Lecter refines his manners and tastes further by killing unpleasant individuals, and, thus, ridding society of boredom, stupidity, and rudeness. Slaughtering and sometimes eating the "free-range rude" (*Hannibal* 831) including Paul Momund (*Hannibal Rising*), Frederick Chilton (*Red Dragon, The Silence*), and Paul Krendler (*The Silence, Hannibal*) apparently "purges him of lesser rudeness" (*The Silence* 412).

Along these lines, another of Freud's concepts, which is elaborated in his study "Totem und Tabu" (1913), needs to be addressed. He refers to the primal horde ("Urhorde") as constitutive of the two great taboos modern society has to face: incest and the killing and eating of the primordial father, or totem. While the topic of incest is presented only indirectly in Harris's books through the parent or sibling fixation of most characters, killing and cannibalism figure prominently throughout the story. The protagonist Dr. Hannibal Lecter, in fact, represents the perfection of cannibalism: He not only prepares body parts and organs of his victims according to the latest *haute cuisine* trends, he also lets his dinner guests (unknowingly) participate in the meals.

While thus using his teeth in rather unconventional ways for a human being, they also serve as the marker of Lecter's vampiric identity.[4] Whenever Lecter is described, his white teeth and pallor are usually mentioned first – along with other features: Dark red eyes that glow in the dark (*Hannibal* 876) and dark hair with a widow's peak (*The Silence* 527). The importance of the senses of sight, smell, and taste, which enable him to sublimate rudeness, also render him super- or rather preternatural. Moreover, his figure's proximity to vampires also complicates the involvement of the novels with mirrors and mirror images, which will be addressed in the following section.

Hannibal in the Lacanian mirror

The meaning of Lacan

Jacques Lacan, French scholar and practitioner of psychoanalysis, is widely perceived as the most flamboyant figure of Post-structuralism. He assertively regarded himself as the authorized successor of psychoanalysis but also as scholarly entitled to "remake" and thus purify psychoanalysis with the help of Structuralism and linguistics. He became legendary for his *Écrits* (1966) and his seminars, which he published in a series format from 1953 to 1979. Each seminar deals with one major revision or "purification" of classical psychoanalysis. Lacan became famous for the introduction of the imaginary, the symbolic, and the real as the three orders to more or less replace the Freudian tripartite division and to re-determine childhood development in terms of linguistic structures. Another revision along these lines included the re-introduction of Roman Jakobson's metonymy for displacement and metaphor for condensation.

When Lecter remembers his sister Mischa, teeth play (again) a crucial role: Whereas classical psychoanalysis links the symbol of teeth, losing teeth, or pulling teeth with sexuality, it is the recurring motif of Lecter's sister's baby teeth that constitutes the core element of his unresolved childhood trauma. Thus, in a Lacanian sense Mischa's baby teeth figure as metaphor, or condensation, of her former presence. This metaphor represents the key to his unconscious.

The imaginary mirror stage

According to Lacan, the imaginary order indicates the pre-linguistic phase of a child, its realm of images. The term imaginary derives from the word "image," yet it also refers to Jung's famous "imago." Referring to the development of an adult winged insect (such as the moth in *The Silence of the Lambs*), it was additionally applied to point out the parents' image in the child's mind, who would keep this image forever. In the Lacanian imaginary the child forms its ego identity during its first encounter with its self-image in a mirror at the age of six to eighteen months. This revelation is immediately followed by a feeling of frustration when the child fails to recognize its actual lack of mastery and control over its body parts – opposite to the wholeness the mirror image simulates.

Instead of employing a mirror to establish some sense of self, Lecter functions as a mirror for others. He reflects those people who see him in his cell in the maximum security ward, where the bars and the net (see *Red Dragon* 69) serve as some kind of permeable mirror surface: While doctors and investigators believe they might elicit valuable information from Lecter to accomplish their mission, he carefully selects to whom he reflects. So he offers Will Graham (*Red Dragon*) and other fragmented persons who approach him a mirror image of themselves, when for example he states: "We're just alike" (*Red Dragon* 75). Lecter also serves as a mirror to Clarice Starling (*The Silence*); he yields information to help her repair her fragmented self and to further her professional and linguistic development. However, the images he offers her reveal a more complementary nature. During their first encounter Starling gazes at Lecter and "in his hands and arms she saw wiry strength like her own" (*The Silence* 404). This likeness does not trouble or frighten her, and toward the end of the story she even dares to touch "the monster": "For an instant the tip of her forefinger touched Dr. Lecter's. The touch crackled in his eyes" (*The Silence* 611). With him as a constantly readjusting mirror, Starling (re-)establishes her self while she provides an image of his lost sister for him and frees him of his own trauma. Considering the vampiric allusions of having no mirror image, Hannibal's figure thus questions the idea of an infantile mirror stage as constricted to a moment in childhood in order to be self- or identity-building.

The symbolic order and the name of the father

Other than the imaginary, the symbolic order indicates the entrance into the realm of language. Since language is associated with laws and rules, it simultaneously represents the introduction of the father as the institution of regulatory, patriarchal power. Lacan's phrase "the name of the father" with its strong religious allusions first hints to language ("name") and second to "the father," which yet is not the father but a name, a word – a reference.

When looking at the Lecter series we find its eponymous protagonist as first influenced and probably rivaled not only by his actual father and father figures like his uncle (*Hannibal Rising*) but by the weight of his own name and his predecessors who passed on the name: "Hannibal the Grim (1365–1428) built Lecter Castle in five years [...] Five hundred years later Hannibal Lecter, eight years old and eighth of the name, stood in the kitchen garden" (*Hannibal Rising* 5). As a reaction to the loss of his family he withdraws from language and, hence, from the law-making power of the father. Soon he understands his position as the last to survive: "Hannibal Lecter, last of his line [...]. He was not Hannibal the Grim in any way he understood" (*Hannibal Rising* 65–66). From then on he *is* the law, and even without speaking he owns language by thought alone and changes into a powerful and painless individual, always in control. Hannibal never succumbs to any(body's) rule whatsoever, he "does not observe the pecking order" (*Hannibal Rising* 74), and he lives and acts according to his individual sense of righteousness, which includes the deliberate execution of retributive justice.

In representing a patriarchal identification figure, he protects the weak, he never lies, he is smart, attractive and civil, he is fearless and strong, and he only kills when his principles of justice are violated or when his primal survival instinct is threatened. Even though being very corporeal, Hannibal represents the signifier without a clearly determinable signified, he *becomes* the name of the father. Even though his name and image surely attain omnipresence, as an "unknowable" phenomenon he cannot be determined even when in custody. Dr. Hannibal Lecter reigns the imaginary as well as the symbolic realm.

Conclusion

The psychoanalytical approach in Literary and Cultural Studies was firmly established by the end of the twentieth century, while fictionalizations of psychology and psychoanalysis have been manifest in Western culture ever since. The Hannibal Lecter novels (re-)present such reflections about the human psyche, and their main protagonist is a psychiatrist. The novels also feature fictionalizations of psychoanalytical concepts throughout: Thus, their very structure and content render them suitable for a psychoanalytical approach.

The Lecter books and movies were criticized especially by feminist scholars, not least due to the depiction of misogynistic murders and the voyeuristic gaze at slashed female bodies. Moreover, the 2006 novel *Hannibal Rising* was attacked by readers, reviewers, and scholars. It thus shared some of its fate with psychoanalysis, perhaps because Lecter's trauma is not founded, as agreed on by psychiatrists and psychologists, in the family, neither is it conditioned by family conflicts. It is precisely the other way around: The early absence of family and the traumatic intrusion of outsiders cause his metamorphosis into a cannibalistic killer. The proper development during formative years of his childhood is disrupted. He is turned into a monster – and this aspect has been famously visualized since the first Lecter movie, Michael Mann's *Manhunter* (1986), was released. The last book, however, reverses much of the first books' descriptions, it not only sheds a different light on Lecter, but it also deconstructs one of the major premises of psychoanalysis itself.

Notes

1 Real-life FBI profiler John E. Douglas, on whom allegedly Harris's character Jack Crawford was based, claims that Harris's work has initiated a blurring of fact and fiction: "There can be little doubt that if one person were to be given credit [...] for placing behavioral science [...] squarely on the map and in the public imagination, that individual would have to be Thomas Harris [...]. So completely have they [the novels and films] become part of the collective psyche, that I recently heard myself referred to on a television talk show as 'that *Silence of the Lambs* guy'" (Douglas and Olshaker 291).

2 Retconning is a technique frequently used in TV shows or book series: "Retroactive continuity" means for example to change information about a character in a later episode to lend some sort of consistency to the information given in the story.

3 In her study of the movie *The Silence of the Lambs*, Elizabeth Young explores how the "link between serial content and serial form helps to explain some of the film's considerable impact" (5). Other scholars, like Lefebvre and Haggerty, have located the phenomenon of serial killing – whose seriality is reflected in popular cultural products like TV or book series – in a decidedly (post-)modern, (post-)capitalist consumerist context.

4 Psychoanalysis has always been interested in the figure of the vampire, not least due to his phallic fangs. Peter Messent observes that "Freud characterizes the 'oral phase of sexual development' as 'cannibalistic existence'" (27).

Works cited

Douglas, John E., and Mark Olshaker. *Obsession: The FBI's Legendary Profiler Probes the Psyches of Killers, Rapists and Stalkers and Their Victims and Tells How to Fight Back*. London: Simon & Schuster, 1998. Print.

Freud, Sigmund. "Das Unheimliche." 1919. *Studienausgabe*. Vol. IV. *Psychologische Schriften*. Ed. Alexander Mitscherlich et al. Frankfurt am Main: Fischer, 2000. 241–74. Print.

---. *Die Traumdeutung*. 1900. *Studienausgabe*. Vol. II. Ed. Alexander Mitscherlich et al. Frankfurt am Main: Fischer, 2000. Print.

---. "Totem und Tabu." 1912–13. *Studienausgabe*. Vol. IX. *Psychologische Schriften*. Ed. Alexander Mitscherlich et al. Frankfurt am Main: Fischer, 2000. 287–444. Print.

Gallop, Jane. "Reading the Mother Tongue: Psychoanalytic Feminist Criticism." *Critical Inquiry* 13.2 (1987): 314–29. Print.

Garner, Shirley Nelson, Claire Kahane, and Madelon Sprengnether, eds. *The (M)other Tongue: Essays in Feminist Psychoanalytic Interpretation*. Ithaca, NY: Cornell UP, 1985. Print.

Haggerty, Kevin. "Modern Serial Killers." *Crime, Media, Culture* 5.2 (2009): 168–87. Print.

Harris, Thomas. *Hannibal*. 1999. *The Hannibal Lecter Omnibus*. London: Heinemann, 2001. 743–1220. Print.

---. *Hannibal Rising*. New York: Dell, 2006. Print.

---. *Red Dragon*. 1981. *The Hannibal Lecter Omnibus*. London: Heinemann, 2001. 1–385. Print.

---. *The Silence of the Lambs*. 1988. *The Hannibal Lecter Omnibus*. London: Heinemann, 2001. 386–742. Print.

Lacan, Jacques. *Écrits: A Selection*. 1966. Trans. Bruce Fink. London: Norton, 2004. Print.

Lefebvre, Martin. "Conspicuous Consumption: The Figure of the Serial Killer as Cannibal in the Age of Capitalism." *Theory, Culture & Society* 22.3 (2005): 43–62. Print.

Messent, Peter. "American Gothic: Liminality and the Gothic in Thomas Harris's Hannibal Lecter Novels." *Dissecting Hannibal Lecter*. Ed. Benjamin Szumskyj. Jefferson, NC: McFarland, 2008. 13–36. Print.

Packer, Sharon, and Jody Pennington, eds. *A History of Evil in Popular Culture: What Hannibal Lecter, Stephen King, and Vampires Reveal about America*. Santa Barbara, CA: ABC Clio, 2014. Print.

Simpson, Philip. *Making Murder: The Fiction of Thomas Harris*. Santa Barbara, CA: ABC Clio, 2010. Print.

Young, Elizabeth. "*The Silence of the Lambs* and the Flaying of Feminist Theory." *Camera Obscura* 9.27 (1991): 4–35. Print.

15 Social theories in Cultural Studies

Habermas, Bourdieu, Latour, and upward mobility

Georgiana Banita

"Practice elocution, poise and how to attain it"

When Mr. Gatz appears unexpectedly at the end of F. Scott Fitzgerald's *The Great Gatsby*, he shares fond memories of "Jimmy" with Nick Carraway, the novel's narrator and only loyal friend to his recently deceased son, Jay Gatsby. On the last flyleaf of a book Gatsby was reading as a boy, they find a schedule the ambitious youngster had compiled with the aim of "improving his mind"; for one hour each day, among other tasks, he planned to "[p]ractice elocution, poise and how to attain it" (184). The schedule recalls self-help books published in the early decades of the twentieth century, such as *Pep: Poise – Efficiency – Peace: A Book of Hows Not Whys for Physical and Mental Efficiency* (Hunter), which sought to train America's youth for success in an increasingly regimented and demanding labor market. As Gatsby's estrangement from his family demonstrates, in order to fulfill their ambitions, the young, hungry masses often embraced desires that were contrary to the habits and wisdom of their elders. Donald E. Pease calls this the "revolutionary mythos" at the heart of national identity (3–80) – a perpetual anti-historical break with the past dramatized in countless American narratives of social progress (see Chapter 11). In *People of Paradox*, Michael Kammen elevates this rebellious myth to the status of a national religion: "The United States may very well be the first large scale society to have built innovation and change into its culture as a constant variable, so that a kind of 'creative destruction' continually alters the face of American life" (115).

Social theory can enrich and clarify representations of the American Dream of social mobility, precisely because this high-octane-driven dream has always been built on the imitative nature of the revolutionary efforts of its believers. In other words: More often than not mobility turns out to be a form of class-passing (see Foster). Just as "race" and gender passing reveal the constructedness of "race" and gender, class-passing exposes American individualism as a mass-produced fantasy of desire that disguises a virulent undercurrent of deception, denial, and self-hatred. Gatsby memorably demonstrates the entwinement of social mobility with performance and performativity – with the radiant but brittle charm of eternally insecure interlopers who already pretend to be what they eventually want to become.

In the following pages, sociological reflections by Jürgen Habermas, Pierre Bourdieu, and Bruno Latour will provide a battery of concepts for analyzing the mimetic mechanism of this key American experience. Taken together, these concepts circumscribe the tensions between individual agency and social hierarchies by showing how they are mutually constitutive; how, in other words, personal ambition is motivated by the desire to attain social standing, which is in turn defined by a personal interpretation and performance of social rank. Starting from a distinction between ascription (inheritance of rank) and achievement (class mobility), they prove that such categories cannot in fact exist independently of each other. Class, in other words, might be what each individual makes of it, that is, it might materialize from desire: Wanting it (and donning the appropriate hat) would then amount to having it. The texts I have selected to test these theories – Fitzgerald's 1925 novel *The Great Gatsby*, Woody Allen's 2013 film *Blue Jasmine*, and the AMC series *Breaking Bad* (2008–2013) – do not trot out clichés about how anyone can achieve the American Dream by pulling themselves up by their bootstraps. In fact they partly venerate, partly demonize their protagonists, whose goal is to become someone else. The fascinating ambivalence of these texts stems from how we react to their new incarnations and from how the parvenus themselves struggle to control it. The fabric that holds their dreams together is a fetishism for wealthy accoutrements, which continues to serve as a touchstone for gauging cultural anxieties about the possibility and desirability of social advancement in America.

Keeping up with the Joneses: Defining social and cultural reproduction

The social model I explore here is predicated on the perpetuation and legitimation of hierarchies that reproduce social inequality – despite the appearance of mobility and meritocracy. They do this – and here I use Bourdieu's terminology to which I will return later – through a persistent bias in favor of inherited cultural capital (education, taste, expression), largely understood as the embodied form of social capital (connections to the right circles) and an extension of economic capital into the symbolic realm, including credentials, belongings, tastes, and mannerisms. These are so closely linked with privilege and class that owning or manifesting such features cannot be distinguished from class itself. The dramatic momentum of American mobility narratives derives precisely from this incongruity between class as an abstract, desirable good and the actual "goods" that constitute and define social mobility, between vague notions about social status and its embodiment in cultural capital.

Social theories of upward mobility seem somewhat disconnected from the popular image of this phenomenon. The prevailing narrative of these theories assumes a long duration of rise or decline, whereas most iconic stories of social mobility involve abrupt shuttles between social worlds. The difficulty of social ascent stems partly from the disparity between the slowly moving cogs of social institutions on the one hand and the intensity of individual ambition on the other – between, in the terms proposed by Habermas, bureaucratic systems and the "lifeworld" of ordinary experience. Habermas associates an instrumental rationality with the institutions and bureaucracies around which classical sociology and social reproduction operate (that is, a technocratic, abstract logic), and a communicative rationality with the lifeworld of everyday practice and cultural reproduction (that is, a logic growing out of the cooperations and conversations of living persons).

Communicative action includes symbolic contents, social spaces, and historical time. The interactions woven into the fabric of everyday communicative practice constitute the medium through which culture, society, and persons are reproduced. These reproduction processes cover the symbolic structure of the lifeworld (138).

Significantly, Habermas envisions communicative action not merely as transporting meaning about the lifeworld, but above all as a form of interaction through which group memberships, identities, and socialization processes are negotiated. What places Habermas as a useful springboard for introducing Bourdieu (another social scientist often referred to in the humanities) is his notion of the lifeworld less in terms of psychological makeup and consciousness than as "a culturally transmitted and linguistically organized stock of interpretive patterns" (124). The shared norms and values that create group solidarity in the lifeworld are not always attained through rational communication but by manufacturing consensus, acceptance, and socialization in the lifeworld of one's choice. In Habermas's words: "[C]ommunicative action presents itself as an interpretive mechanism through which cultural knowledge is reproduced," whereby any "reproduction of the lifeworld consists essentially in a continuation and renewal of tradition, which moves between the extremes of a mere reduplication of and a break with tradition" (139). The sedimented cultural codes inherent in the lifeworld (for instance, concepts such as love, the nation, or class) are up for grabs – open for negotiation and reproduction through discursive mechanisms. Individuals internalize cultural knowledge by convincing others that they rightly possess this knowledge or by accepting that others do. It is through such processes of reproduction or transmission that cultural behaviors and experiences are constructed and defined.

Cultural reproduction describes the affirmation of cultural traditions by virtue of inclusions and exclusions negotiated around arbitrary nobility markers that perpetuate themselves through the socially uneven distribution of cultural capital (education, manners). Bourdieu was the first to amply theorize this process, focusing especially on the role of education in reproducing the culture and power of the dominant classes. From among Bourdieu's concepts I want to dwell on "cultural capital" (the sum of possessions, skills, and authority markers that index social standing) and "habitus" (the deeply ingrained, "natural"-seeming, yet culturally developed tastes and sensibilities that shape cultural capital) because they are at the center of a debate around the application of Bourdieu's theories to the relationship of individual agency and social determination in US culture.

Bourdieu is interested in how communicative and behavioral patterns perpetuate specific communities and he emphasizes the education system as seminal to cultural hierarchy (see Bourdieu and Passeron). Education, Bourdieu argues, discriminates positively in favor of natural inheritors of cultural capital, which is thereby self-sustaining. He singles out cultural practices of consumption – rather than production or labor – as the chief supporting beams of social hierarchies. His key argument is that symbolic consumption – i.e., the conspicuous recourse to objects and practices endowed with connotations of prestige and power – does not merely reflect social position, but actively generates it. The reproduction of social roles cannot thus be distinguished from their cultural production. What Bourdieu calls "habitus" organizes this consumption of objects, constructing desire toward consecrated products (going to the opera house) and rejection of objects that are not socially valued (visiting a beer tent). The key to cultural capital is that it involves the complicity of both dominant and dominated actors who must agree on what has cultural cachet and what does not; this often leads to games of credibility, enactment, and impersonation whereby individuals try out and act out a new habitus by going through the motions of its material rituals: obtaining a particular degree, consuming certain foods or art forms.

Indeed, many responses to Bourdieu's method have picked up on its negative aspects of copy and imitation. Yet it is precisely these features that make social reproduction pertinent to US culture, because the acquisition of imitative social skills is central to US national mythology and not merely a matter of individual caprice. The authenticity and tangibility of the American character – and of the characters I analyze here – emerge from a mixture of inherited and emulated routines. Character is thus not static but elastic, a matter of duplication, adaptation, and becoming. Jay Gatsby, Jasmine French, and Walter White refute the negative definition of social reproduction as mechanical "cultural plagiarism" and lean toward a more vibrant reading that blends crafted self-fashioning with the magical excitement of social fulfillment and financial success.

These Americans become wealthy through association and collaboration; or, as Nick Carraway puts it in *The Great Gatsby*, they are "rich together" (6–7), forming a network of consumption and mutual regard. Read with Latour's theory of action, upward mobility is far from an individual story but a vivid intersection of multiple agencies. For Latour, action "is not done under the full control of consciousness; action should rather be felt as a node, a knot, and a conglomerate of many surprising sets of agencies," which he refers to as "actors" forming an "actor network" (*Reassembling the Social* 44). We recognize in this light the contingency of upward mobility and the fortuitous events that allow individuals to extricate themselves from one system and join another.

The vagaries of social success lend themselves especially well to a reading that stresses complexity and repudiates the rigid categories of classical sociology. Latour insists that sociology should not be concerned with external, collective formations (such as "the proletariat" or "the gentry") as much as with the practices of imitation through which social phenomena come into being. His approach moves away from social facts as distinctive substance, describing instead various forms of association. In essence, his actor-network-theory (ANT) describes and analyzes various entanglements in which humans and non-humans are involved. It is a theory that defies clarity and encourages heterogeneous thought.

As we shall see, the Heisenberg Uncertainty Principle and its popular interpretation (focused on the relative and indeterminate perception of not only subatomic particles but also morality and individual circumstances) has a similar effect when it is invoked in *Breaking Bad* by another "Heisenberg," the drug world alias used by Walter White. In Latour's words, "the social is a certain type of circulation that can travel endlessly, without ever encountering either the micro-level – there is never an interaction that is not framed – or the macro-level – there are only local summings up which produce either local totalities or total localities" ("On Recalling ANT" 19). Habermas's lifeworld driven by communicative consensus, Bourdieu's replicative socialization, and Latour's complicated actor network help gather and galvanize disparate moments in the cultural history of social mobility in the United States, from the Great Depression to the global financial crisis of 2007–2008.

Class acts: Jay Gatsby and Jasmine French

Underneath Jay Gatsby's seemingly carefree lifestyle, two tectonic plates collide: the heavily stigmatized social position of his birth to an impoverished German American farming family in rural North Dakota and the frail glamour in which he wraps everything and everyone around him. In Fitzgerald's novel and its two major film adaptations (Jack Clayton's in 1974 and Baz Luhrmann's in 2013), Gatsby's life has been reduced to instrumentalized fiction: war bravery, Oxford stint, business credentials, and of course wealthy ancestry. Importantly, we do not actually see much of the hurdles that Gatsby has had to catapult himself across to live in his decadent Neuschwanstein across the bay from the home of his well-heeled beloved, whose pier emits a distant glow that literally "greenlights" his high society ambitions. Daisy Buchanan's half-coarse, half-sophisticated charm – "[h]er voice is full of money" (Fitzgerald 127) – correlates with his own half-sordid, half-romantic fantasies. Daisy herself is nothing but an object of symbolic consumption, a flashy, attention-getting indicator of privilege. Gatsby accumulates social power through his attachment to her, especially when she is not physically there, which reinforces the enchanted and insubstantial nature of her value.

Things come to a head when Gatsby must compete with Daisy's husband, Tom Buchanan, for the woman's affections, exposing the yawning gap between their respective social backgrounds. Tom, who can boast of a distinguished pedigree and elite education, does not think much of Gatsby's route to social reproduction through forgery. Gatsby's painstakingly achieved index of worth is being challenged and disentangled from the mere display and consumption of cultural goods: parties, flashy automobiles, cartloads of flowers, and pink suits. What Fitzgerald's novel and especially the screen adaptations illustrate very well is the grandeur and affectation of the simulation-prone sensibility that Bourdieu refers to as habitus, from sartorial styles to speech patterns, which guarantees Gatsby's upper-class community integration and proximity to his habitus-endowed (even habitus-obsessed) beloved. The films' visual exuberance does not merely enliven our experience of the novel and Gatsby himself; it plays on the truculent materiality of his consumption habits. Luhrmann goes overboard with gaudy, candy-colored sets and costumes while Clayton plays more subtly with soft focus to outline Gatsby's world – "material without being real" (Fitzgerald 172). Photos of Daisy are scattered among his monogrammed belongings, the woman herself nothing but marked property. In a particularly fetishistic scene, Daisy sensually touches luxury objects in his house before settling on Jay's hand that quietly waits for her as if cast in gold.

Much has been made of the novel's regressive conclusion – the "boats against the current, borne back ceaselessly into the past" (Fitzgerald 192). Gatsby tries to recapture his past (and overly idealized) romance with Daisy; but at a deeper level the past is also trying to recapture him – not the same past he desperately seeks to retrieve, but the submerged roots of his modest background. When the car driven by Daisy accidentally runs over and kills Tom's working-class lover Myrtle, the blame for every imaginable transgression falls on Gatsby, whom Myrtle's husband, Wilson, sets out to execute. Clayton's adaptation of the novel is more Bourdieusian than Luhrmann's because it dwells more on Wilson's house invasion and the sudden appearance of Gatsby's father as the irruption of a sordid past into the extravagant present. Despite attempts to rewrite his own story and to mold a new life trajectory through social reproduction, the narrative of his rise, including its beginnings, remains part of Jay's lifeworld and social habitus. Fitzgerald portrays an archetypal American dreamer who studied inventions as a child and reinvented himself in the end, yet the narrative ultimately uncovers the limitations of such reinvention.

In *The Great Gatsby* we see upper-class mannerisms being learned; in Woody Allen's *Blue Jasmine* we see them being unlearned. The film tells a reverse Cinderella story of the kind that explains why social mobility narratives often feature sinister and mean-spirited protagonists. New York Upper East Side princess Jasmine French is simply the woman who never wants to get off the high horse she rode in on – but must. After her husband, Bernie-Madoff-like embezzler Hal, is arrested and loses his assets, she moves from New York to San Francisco to be with her poorer sister. She is dragged kicking and screaming into a stigmatized social position in deep contrast to the expectations she has concocted for herself. Unlike Gatsby, who remains shrouded in mystery and elegance, Jasmine unravels for all to see once her wealth and prospects are gone. The discrepancy between the mannerisms she has acquired as a rich socialite and the squalid conditions of her downfall masterfully highlights the stark polarities of social reproduction and the disorientation that sets in when upward mobility leads to a dead end or downward spiral.

Yet even though her porcelain façade cracks a few times during the film (as when she is sexually assaulted by the horny dentist she works for), she is never anything short of regal. The film plays off of the audience's familiarity with the aristocratic and ethereal Cate Blanchett, whose screen life as anything but a queen, immortal elf, or some other kind of unearthly heroine is to us – and tragically to Jasmine herself, in the subtext of the film – utterly unimaginable. The behavior she parroted in the exclusive circles she used to frequent has become second nature to her. In her sister's homey apartment, Jasmine's catwalk felinity and verbal refinement seem impossibly out of place – she might as well be speaking Elvish (especially when sedatives and alcohol interfere with her ability to speak intelligibly). But there is, of course, nothing organic about her upper-class comportment. Both back in New York and now in San Francisco, she defines herself in relation to the status and habits of the people around her. And in both cities she must rely on prevarication to survive: In the first instance, she puts on a vacuous "pretty woman" persona, in the second, she glamorizes her past and uses old Chanel outfits stained with sweat and tears to make herself prole-proof among her sister's working-class entourage. Her constantly redefined fantasies are an instructive lens through which the underbelly of social reproduction narratives is brought to light. Jasmine wants to be an interior decorator, but she herself lacks an interior that she can design, personalize, and present to the world. This is not a personal flaw that Jasmine masks with falsehoods, for which she is ultimately punished, but the hyperbolized manifestation of a blankness that Bourdieusian social theory locates at the very core of class performance and perception. Jasmine is looking to become something substantial, yet her mimicry can more aptly be described as social karaoke – a parody of social reproduction undermined by the increasingly psychotic tone of Jasmine's soliloquies.

With both Gatsby and Jasmine, *what* they consume is less significant than *how* they do it. He likes jazz, as long as it is played on an organ in his home. He throws lavish parties, but prefers to watch them from a distance. He owns countless shirts imported from Europe, but they do not quite unfold their capital until he scatters them all over the house, putting them on show when Nick and Daisy come to visit. In addition to all the commodities in her life, Jasmine devises an entire range of self-important maneuvers (always busy, never at anyone's beck and call) that advertise her own symbolic value as a rare, prized commodity.

In his seminal article "Does Cultural Capital Structure American Consumption?" Douglas Holt argues that for an American context Bourdieu's theory should be reformulated to stress consumption practices rather than

objects (indeed "how" rather than "what"). What Bourdieu's French consumers prefer in terms of fine art does not match the interests of US elites.
The reputational currency at work in Gatsby and Jasmine testifies to the idea
that American cultural capital becomes objectified in practices rather than
items alone. *Breaking Bad* in fact completely undermines the indexicality of
cultural goods as class markers by obfuscating the ways in which individuals
gravitate toward their desired hierarchical location.

Walter White and the principle of social uncertainty

Fitzgerald and Allen already paint a compelling picture of imitational, associa-
tional sociality in *The Great Gatsby* and *Blue Jasmine*, refuting the implication
of historical homogeneity and invariability of upward mobility in the United
States. But the way Latour problematizes the social echoes especially well
with *Breaking Bad*'s overt critique of social mobility in a society that is simply too
fragmented to allow for a clear hierarchy and path of ascent. Precisely because
their social roles are so carefully contextualized, we warm to the behavior of
Gatsby, Jasmine, and Walter and revile it at the same time. Sociology, Latour
maintains in the same vein, should not be used as a weapon of privilege to
simply debunk the people being studied, when their lifeworlds require greater
analytical empathy ("Why Has Critique Run out of Steam?").

Walter White finds himself plagued by illness and concerned about his
family's welfare after receiving a deadly cancer diagnosis. To even assume
privilege as the starting point of a social odyssey, *Breaking Bad* suggests, is a
misleading premise. And because it starts at a point free of illusions and
megalomania – not with some grand, Ahab-type individualist but a chemistry
teacher and part-time car wash cashier – *Breaking Bad* embeds the shopworn
American narrative of unbridled ambition and success into a filigreed social
structure that stresses labor and class politics, border and multicultural
discourses, the complex connotations of (drug) consumption in American
culture, the sense of diminished masculinity in the post-Frontier age, and the
hollowness of Bourdieusian theories around education as a springboard of
class advancement.

Latour's actor-network-theory combined with the epic arc of the serial
format is probably best placed to help us understand why Walter's trajectory
cannot be reduced to the narrative of individual agency in crisis. While
Gatsby and Jasmine focus on the food in recounting the challenges of climbing
up the food chain, *Breaking Bad* is more interested in the chain – the chain of
Walter's involvement with drug gangs and the wider social impact of his
"work." All three protagonists turn a blind eye to the consequences of their
actions, but it is only with Walter that these consequences are not merely
localized (as in Gatsby's doomed personal relationships) or implied (the same
way the global financial crisis and its bankrupt ethics underlie the plot of *Blue
Jasmine*), but truly systemic, in the sense that Walter's business actively harms
millions. Gatsby is a bootlegger who organizes parties where people get drunk

and sometimes start brawling, so even Gatsby does not exist in a social vacuum. Neither does Jasmine, although the financial politics of the film are tempered somewhat by the revelation that Jasmine willingly turned her husband in to the FBI to pre-empt the humiliation of a divorce. But Walter feeds class-A drugs to underprivileged hordes of disillusioned Jays and Jasmines, people unable to accept whatever cruel hand they have been dealt.

Latour's adherence in his critique of classic sociology to a notion of diffuse social agency – with a complex human and non-human network pulling the strings of individual behavior – resonates powerfully with the series' moral equivocation symbolized by the Heisenberg Uncertainty Principle, from which the protagonist's drug lord alias is derived. When the myth materializes, it has nothing to do with classical self-reliance and industry. It is upward mobility with a vengeance, born out of the impossible myth of hard work and meritocracy. Walter self-consciously performs an identity he does not believe in, one that mocks the Emersonian ideal of self-reform. In the spirit of Latour's indeterminacy, rather than take social reproduction for granted, the series examines the fissures and failures of cultural masquerade. Walter mimics social mimicry, rewriting the narrative of social aspiration by throwing doubt on what is worth aspiring for – the parties, Daisies, and Chanels of textbook social ambition.

Conclusion: the cultural capital of the social mobility narrative

Through the prism of theories that uncover the underlying structures and mechanisms of social life, *The Great Gatsby*, *Blue Jasmine*, and *Breaking Bad* expose the excesses and failures of social reproduction. They confirm that social mobility remains a fallacy – temporarily boosted by widespread professional employment in the early and mid-twentieth century, but in essence already stalled and flawed as a concept in a static society with little room for permutation. As Gregory Clark argues in *The Son also Rises: Surnames and the History of Social Mobility*, variation in overall life chances and status can largely be predicted by lineage. Clark studied data on surnames as an indicator of social status and found that many distinguished surnames are still disproportionately represented among today's elites. Cultural reproduction in this scheme cannot make a dent in the impact of ancestry and genetics on life outcomes. The "revolutionary mythos" Pease writes about does not necessarily accelerate mobility in the "land of opportunity." Cultural reproduction cannot be ruled out as a factor in how elite groups are perpetuated, yet it may hold little potential in altering social mobility among the poor. However, its symbolic quality as an incontrovertible badge of American identity and cultural engine of national history remains unchanged. The texts discussed here admit that low status will keep one down, helpless against the backward current of ancestry. Yet taken together, they do perform the emboldening effect of social mobility as both a social concept and a quintessentially American cultural tradition.

The starry-eyed narratives of success that Jay and Jasmine tell themselves and others echo Bruce Robbins's diagnosis that such stories are "rhetorical weapons designed for the ruthless seizure of moral advantage" (x). I want to end this chapter on a different note, one inspired by Robbins's point that "upward mobility is also a story" in which "the initial state of economic deprivation represents a perverse sort of capital, capital that can only be realized by being shown off to others" (xi). Part of the reason why Bourdieu's fine art cannot compete against the opulent consumption favored by American elites may have something to do with this inverse ostentation. In other words, social capital also accrues from the story of social reproduction itself. There is a greater social reward for the acquisition of status symbols than from their mere consumption from a position of inherited, uncontested privilege. And because the meteoric rises and falls of these stories are so alluring, socially mobile impostors can even be seen as imaginative resources on which readers and audiences draw to shape themselves into individuals and expand their own social networks. The imitative drive thus culminates at the reception level when the audience is asked to identify with the faux class winner. Readership and spectatorship thus mobilize a form of (simulated) social reproduction and class-passing, too.

Read with Habermas, Bourdieu, and Latour, narratives of social reproduction cement the notion that one's position within the social spectrum is largely constructed. Many American stories of aspiration and failure paint a gloomy picture of drive and ability, subjecting them to the fickle lottery of accident and lineage. But the specific cultural embodiments of social reproduction legible within these histories teach us how they may have had a different outcome – and how they could now be rewritten. Against facile and complacent glamorization of opportunity, they ensure that the problematic of upward (and for that matter downward) mobility stays subject to scrutiny and contest. The flexibility of theories around social reproduction and even the contested nature of sociology as a discipline help us understand the tensions and irresolution that keep the myth of upward mobility alive, generation after generation.

Works cited

Blue Jasmine. Dir. Woody Allen. Perf. Cate Blanchett, Alec Baldwin, and Sally Hawkins. Sony Pictures Home Entertainment, 2013. DVD.

Bourdieu, Pierre. *Distinction: A Social Critique of the Judgement of Taste*. Trans. Richard Nice. Cambridge, MA: Harvard UP, 1984. Print.

Bourdieu, Pierre, and Jean-Claude Passeron. *Reproduction: In Education, Society and Culture*. Trans. Richard Nice. London: SAGE, 1977. Print.

Breaking Bad. Writ. Vince Gilligan et al. Perf. Bryan Cranston et al. AMC 2008–13. DVD.

Clark, Gregory. *The Son also Rises: Surnames and the History of Social Mobility.* Princeton, NJ: Princeton UP, 2014. Print.

Fitzgerald, F. Scott. *The Great Gatsby.* 1926. London: Penguin, 2010. Print.

Foster, Gwendolyn Audrey. *Class-Passing: Social Mobility in Film and Popular Culture.* Carbondale: Southern Illinois UP, 2005. Print.

The Great Gatsby. Dir. Jack Clayton. Perf. Robert Redford, Mia Farrow, and Bruce Dern. Paramount Home Video, 2003. DVD.

The Great Gatsby. Dir. Baz Luhrmann. Perf. Leonardo DiCaprio, Carey Mulligan, and Joel Edgerton. Warner Home Video, 2013. DVD.

Habermas, Jürgen. *The Theory of Communicative Action.* Trans. Thomas McCarthy. Vol. 2. *Life World and System: A Critique of Functionalist Reason.* Boston, MA: Beacon P, 1987. Print.

Holt, Douglas B. "Does Cultural Capital Structure American Consumption?" *Journal of Consumer Research* 25 (1998): 1–25. Print.

Hunter, William Crosbie. *Pep: Poise – Efficiency – Peace. A Book of Hows Not Whys for Physical and Mental Efficiency.* Chicago, IL: Reilly & Britton, 1914. Print.

Kammen, Michael G. *People of Paradox: An Inquiry Concerning the Origins of American Civilization.* 1972. Ithaca, NY: Cornell UP, 1990. Print.

Latour, Bruno. "On Recalling ANT." *Actor Network Theory and After.* Ed. John Law and John Hassard. Oxford: Blackwell, 1999. 15–25. Print.

---. *Reassembling the Social: An Introduction to Actor-Network-Theory.* New York: Oxford UP, 2005. Print.

---. "Why Has Critique Run out of Steam? From Matters of Fact to Matters of Concern." *Critical Inquiry* 30.2 (2004): 225–48. Print.

Pease, Donald E. *Visionary Compacts: American Renaissance Writings in Cultural Context.* Madison: U of Wisconsin P, 1987. Print.

Robbins, Bruce. *Upward Mobility and the Common Good: Toward a Literary History of the Welfare State.* Princeton, NJ: Princeton UP, 2007. Print.

16 Justice, ethics, violence

American Studies and the ethical controversy

Zuzanna Ladyga

"What kind of a turn is the turn to ethics? A right turn? A left turn? A wrong turn? A U-turn? Whose turn? Whose turn is it to turn to ethics? And why? Why now?," asked the editors of *The Turn to Ethics*, a book whose publication in 2000 pronounced the shift that dominated critical discourse in the last decade of the twentieth century (Garber, Hanssen, and Walkowitz vii). Since the late 1980s, the word "ethics" has appeared frequently in Literary and Cultural Studies, often supplanting "ideology" and "politics." Critics have written about "ethics of pardoning" in Shakespeare, "ethics of projections" in *The Crying of Lot 49*, "ethics of masculinity" in *Fight Club*, "communal ethics" in the films of Lars von Trier, and even "ethics of vigilantism" in *Batman*.

To most students of American culture, such uses of the term ethics are utterly confusing, because authors using the buzzword rarely explain whether they employ "ethics" in the sense of moral norms or in some other, more complex sense. Most young scholars are perplexed by the air of controversy permeating the discussions of ethical problematics. The aim of this chapter is therefore to offer some clarification on different uses of "ethics," and to address the issue of the contemporary ethical controversy by tracing the genealogy of the e-word in the discourse of American Literary and Cultural Studies. I will also provide you with an example for ethical analysis.

Although in everyday discourse ethics is synonymous with moral norms, from the historical perspective morality is neither the only nor the most important meaning of the philosophical term. In fact, as far as classical thought is concerned, ethics was initially not conceived of in terms of moral standards at all. The Greeks understood it rather as *epimeleia heautou*, a habit of "taking care of oneself," an aesthetic exercise in self-awareness and self-betterment of one's body and mind, practiced in order to surpass oneself and attain higher knowledge of truth (see Foucault). In the words of Seneca, the idea was to live well, "to find joy in the best part of yourself," thus finding inner freedom and plunging into the cosmic Whole (Foucault 66). As an individual, personal practice, ethics was not linked to any institutional, religious, or legal system, and hence was never associated with doctrinaire attempts to normalize (i.e., control) the population – on the other hand, the possibility of taking care of oneself in this way was restricted to only a fraction of the population. Therefore classical ethics differed from how we tend to understand it today: first in its focus on the self rather than the community, and second in the postulate of equivalency between the value of life and aesthetic value – an equivalency erased from the system of modern philosophy, which since the eighteenth century distinguishes between ethics and aesthetics.

The notions of "self-care" and aestheticization of life seem particularly relevant to the discussion of ethics in the context of American culture because through its Puritan legacy this culture evolved and sedimented around the ideas of self-examination and self-perfection, which are very close to the ancient concept of ethical practice. The philosopher Stanley Cavell sees the ancient paradigm as central also to Emerson's philosophy of self-reliance, which is "the mode of the self's relation to itself" in pursuit of superpersonal wisdom (134). From the vantage point of Cavell's insight, the entire grand narrative of American individualism, perpetuated by the pastoral tradition of Romanticism and illustrated so vividly by Walt Whitman's performative celebrations of his self in *Leaves of Grass* (1855), can also be interpreted as resonant with the forgotten ancient logic of the ethical way of life. Similarly, the pursuit of philosophical sublimity by way of caring about the form of one's existence seems echoed in the pragmatist doctrines of William S. Pierce and William James (see De Waal and Skowroński).

This brief catalogue of examples of the American ethos of care for oneself is not to divert you from the topic of ethics in American Studies. In *The Great Tradition*, one of highly influential New Criticism's founding texts, the English scholar F.R. Leavis asserted that the greatness of a writer lies in the intensity of his work's moral concern and that literary criticism must address questions of "emotional hygiene and moral value" (Leavis, "Thought and Emotional Quality" 55). The word "moral" appears 191 times across 231 pages of *The Great Tradition*.

The normative measures of the New Critical method were a response to the turn-of-the-century democratization of the student population in British universities and the pedagogical demands of the new generation of students who, coming from less-educated backgrounds, could neither speak Latin or Greek nor communicate in the jargon of classical rhetoric (see Eagleton). Therefore, the definition of ethics promoted by the New Critical approach was limited to the modern Kantian sense of "objective knowledge of moral values" while staying oblivious to the ancient idea of "taking care of one's life." Simply put, New Criticism conflated ethics with moral universalism, treating it as not something one discovers and cultivates in oneself, but something one cogitates and dutifully observes.

The application of this kind of universalism in the first half of the twentieth century to the culturally divergent American context inevitably brought about the first crisis in critical discourse on ethics. Some of New Criticism's initial success may be attributed to the specific political climate in the United States, which discouraged any form of historical or ideological criticism, especially after 1945, through the McCarthy era and the Cuban missile crisis to the onset of the Vietnam War. Ironically, however, the same political climate was also the source of New Criticism's demise. In the atmosphere of 1960s politics, the American academia underwent rapid "politicization," which in turn triggered the emergence of critical trends that radically contested the assumptions of moral criticism (Gibson 288; see Chapters 1 and 13).

One effect of the politicization of scholarship was the emergence of Feminist and later Ethnic, Critical Race, and Postcolonial Studies, whose common impulse was to de-normativize the discipline of criticism, seen as the stronghold of the most conservative and repressive dogmatism. By critical interventions into the white/male/middle-class/heterosexual field of critical expertise, Feminist Criticism destabilized the concept of ethics as a system of moral laws. However, it was not by rehabilitating the old notions of ethical caring for one's identity, but by radically opposing ethics to politics, and thus unwittingly perpetuating the New Critical reductionist view of ethics. Another effect was the post-structuralist revolution, initiated in America with the "Structuralist Controversy" Conference at Johns Hopkins in 1966 (see Chapter 13). With the notions of freeplay of signification, *différance*, and Deconstruction, Post-structuralism challenged everything the New Critics ever proclaimed.

Since the history of American Studies is usually told from the perspective of the English-speaking world, the seminal role of Emmanuel Levinas in the formation of French Post-structuralism is rarely recognized (Peperzak; Cohen; Ziarek). A glance at the history of theory in France reveals, however, that not only did Levinas's radical ethics inspire such thinkers as Sartre, Lacan, Lyotard, and Deleuze (see May), but it also served as the primary motivation behind the evolution of Derrida's deconstructive practice (see Critchley).

What was so inspiring and radical about Levinas's ideas? Levinas's first radical gesture was his critique of philosophy's hegemonic confidence in its (allegedly transparent) notions and categories. His second, more ground-breaking notion was the reorientation of ethics as a language-based realm of relations with the Other. To understand the character and the implications of these ideas let us take a look at the main tenets of Levinas's thought.

Levinas's interest in ethics developed in the 1950s, culminating in his first major treatise *Totality and Infinity* (1961), where he criticized the Western philosophical tradition for its excessive preoccupation with being and the self as the subject at the center of cognition (21–22). This, Levinas claims, is philosophy's greatest error, because by privileging the self (or "the Same" as he calls it after Plato), philosophy remains blind to the violence inherent in the self's cognitive relation to the world. It fails to recognize that every cognitive act is somewhat usurpatory toward reality.

Just how problematic this omission is becomes apparent when we think about the self's relations with other human beings. After all, is it possible in relations with others to fully capture and understand their alterity? Can we bypass their existence within the limits of our cognitive horizon? Levinas's answer is a resounding no, as he perceives the alterity of the Other to be infinite and insurmountable. Therefore, opposing the traditional view that the self can reduce all otherness to itself, Levinas situates at the center of his philosophical thought the idea of the infinitely Other. The Other's alterity escapes the grasp of the self (Same), hence the acts of interacting with the Other are not so much cognitive as ethical, their ethics stemming from the fact that the Other imposes a responsibility to respond to his/her otherness.

Simply put, the self does not *precede* the encounter with the Other in the sense that it does not control the situation; rather, the self is actually established at the very event of this encounter and, at the same time, put into question by the presence of the Other. Levinas warns us however not to think of this event as interpersonal or dialogic – as a relation in which both parties are equal. The ethical encounter is "asymmetrical" insofar as the Other's presence "commands" the self to respond, his infinite alterity destabilizing entirely the self's sense of continuity, congruity, and cognitive capacities (*Totality and Infinity* 215, 197). In this way, radical ethics is the philosophy of infinity and thus the "first philosophy," inasmuch as it precedes all other philosophical endeavors of the self.

To illustrate the exceptional character of the ethical encounter, Levinas introduces the notion of the "face," a concept supposed to make us break with the habit of thinking of the Other in terms of some abstract entity. The face is a unique singular "epiphanic expression" of the Other (51). Levinas says that the face "speaks" to the self by "undoing the form" in which it speaks, which is to say that the face does not "communicate" meanings "decodable" through grammatical or cultural rules; it signifies in a different mode than that of a symbolic social mask (66). The "manifestation of the face is already discourse" – an act of language – which refutes the self's interpretation and comprehension (66).

The main problem discussed in *Otherwise than Being*, Levinas's second treatise, is how the encounter with the Other can happen as language and still be unique and singular, even if language is guarded by rules and conventions that are the same for us all. Language may be the same, answers Levinas, but its uniformity inevitably becomes disrupted and put into question in individual utterances. There exists the standardized, legitimized language, which Levinas terms "the Said," but there are also discursive instances when the conventionality of the Said is undermined, disturbed by what he calls "the ethical Saying." The Saying is ethical in character, because it occasions in language the same that the Other's face does to one's horizon of knowledge: It destabilizes signification and cognizance. It signifies as trace of undecidability.

Back to the United States: When the 1960s gave birth to the currents of feminism and Post-structuralism, each of the disciplines developed a different ideological agenda against New Critical moralism. Feminism juxtaposed it to politics; Post-structuralism to the limitless play. As stated earlier, feminists destabilized the concept of ethics as a system of moral laws, therefore unwittingly perpetuating the New Critical reductionist moralism. This was further complicated when, in the following decades, the transatlantic intellectual exchange resulted in a more pronounced presence of ethical terms in American feminist discourse. The latter gradually incorporated the figure of the Other from French critics such as Luce Irigaray or Hélène Cixous who were immersed in discussion with Levinas's ethics (Chanter). In the American feminist context, however, Otherness was emphatically subsumed under the category of politics. And just as in the case of feminist discourse, in American Post-structuralism, too, the New Critical urge to moralize is cross-dressed as something else, while the notions of ethics-as-care-for-oneself or ethics-as-a-response-to-the-Other are subdued.

Even today, while interest in ethics spreads across disciplines, in the American context, the phenomenon meets with strong resistance. Critics worry that the ethical turn signals "a regression from the *engagé* mode of criticism" (Guillory 30) and "an escape from politics" (Butler, "Ethical Ambivalence" 15). That this does not have to be the case – provided that ethics is not equated with morality – is illustrated by the work of such affect theorists as Lauren Berlant or Judith Butler, whose eventual reconciliation with ethical problematics is provided below in the analysis of Errol Morris's 2008 documentary *Standard Operating Procedure* about the infamous photographs of tortured detainees in the Abu-Ghraib military prison, which leaked into the press in 2004.

Standard Operating Procedure (2008) by Errol Morris

In *Standard Operating Procedure*, Morris investigates the background narrative of the Abu-Ghraib scandal by conducting interviews with soldiers who had tortured Arab detainees and/or took pictures of the acts of torture and of their fatal consequences. The plot of the film intertwines actual photos of the Abu-Ghraib crimes with fragments of face-to-face interviews with the oppressors. Significantly, the interviews are shot with the use of Morris's trademark device, Interrotron – a combination of camera, mirrors, and teleprompters that allows for the interviewer and the interviewees to face each other directly (without having to look through and into the camera) as well as for the film viewers to see the perpetrators as if eye-to-eye. Largely due to this cinematic strategy, Morris's film manages to avoid a condemnatory, moralistic tone and perhaps even redeems some Abu-Ghraib perpetrators as young, naive victims of the inhumane military system (Butler, *Frames of War* 81).

Butler has been engaged with the ethical problematics and an intense discussion with Levinas for over a decade. Initially Butler rejected Levinas's ethics ("Ethical Ambivalence" 2000). But in 2006 she explained her reconciliation with Levinas: "[I]t is worthwhile to reconsider Levinas in the context of today, because he gives us a way of thinking about the relationship between representation and humanization" (*Precarious Life* 140). What triggered Butler's interest was none other than Levinas's controversial notion of the face. Butler was particularly interested in the following controversial passage from Levinas's "Is Ontology Fundamental?":

The Other is the sole being I can wish to kill. I can wish. And yet this power is quite the contrary of power. The triumph of this power is its defeat as power. At the very moment when my power to kill realizes itself, the other [...] has escaped me. [...] I have not looked at him in the face, I have not encountered his face. The temptation of total negation [...] – this is the presence of the face. To be in relation with the other [...] face to face is to be unable to kill. It is also the situation of discourse. (*Ethics and Infinity* 9)

Butler capitalizes on an ambivalence Levinas sets at the core of the concept of the face, namely the ambivalence between the primary obligation to respond to the Other's pain, to become his/her "hostage" to the point of suffering and, on the other hand, a violent impulse to kill, to eliminate the uncanny indecipherability of the Other's face. It is precisely because of this ambivalence that Butler finds the notion of the face of the Other relevant for our times and also its uses of the face within contemporary media:

We may have to think of different ways that violence can happen: one is precisely *through* the production of the face, the face of Osama bin Laden, the face of Yasser Arafat, the face of Saddam Hussein. What has been done with these faces in the media? [...] These are media portraits that are often marshaled in the service of war, as if bin Laden's face were the face of terror itself, as if Arafat were the face of deception, as if Hussein's face were the face of contemporary tyranny. (Butler, *Precarious Life* 141)

So, the image of the face, as Butler puts it later in *Frames of War* (2009), is one of the modes of normativizing the production and reception of evil and violence, which come to "regulate affect, outrage, and ethical response" (78). This observation is of significance for the examination of the Abu-Ghraib archive, the images of torture and violence, the images of oppressors and their victims, of the faces exposed to a camera and hooded in sandbags. How are other faces framed and reframed? The Abu-Ghraib photographs and their re-contextualizations in films such as Morris's *Standard Operating Procedure* employ the image of the face to structure our affective response of anger, irritation, and sympathy. Therefore, it seems vital to explore the technologies of affect (and its commodification) as well as their consequences, such as the pastoral rhetoric of compassionate conservatism and the syndrome of "compassion fatigue" (Moeller), which Susan Sontag called the "numbing effect" of torture photography (77).

What is wrong with compassion? In *The Female Complaint* Berlant designates compassion not as an organic emotion but as an acquired reaction signifying the power of the one who feels sympathy over the underprivileged object of his feeling. In other words, compassion is a historically complex social and aesthetic technology of the relationship between the sufferers and the spectators who enjoy the privileged social role of potential ameliorative actors. According to Berlant, this model of a relationship was consolidated in American culture by nineteenth-century sentimental literature and its figures of sensitive white female slave owners (*Uncle Tom's Cabin*, 1852), whose excessive receptivity to pain and suffering never realizes its political potential, but instead gets lost in spectacular outbursts of exaltation. Since then, sentimentality has been used to hardwire not only the history of slavery, but the general habit of the American culture industry to regulate affect by means of the "emotional citation" of the old modes of pain, identity, and identification (Berlant, *Female Complaint* 47).

Berlant's concept offers a useful perspective for discussing images of torture and the power of the pornographic gaze over corporeal vulnerability. It accounts for how our responses to the images of faces of victims and victimizers end up being affective citations (repetitions of expected reactions), how they reenact the paradigm of mandatory empathy for the victims and a "wish to kill" the figures of their oppressors. The gender issue is of crucial importance here. After all, the patriarchal, heteronormative logic of the compassion paradigm blames women as agencies of its perpetuation. The crying, receptive creatures, as Emerson used to call women ("Woman"), care more and at the very same time epitomize passivity and inability to start political action.

An example of affective citation is art historian W.J.T. Mitchell's analysis of Morris's *Standard Operating Procedure* in his *Cloning Terror*. Mitchell's interpretation suggests that the image of the Hooded Man (Abdou Hussain Saad Faleh) from Abu-Ghraib is a biopolitical icon. This "bioimage" has permeated public consciousness so thoroughly because of its resonance with the image of Christ's crucifixion. Mitchell claims to have been prompted to the Christological reading by one the Abu-Ghraib guards, Specialist Sabrina Harman, who in Morris's film confesses to have come up with the idea of taking photos on seeing one humiliated hand-cuffed prisoner who "looked like Jesus Christ."

Mitchell's bow to Harman is, of course, purely rhetorical, but it develops into an argument that establishes a crucial link between the idea of compassion and the face. While commenting on the hooding and digital blurring of human faces in the Abu-Ghraib photos reframed by Morris, Mitchell asserts that it is "precisely the *anonymity* of the victim's faces that is the key to the power" of those images (135): "[M]ost notable is the *invisible potential* of the facelessness to suddenly turn into **facing*ness***" (141; bold mine). It is this potential that translates into a power to "awaken the desire for a justice to come" (122). Mitchell seems to imply that the invisible potential is a potential for self-reflection, represented in Morris's film by the "uncanny resemblance/ mirroring" (115) between the figures of the tortured and the executioners, who are also tortured in the sense of being entangled in the transgressive manipulation of their moral standards by the American state. Contrasting the surrealism of Morris's slow motion "noir-ish" reenactments of prison scenes accompanied by Danny Elfman's melodramatic soundtrack on the one hand

and the Interrotron's intimacy with the faces of the beleaguered GIs who took the photos on the other, Mitchell reads Morris's visual strategy as an attempt at immersing the viewer in the nightmarish atmosphere of the prison. The point is to make the spectator a "sympathetic observer and even a collaborator in the tenuous search for truth and justice" (Plantinga 48).

Crucially, the word "sympathetic" appears not in the context of the Hooded Man, but in the context of Morris's Interrotroned interviewees. One of the revelations of the film is in Mitchell's view the rehabilitation of Sabrina Harman from the "leering thumbs-up girl, reminiscent of the delighted spectators in American lynching photographs, into a woman of conscience who recognized a crime taking place and determined to record it for the world" (134) – from a character toward whom you feel a murderous instinct to the person whose suffering as a victim of circumstance you want to embrace with charity. Situating the woman behind the camera, Morris commits to an affective citation, which later mutates into a meta-citation of which Mitchell's representation, however brilliant, is a prime example. Why is that a problem? Because, as Berlant says,

> when sentimentality meets politics, it uses personal stories to tell of structural effects, but in so doing it risks thwarting its very attempt to perform rhetorically a scene of pain that must be soothed politically. [...] The ethical imperative toward social transformation is replaced by a civic minded but passive ideal of empathy. ("Poor Eliza" 641)

The power to awaken "the desire for a justice to come," generated by the pictures of hooded prisoners, is neutered by the figures of the perpetrators, not because they are perpetrators but because they are women – their characters being automatically perceived through the sentimental prism of compassion. The effect is what Sontag identifies as powerlessness of the photographs as well as of their spectators (62, 78).

Morris's apparatus of Interrotron allows the spectator to encounter the interviewees *as if* face-to-face as they look directly into the camera. In *Standard Operating Procedure*, just as in all other documentaries by Morris, the Interrotron is supposed to provide an "unnerving concentration of the face, with the subject staring and speaking directly into the camera, which records every movement and twitch of his interviewees" (Gourevitch and Morris 52–53). The desired effect is that in such scenes (as when Sabrina Harman confesses why she smiles in the photographs featuring her next to humiliated prisoners of Tier 1A or when Lynndie England comments on an image of her holding a lying, naked prisoner on a leash) the Interrotron creates intimacy and occasions an ethical encounter with the interviewees (Gerbaz). On the one hand, we face the faces; on the other, we forget the technology that occasions this encounter.

What could be the consequences of that omission of the technical apparatus in terms of affect regulation? Let us look at one study of the Interrotron's effect by Linda Williams in her "'Cluster Fuck': The Forcible Frame in

Morris's *Standard Operating Procedure.*" In the essay, Williams examines the microphysiognomy of Private Lynndie England's face when for the first time addressing directly her participation in the prisoner abuse:

> After another camera blink and another reframing, England comes as close as she ever will to explaining her acquiescence. Finally looking directly at us, with her eyes widening for emphasis, she faces the fact of her own acquiescence, saying with more force than anything she has said so far: "I mean [pause] it was OK."
>
> The microphysiognomy of England's face as revealed in the Interrotron does not dramatically catch her lying, nor does it catch an overt admission of guilt. [...] Rather, she is viewed as an ethical being wrestling with her acquiescence to an unethical situation.

What is at stake in such an inquiry is not the question of moralizing representation, let alone behavior. What is at stake is an analysis of the ethics involved in the encounter with the Other, the response demanded by the face, and the concomitant care for the self beyond automated compassion. It would be one thing to say that the most important ethical lesson of the film is to discourage us from judging England or Harman. It is quite another to claim that the face disempowers us from the act of judgment as such. Levinas says that the face "speaks" by "undoing the form" in which it speaks (*Totality and Infinity* 66), which is to say that the microphysiognomy of England's face does not tell us any more than her face in the actual Abu-Ghraib photos. In fact, it tells us less, since it engages the spectator in the automatisms of compassion, which prompt to see her hardened tone of voice, her nervousness, her pressed lips, and her story about being just a pregnant prisoner of love for her superior through the sentimental lens of charity slashed with anger.

Works cited

Berlant, Lauren. *The Female Complaint: The Unfinished Business of Sentimentality in American Culture.* Durham, NC: Duke UP, 2008. Print.
---. "Poor Eliza." *American Literature* 70.3 (1998): 635–68. Print.
Butler, Judith. "Ethical Ambivalence." *The Turn to Ethics.* Ed. Marjorie Garber, Beatrice Hanssen, and Rebecca L. Walkowitz. New York: Routledge, 2000. 15–28. Print.
---. *Frames of War: When Is Life Grievable?* New York: Verso, 2009. Print.
---. *Precarious Life: The Powers of Mourning and Violence.* New York: Verso, 2006. Print.

Cavell, Stanley. *The Senses of Walden: An Expanded Edition*. Chicago, IL: U of Chicago P, 2013. Print.

Chanter, Tina. *Ethics of Eros: Irigaray's Re-Writing of the Philosophers*. New York: Routledge, 1995. Print.

Cohen, Richard A. *Ethics, Exegesis and Philosophy: Interpretation after Levinas*. Cambridge: Cambridge UP, 2001. Print.

Critchley, Simon. *The Ethics of Deconstruction: Derrida and Levinas*. Edinburgh: Edinburgh UP, 2014. Print.

De Waal, Cornelis, and Krzysztof Piotr Skowroński, eds. *The Normative Thought of Charles S. Peirce*. New York: Fordham UP, 2012. Print.

Eagleton, Terry. *Literary Theory: An Introduction*. Minneapolis: U of Minnesota P, 1996. Print.

Emerson, Ralph Waldo. "Woman." *The Complete Works*. Vol. XI. New York: Houghton, Mifflin. 1904. Bartleby.com. 2014. Web. 20 Mar. 2014.

Foucault, Michel. *The History of Sexuality*. Vol. 3. *The Care of the Self*. Trans. Robert Hurley. Reprint ed. New York: Vintage, 1988. Print.

Garber, Marjorie, Beatrice Hanssen, and Rebecca L. Walkowitz. "Introduction: The Turn to Ethics." *The Turn to Ethics*. 2000. Ed. Marjorie Garber, Beatrice Hanssen, and Rebecca L. Walkowitz. New York: Routledge, 2013. vii–xii. Print.

Gerbaz, Alex. "Direct Address, Ethical Imagination and Errol Morris's Interrotron." *Film-Philosophy* 12.2 (2008): 17–9. Print.

Gibson, Andrew. "Ethics." *The Johns Hopkins Guide to Literary Theory and Criticism*. Ed. Michael Groden, Martin Kreiswirth, and Imre Szeman. Baltimore, MD: Johns Hopkins UP, 2005. 287–96. Print.

Gourevitch, Philip, and Errol Morris. "The Woman behind the Camera at Abu Ghraib." *The New Yorker* (24 Mar. 2008): 44–57. Print.

Guillory, John. "The Ethical Practice of Modernity." *The Turn to Ethics*. Ed. Marjorie Garber, Beatrice Hanssen, and Rebecca L. Walkowitz. New York: Routledge, 2000. 29–46. Print.

Leavis, F.R. *The Great Tradition: George Eliot, Henry James, Joseph Conrad*. 1948. New York: Faber & Faber, 2011. Print.

---. "Thought and Emotional Quality." *Scrutiny* 13 (1945): 53–71. Print.

Levinas, Emmanuel. *Ethics and Infinity: Conversations with Philippe Nemo*. Trans. Richard A. Cohen. Pittsburgh, PA: Duquesne UP, 1985. Print.

---. *Otherwise than Being: Or Beyond Essence*. Trans. Alphonso Lingis. Pittsburgh, PA: Duquesne UP, 1998. Print.

---. *Totality and Infinity: An Essay on Exteriority*. Trans. Alphonso Lingis. Sixteenth ed. Vol. 1. Pittsburgh, PA: Duquesne UP, 2002. Print.

May, Todd. *Reconsidering Difference: Nancy, Derrida, Levinas, and Deleuze*. U Park: Pennsylvania State UP, 1997. Print.

Mitchell, W.J.T. *Cloning Terror: The War of Images, 9/11 to the Present*. Chicago, IL: U of Chicago P, 2011. Print.

Moeller, Susan D. *Compassion Fatigue: How the Media Sell Disease, Famine, War and Death*. New York: Routledge, 1999. Print.

Peperzak, Adrian. *Ethics as First Philosophy: The Significance of Emmanuel Levinas for Philosophy, Literature and Religion*. New York: Routledge, 2013. Print.

Plantinga, Carl. "The Philosophy of Errol Morris: Ten Lessons." *Three Documentary Filmmakers: Errol Morris, Ross McElwee, Jean Rouch*. Ed. William Rothman. Albany: State U of New York P, 2009. 43–60. Print.

Sontag, Susan. *Regarding the Pain of Others.* New York: Picador, 2004. Print.
Standard Operating Procedure. Dir. Errol Morris. Sony Pictures Classics, DVD. 2008.
Williams, Linda. "Cluster Fuck: The Forcible Frame in Errol Morris's *Standard Operating Procedure.*" *Camera Obscura* 25.73 (2010): 29–67. Web.
Ziarek, Ewa Plonowska. *An Ethics of Dissensus: Postmodernity, Feminism, and the Politics of Radical Democracy.* Stanford, CA: Stanford UP, 2002. Print.

17 Feminist criticism

Justine Tally

Late in 1964 with thousands of young people both Black and white in the South to participate in Freedom Summer, teaching and registering Black people to vote, two volunteer members of the Student Nonviolent Coordinating Committee (SNCC) composed an internal flyer entitled "Sex and Caste: A Kind of Memo," reflecting on the status of women working within the Civil Rights Movement, based on their own experiences and those of other women. Casey Hayden and Mary King, having learned to think seriously about issues of equality among the "races," questioned the lack of leadership roles for women (who were dedicating their time and energy and risking their lives) and their relegation to more "traditional" supportive roles in favor of the male leaders.

Credited with kick-starting the renewal of the Women's Movement, today some of Hayden and King's words prompt a smile: "Objectively, the chances seem nil that we could start a movement based on anything as distant to general American thought as a sex caste system." With the gift of hindsight and understanding today, and with a feminist consciousness so widespread that we simply have taken many of the battles and achievements of women for granted, we are now much more accustomed to seeing women take on high positions of leadership and power across the board: socially, economically, culturally, and politically. It has been said that the one great gap in the visions of George Orwell and Aldous Huxley, the one most important thing that has come between us and their dystopian projections of "brave new (totalitarian) worlds," has been precisely the rise of the Women's Movement, which changed the gender equation and catapulted women into the workforce and the echelons of power.

In a way it is curious that neither Orwell nor Huxley could imagine such an adjustment in the gender equation. After all, women had been making their discontent felt from the very beginning of the New Republic when Jane Adams complained to her husband John that the new Constitution effectively blocked over half the population (women, African Americans, and Native Americans) from full participation in the political life of the new country. The landmark convention of women at Seneca Falls (1848), organized by Elizabeth Cady Stanton and Lucretia Mott, produced its "Declaration of Sentiments" and an accompanying list of resolutions, which were instrumental in gaining limited rights for married women, beginning with the revised property laws in New York that same year. The powerful Susan B. Anthony joined forces with Stanton in 1851 and campaigned tirelessly for women's suffrage throughout the nineteenth century, though women did not achieve the right to vote in the United States until 1920.

Representing the rights of African Americans – both men and women – Frederick Douglass spoke out for women's rights right up until the day of his death in 1895. The journalist Ida B. Wells was also instrumental both in the campaign against the lynching of Black men (often on trumped-up charges of insulting a white woman) and the rights of Black women, though she was effectively betrayed by Anthony and Stanton when asked not to participate in rallies to be held in the South so as not to offend white women whose support they very much needed for their national campaign for women's suffrage.

In the twentieth century both World Wars saw a massive influx of women into the work place as men were drafted to fight in Europe and the Pacific theater, but their forced retreat to domesticity upon the return of their men created a suppressed form of unhappiness in the suburban bliss of the affluent 1950s. Simone de Beauvoir – a French intellectual, philosopher, and women's activist – famously captured the imbalance in gender relations in her landmark book *The Second Sex* (1949),[1] now widely regarded as the foundational tract of second-wave feminism. Across the ocean in the United States, Betty Friedan published *The Feminine Mystique* (1963), also credited as a starting point for the regeneration of the Women's Movement. Although Friedan had originally planned her analysis (based in part on interviews with unhappy housewives) as a magazine article, no magazine would publish her critique of what she called "the problem that has no name" – the wide-spread discontent of women in the 1950s and early 1960s (see Chapter 3). What is clear is that the post-war era generated a time of unease about women's role in society.

Though second-wave feminism was sparked among young white women in the Civil Rights Movement in the 1960s, Black women were estranged once more from an organization that they referred to as the White Women's Movement. And yet, Sara Evans's book *Personal Politics: The Roots of Women's Liberation in the Civil Rights Movement and the New Left* (1979) documented, via interviews with young white female activists, the importance of Black women in the South as role models. Rejecting the model of their own suburban mothers and their stifling lives, they were inspired by the courage and serenity of Black women, who risked everything to shelter and feed them when they were threatened by the locals.[2] Nevertheless, in the esteem of many of these Black women, racism trumped sexism as their major concern. This is not to ignore the fact that sexism was alive and well in the Black community, but once again Black women were estranged from what they perceived as essentially just another form of exclusion. In the words of Toni Morrison:

> The early image of Women's Lib was of an élitist organization made up of upper-middle-class women with the concerns of that class [...] and

not paying much attention to the problems of most black women, which are not in getting into the labor force but in being upgraded in it, not in getting into medical school but in getting adult education, not in how to exercise freedom from the "head of the house" but in how to *be* head of the household. ("What the Black Woman Thinks" 22)

It took a long time and the work of many Black female critics to make their concerns heard and have them accepted by the white majority.

In the 1970s, Women's Studies departments sprang up at universities around the country and the first thrusts of these new curricula were concerned with the "rescue and recovery" of women writers from the past who had been neglected by academic (read "traditionally male") syllabi. To these first efforts we owe recently "canonized" authors such as Rebecca Harding Davis, Charlotte Perkins Gilman, Kate Chopin, and a long etcetera, whose works were often first published by the Feminist Press (founded by Florence Howe) and have now become staples of university courses. Alice Walker recalls leaving certain texts by Black authors on her desk so that her office mate, busily ensconced in writing a book about female authors, would recognize the neglect of other women in her survey ... to no avail. Walker herself stumbled across Zora Neale Hurston and almost single-handedly restored the Harlem Renaissance author and anthropologist to prominence as a "foremother" of Black writers. Walker also not only wrote novels about sexism in the Black community (to the disgruntlement of male Black writers and critics), but also drew on her own heritage to coin "womanism" in an attempt to bring the feminist issues to the table: "Womanist is to feminist as purple to lavender" (Walker xii; see Chapter 22). And in 1979 Mary Helen Washington made a clarion call to Black female literary critics to turn their attention to their own writers; such was the critical support and acclaim that the 1980s saw the rise of what was called "The Black Women Writers' Renaissance" and the eventual recognition of Toni Morrison with the Nobel Prize in Literature in 1993, only the eighth woman recipient and the first African American.

Even with all the possibilities opened up over the years, there is still a tendency to distinguish between "Anglo-American feminism" and "French feminist theory." The former has in general terms tended toward activism and political concerns ("the personal is political"), concentrating not only on who has been silenced by the dominant patriarchal culture but also on what the silences themselves tell us in the work of female authors. Who is speaking for whom and by what authority? What is it that is not being said? And how does the recognition of those silences shade the interpretation of these authors' work? How much is the portrayal of women in popular culture, for example, set out for the male gaze rather than responding to and fomenting a healthy integrity in women? And how are women in powerful positions in society making a difference? What has it meant that more and more women directors are making their mark in the cinema and on TV? The questions are endless and the research ongoing, itself prompting yet more questions and focusing on ushering in a more egalitarian society for all its members.

French feminist theory, on the other hand, is traditionally steeped in psycho-analysis and explores the *différence* manifest in language and culture that is specific to women. Frequently criticized for being "essentialist" (and therefore coming dangerously close to the biological arguments that were traditionally used to keep women "in their place" in society), the explorations into a speci-fically female "psyche" nevertheless opened up a new way of understanding difference and marginalization. Not only were women different from men, but they engaged others in a semiotic communication that might well be beneficial to all human beings if acknowledged and given value. Luce Irigaray posited "a feminine myth of origin" founded on "the daughter's relation to origin and her mother, as the foundation for an alternative modality of libido" (Buck 133). For this critic, women were engaged in a special *parler femme* that originated in the *sémiotique.* That is, before the child enters into the Lacanian "symbolic," which is language (see Chapter 14), s/he communicates with the mother through the senses, even while still in the womb: Touch, smell, taste, sound, all carry meaning long before the child learns to speak and constitute a special relationship between the mother and her progeny before the "Oedipal" moment governed by the "Law of the Father." Hélène Cixous speaks of a feminine way of writing, *écriture féminine,* that is both an attempt at reclaiming the semiotic and a tool for understanding the "gaps" or "cracks" and silences in women's writing: "By writing her self, woman will return to the body which has been more than confiscated from her [...]. Censor the body and you censor breath and speech at the same time" (350–51). There-fore, liberating the body and returning to the semiotic is the first step to recovering the integrity denied by the patriarchy. Julia Kristeva, though also steeped in psychoanalysis, is more Marxist in her conception of women as a subordinated group of society. For her, both the male and female child are equally participative in the realm of the semiotic, what Kristeva calls the *chora,* and that type of communication is not gender-bound. This does not make it less crucial, however, in the search for wholeness for both sexes.

In her seventh novel, *Paradise,* Toni Morrison undertakes a narrative experiment, which engages many of the theories and techniques put forward by feminist theorists. Though many reviewers were initially disappointed in the novel, reading it through such a theoretical framework can illuminate the text in new and startling ways.

Paradise deals with the confrontation between the men of Ruby, the "perfect" all-Black town, governed by the Law of the Fathers whose women are stifled in their "propriety," and the former Convent, now inhabited by a motley group of wayward women, all traumatized by the abuse by males in their former lives. As the men of Ruby begin to feel like they are losing control over their women and the young people in their "eight-rock" (pure Black) town, they scapegoat the Convent women for living without men, for being "slack" (not conforming to the men's idea of appropriate feminine behavior) and for supposed sexual impropriety. Indeed the Convent women constitute what Elaine Showalter would denominate the "wild zone" of women on the margins of society, who grow their corn and vegetables in circles, not straight rows, and offer succor and kindness to everyone in need. The novel opens with the massacre of these women, "[t]hey shoot the white girl first," and though "race" is dramatically signaled, the text never divulges who the "white girl" might be, and ultimately, why it would even matter.

This female community is headed by Connie (later Consolata), a former street-urchin rescued from Brazil by Mother Mary Magna and brought to the Convent. Connie takes in all those young women who arrive there in need of care and love and offers them absolute freedom to come or go as they please. Such is the comfort they find that no one wants to leave. Having been used and abused as a child, Connie is steeped in the ways of the nuns, but as an adult finds passion with Deacon, one of the leaders of Ruby who is married to Soane, who eventually forges a close friendship with Connie. The romantic relationship is short-lived and Connie returns to church and Mary Magna, the "sha-sha-sha" of her passion for Deacon replaced with the "sh-sh-sh" of erotics denied. A piercing light leaves her partially blinded and overly sensitive to light. Yet when Mary Magna dies in spite of all Connie's ministrations and her "reaching in" to save her, she loses all sense of self, literally "dis-Consolate," and retreats to the cellar hoping to die. Disappointed to still be alive and still wearing her sunglasses as she cannot tolerate the light, she sits in the garden at twilight. It is only when her male visitor appears that she begins her quest for wholeness.

In fact Connie's weak eyesight moves us into the realm of French feminist theory, for while the male economy and libido is founded on "sight," the female erotic prioritizes touch. Connie's role as "visionary," her "seeing in," also positions her outside the patriarchy and moves her within the realm of the maternal. Though some reviewers complained about the "contrived" conversion Connie undergoes after meeting the stranger in the garden "who causes her to begin speaking in the cadences of her childhood tongue, and who, more significantly, looks like a male version of her[self], with his long tea-colored hair and his eyes 'round and green as new apples'" (Stave 6), it is this encounter with her male Other that forms a critical aspect of Cixous's theory of the "erotic bisexuality" of the "presymbolic child," its "polymorphous perversion" (354–58).

The first celebratory act of Connie (now Consalata) after this "visitation" and reclaiming of direction in her life is to cook for the younger women:

> Consolata tilts the fowl and peers into their silver and rose cavities. She tosses in salt and scours it all around, then rubs the outer skin with a cinnamon and butter mixture. [...] As soon as the hens are roasted brown enough and tender she sets them aside so they can reclaim their liquids. [...]
>
> Consolata is peeling and quartering small brown potatoes. She simmers them in water seasoned with pan juices, bay leaf and sage before

arranging them in a skillet where they turn darkly gold. She sprinkles paprika and seeds of blackest pepper over them. "Oh, yes," she says. "Oh, yes." (255, 257)

The choice of words in these excerpts reinforces the idea of sensuousness and the wholeness of the female experience and sexuality: "silver and rose cavities," "tender," "liquids," "juices," "darkly gold," and sighs of "[o]h, yes." Moreover, Consolata successfully incorporates her Other, reconciles the split between body and mind imposed by Western patriarchal discourse, and deconstructs its "virgin/whore" dichotomy:

A woman who teach me my body is nothing my spirit everything. [...] My bones on his the only true thing. So I wondering where is the spirit lost in this? It is true, like bones. It is good, like bones. [...] Where is it lost? Hear me, listen. Never break them in two. Never put one over the other. Eve is Mary's mother. Mary is the daughter of Eve. (263)

Shirley A. Stave argues that in this passage Consolata's speech "disrupts accepted rules of grammar and syntax and, as such, can be perceived as outside the Symbolic Order" (7), and Consolata's subsequent retreat into the cellar with the four psychically damaged women can be read as an enactment of the return to the presymbolic, or semiotic, or *chora* in Kristeva's terminology.

Once in the cellar Consolata has her charges lie quietly on the floor where she draws their silhouettes. In subsequent visits to the cellar the young women draw projections of their individual traumas onto the outline of their bodies. These scenes in the cellar can be interpreted as a move to presymbolic time, a return to the (M)Other as well as an experiment with Cixous's theory of (literally) "writing the body"; Consolata has these women release their trauma precisely through projecting themselves onto and through their outlined bodies, a visceral reenactment of *écriture féminine*. Moreover, the text simultaneously insinuates Irigaray's preference for the idea of *parler femme* in that we never actually hear what words, if any, the women vocalize in their "loud dreaming" in order to liberate their woman-story. Prompted by Consolata's story, the women begin to give voice to their own: "In loud dreaming, monologue is no different from a shriek; accusations directed to the dead and long gone are undone by murmurs of love" (264).

When the men of Ruby attack the women and storm the Convent, they are unable to understand or to meaningfully return to the *sémiotique*. Storming the house, brandishing their phallic guns – which are "more than decoration, intimidation or comfort. They are meant" (285) – they find that the mirrors upstairs are all covered with chalky paint except for one, which a man ignores. "He does not want to see himself stalking females or their liquid" (9). The reference to these mirrors is significant: Irigaray has written that in psychoanalytical theory, within the symbolic order, "woman is man's 'specularised Other,' her function to reflect back man's meaning to himself, becoming the negative of this reflection" (qtd. in Millard 159); for Kristeva (following Lacan) the passage from the presymbolic (dominated by the mother) is preceded by the "mirror stage," which "opens the way for the constitution of all objects which from now on will be detached from the semiotic chora" (qtd. in Moi 162). The men are unable either to return to or even to relate to the *sémiotique*. After the massacre, Anna Flood and Richard Misner, the minister, walk through the building and down to the cellar. Anna Flood sees "the terribleness K.D. reported, but it wasn't the pornography he had seen, nor was it Satan's scrawl. She saw instead the turbulence of females trying to bridle, without being trampled, the monsters that slavered them" (303). What they do sense are an open door and open window, and Anna also gathers warm eggs, symbol of hope and fertility.

The last lyrical coda, which has puzzled many readers of the novel, actually moves to enact Irigaray's feminine "Myth of Origin":

> In ocean hush a woman black as firewood is singing. Next to her is a younger woman whose head rests on the singing woman's lap. Ruined fingers troll the tea brown hair. All the colors of seashells – wheat, roses, pearl – fuse in the younger woman's face. Her emerald eyes adore the black face framed in cerulean blue. Around them on the beach, sea trash gleams. Discarded bottle caps sparkle near a broken sandal. A small dead radio plays the quiet surf. (318)

Cixous employs the same metaphors to depict what she calls the metaphorical mother and the language of the presymbolic:

> But look our seas are what we make of them, full of fish or not, opaque or transparent, red or black, high or smooth, narrow or bankless; and we are ourselves sea, sand coral, seaweed, beaches, tides, swimmers, children, waves [...]. More or less wavily sea, earth, sky – what matter would rebuff us? We know how to speak them all. (357)

The final scene of Morrison's novel reworks the Christian Pietá as Piedade cradles Consolata in her lap and sings "in ocean hush" of "memories neither one has ever had" (318). For Cixous,

> [t]he voice in each woman, moreover, is not only her own, but springs from the deepest layers of her psyche: her own speech becomes the echo of the primeval song she once heard, the voice the incarnation of the "first voice of love which all women preserve alive" [...] the Voice of the Mother, that omnipotent figure that dominates the fantasies of the pre-Oedipal baby. (qtd. in Moi 114)

After the massacre, as Deacon struggles to come to terms with his role in it, he yearns for reconciliation with Soane. In an act of humility he walks barefoot to the house of Misner, but the text carefully lays out the explicit vertical and horizontal streets of his trajectory, an enactment of Irigaray's suggestion for the healing that must take place between men and women: "The link uniting or reuniting masculine and feminine must be both horizontal and vertical, terrestrial and celestial [...] in which a sexual encounter would be a celebration, and not a disguised or polemic form of the master–slave relationship" (127). Tellingly, Irigaray finds the replica for a complete sexuality in the female body itself: "Superimposed, [the female] lips adopt a cross-like shape that is the prototype of the crossroads, thus representing both inter and enter, for the lips of the mouth and the lips of the female sex do not point in the same direction" (127).

There is no closure here, but a promise for the future. The irony of Deacon's earlier phrase dissolves as he embarks at the end of *Paradise* on a different type of journey: "Women always the key, God bless 'em" (61).

Today the Women's Movement is much more inclusive and, together with the 1960s challenge to the traditional canon of "dead white males" (DWMs), has encouraged a plethora of "minority" writers as well as developing the critical tools to analyze them on their own terms. The emphasis on "multiculturalism" has meant that we can no longer talk in the singular about "feminism." Consequently Feminist Studies has continued to expand into Gender Studies over the decades to include a multiplicity of genders, class, and alternate sexualities, and to encompass the cultural specificities of them all.

Notes

1 The Vatican included it on its "List of Prohibited Books."
2 For a discussion on the revisionary nature of historical memory with respect to these questions of gendered positions within the Women's Movement, see Estes.

Works cited

Buck, Claire. "'O Careless, Unspeakable Mother': Irigaray, H.D. and Maternal Origin." *Feminist Criticism: Theory and Practice*. Ed. Susan Sellers. Toronto: U of Toronto P, 1991. 129–42. Print.
Cixous, Hélène. "The Laugh of the Medusa." *Feminisms: An Anthology of Literary Theory and Criticism*. Ed. Robyn Warhol and Diane Price Herndl. New Brunswick, NJ: Rutgers UP, 1997. 334–9. Print.
de Beauvoir, Simone. *The Second Sex*. 1949. Trans. Constance Borde and Sheila Malovany-Chevallier. New York: Vintage, 2011. Print.
Estes, Steve. "Engendering Movement Memories: Remembering Race and Gender in the Mississippi Movement." *The Civil Rights Movement in American Memory*. Ed.

Renee C. Romano and Leigh Raiford. Athens: U of Georgia P, 2006. 299–307. Print.

Evans, Sara. *Personal Politics: The Roots of Women's Liberation in the Civil Rights Movement and the New Left*. 1979. New York: Vintage, 2001. Print.

Friedan, Betty. *The Feminine Mystique*. 1963. New York: Norton, 2013. Print.

Hayden, Casey, and Mary King. "Sex and Caste: A Kind of Memo." *Freedom Song: The Power of Nonviolent Action and the Works of Mary King*. 1964. http://maryking.info/?page_id=176 Web. 17 May 2014.

Irigaray, Luce. "Sexual Difference." *French Feminist Thought: A Reader*. 1987. Ed. Toril Moi. Oxford: Basil Blackwell, 1989. 118–32. Print.

Millard, Elaine. "French Feminisms." *Feminist Readings/Feminists Reading*. Ed. Sarah Mills et al. Hemel Hempstead: Harvester Wheatsheaf, 1989. Print.

Moi, Toril. *Sexual/Textual Politics*. London: Routledge, 1988. Print.

Morrison, Toni. *Paradise*. New York: Knopf, 1998. Print.

---. "What the Black Woman Thinks about Women's Lib." *What Moves at the Margin*. Ed. Carolyn Denard. Jackson: UP of Mississippi, 2008. 18–30. Print.

Showalter, Elaine. "Feminist Criticism in the Wilderness." *Critical Inquiry*. Special Issue "Writing and Sexual Difference" 8.2 (1981): 179–205. Print.

Stave, Shirley A. "Narrativizing the Unspeakable: Articulating the Mystical in Toni Morrison's *Paradise*." Lecture presented at ALA Conference, Boston, MA. 27 May 2001. Manuscript.

Walker, Alice. *In Search of Our Mothers' Gardens: Womanist Prose*. New York: Harcourt Brace Jovanovitch, 1983. Print.

18 Gender Studies

Challenging heteronormativity

Eva Boesenberg

In the 1980s and '90s, research on gender and sexuality underwent significant transformations. This was already signaled by the terms commonly used to refer to this academic field. In many cases, the designation "Women's Studies" was replaced by "Gender Studies." What's the difference? First, Gender Studies investigate gender as a system, that is, they analyze masculinity as well as femininity – or rather, since some feminist researchers had already done so in the context of Women's Studies, one should say that masculinity now received more sustained attention.

In fact, it would be more appropriate to state that Gender Studies seek to illuminate masculinities and femininities (in the plural) because, second, they moved away from understanding gender in terms of a male/female dichotomy toward models that identify a potentially unlimited number of gender positions, which need not be stable or coherent either. It is here that the intensive interaction with Queer Theory, Transgender, and Intersex Studies perhaps becomes most visible (Stryker and Whittle; Holmes; see also Chapter 19).

Third, Gender Studies tend no longer to work with the sex/gender division established by Gayle Rubin and others, according to which "sex" refers to given, biological bodies, and "gender" is the cultural construction employed to invest sex with meaning in specific social and cultural contexts. Instead, Gender Studies also regard "sex" as a cultural construction. The scholar whose work established this point most effectively and most influentially is Judith Butler.

Gender as performance

In her book *Gender Trouble* (1990), Butler famously argued that gender is the result of particular actions and utterances that *produce* masculinities and femininities (as well as other gender positions) instead of *expressing* them. The impression of "femininity" or "masculinity" is achieved through what she calls "gender performance." Perhaps an analogy to the theater is helpful here. Just as actors in a drama wear certain kinds of clothing, speak and move in particular ways to suggest a character's gender (regardless of their own – in Shakespeare's time, for instance, all roles were played by male actors) – we "perform gender" outside of the theater by following the "scripts" our culture has prepared for male and female genders. Think of romance and marriage, for example: There are fairly clear guidelines for who is supposed to approach whom, for possibly proposing marriage, for the respective responsibilities in a conventional nuclear family, etc.

If we realize that gender is a hierarchical system that benefits some groups and discriminates against others, and we don't want to support such an unfair structure, why don't we just stop what Butler called "doing gender"? We can't, she argues, because being perceived as gendered – gendered male or female, that is – is considered a precondition for being considered human. People whose gender performance is seen as "inappropriate," as not quite fitting, may face consequences ranging from stares and hostile comments to physical attack and murder. In films and literature, they are often portrayed as "monsters."

What is their crime? They depart from a gender arrangement that is heteronormative, but that many people just consider "normal" or "natural." In fact, nobody is "normal." The idea of the "normal" is another social construction – the supposedly "normal" or "natural" positions are simply the powerful ones in a particular society. They come to seem "normal" and "natural" – they are *normalized* and *naturalized* – because they are repeated, again and again, in the media, in political debates, in laws, etc. (see also Chapter 22). This has little to do with statistical averages – what would be a "normal" age, for example? Why would a middle-class position be "more normal" than a working-class one? Why should a man be more "representative" than a woman, given that women outnumber men in most Western societies? The "normal" is really a *norm*, an ideal, a standard of what things should be like, instead of what they are. And since ideas of "the normal" serve to maintain the status quo, to keep certain social groups in power, they have conservative political effects.

Against heteronormativity

So what is a heteronormative model of gender? It suggests that there are two (and only two) genders, male and female, that there is a clear dividing line between men and women, and that these groups do not overlap; that one's gender is the same in each situation and that it does not change during one's lifetime; and that there is a logical and necessary relation between one's (sexed) body, one's gender position, and one's sexual preference. Men, for example, are supposed to possess a body with a penis and desire women. But not all do. Some desire both men and women (bisexual men); some desire only other men (gay or queer men); some are not interested in sex at all, whether or not they have a penis. On the basis of such observations, Gender Studies question all of the assumptions on which the heteronormative model rests.

Perhaps the most obvious challenge to heteronormativity comes from gay men and lesbians. Even if they identify as men and women, they do not desire the "opposite" sex, as they should according to the dominant model of gender and sexuality. Because of this, they are stigmatized and oppressed. But other groups also do not conform to dominant ideas. Judith Jack Halberstam's study *Female Masculinity* (1998) has shown that masculinity is not the exclusive property of males, for example. Females have "performed masculinity," i.e., have lived as men, have been and *are* men, in the past as well as the present. The gender assigned to transsexual persons tends not to match their own sense of their gender, so that they frequently seek gender reassignment by changing their names and their official gender position, sometimes even undergoing hormone treatment or surgery in order for their bodies to express their gender in a way they feel to be more fitting. Transgender, trans* or queer persons may refuse to position themselves as male or female altogether.

Finally, intersex individuals confound a binary gender model (one that accepts only the two positions of male and female) because their bodies are "ambiguous," i.e., they show both, or neither, "male" and "female" characteristics. Doctors and parents generally identify the gender of newborns based on the size of their genitals. If these are longer than 2.5 centimeters, they are considered penises and the baby male; an organ less than 0.9 centimeters is classified as clitoris and the child as female. Genitals longer than 0.9 centimeters but shorter than 2.5 centimeters are not supposed to exist, but they do. In Germany, parents were required by law to categorize their children as "male" or "female" anyway, and until the late twentieth century, many intersex children were operated on – their genitals were mutilated – to make them fit dominant models of gender.

Reflecting on the variable quality of gender and the diversity of gender positions, most scholars in Gender Studies now work with an understanding of gender as a social construction (social constructivism). They also note that gender is experienced differently depending on one's "race," class, sexuality, disability, religion, etc. The concept that expresses this insight is called inter-sectionality. It was first formulated by African American scholars such as Kimberlé Crenshaw, Audre Lorde, and Patricia Hill Collins and suggests that axes of different hierarchies (like gender or "race"), imagined as lines, "intersect" (cut across each other) to produce different social positions and fields. Other theorists speak of the interdependence of different social categories to describe this phenomenon. If I am a white middle-class heterosexual cis- (i.e., not trans) woman, for example, I do experience gender differently than an Asian American middle-class lesbian. Even though we are both discriminated against as women, my problems will not include being denied housing or being called names because of my "race," nor will I be harassed because of my sexual orientation.

Scholars in Postcolonial Studies (see Chapter 21) have also observed that colonial and postcolonial power relations result in differing forms of "femininity" in Western (European and North American) and colonized cultures (Spivak). Some, like Chandra Talpade Mohanty, have even questioned whether it makes sense to use Western concepts to analyze the situation of women in formerly colonized nations at all.

Gender Studies theorists are of at least two minds about the most productive ways of challenging gender oppression. Some, like Butler, call for "undoing gender"; others look for strategies to make existing gender categories more "livable" by constructing them as more flexible and more comprehensive. At the same time, mobilizing established terms such as "women" may be effective for challenging particular forms of sexism. In most Western countries, for instance, the so-called "gender pay gap" still stands at 20 to 25 percent, meaning that women on average earn 20 to 25 percent less than men. To address this unfair situation, it may be a good idea to hold on to the terminology of "women and men" even if one is aware of these designations' problematic effects. This is called strategic essentialism (Spivak).

Trifles?

A play that shows quite clearly how gender is constructed is Susan Glaspell's drama *Trifles* (1916). It revolves around a murder case. A farmer has been found strangled in his bed, and the question is whether his wife did it. The cast consists of five characters. The men – the county attorney, the sheriff, and Mr. Hale, a neighboring farmer who found the body – are there (on the Wrights' farm) on business: They are investigating the crime. The women, Mrs. Hale and Mrs. Peters, the sheriff's wife, have come along to pack some clothing for Minnie Wright, the suspect who is in prison. While the men go upstairs and outside to search for evidence, the women stay behind in the kitchen. While waiting, they notice things the men consider "trifles" – the cold in the room, a badly knotted piece of a quilt, a bird cage with a broken door, and more. On the basis of these clues, they solve the case – but in the end decide to keep their knowledge to themselves.

In the drama, gender is constructed through space – most of the time, the men are upstairs in the bedroom, literally on top of the women. This can be understood symbolically as well – it corresponds to the condescension with which the male characters treat Mrs. Hale and Mrs. Peters. They dismiss their interest in trifles and are quick to judge the absent Mrs. Wright on the basis of her dirty kitchen towels, showing little or no understanding for and appreciation of women's work. This leads to feelings of solidarity between the female characters, who believe that the men cannot be trusted to treat the accused Minnie Wright fairly.

Building on their knowledge of their neighbors and the labor of home-making, they try to make sense of the small unusual things they observe in the kitchen – the trifles of the play's title. These tell them that the Wrights' marriage was cold, like the kitchen – perhaps it had even gone bad because of this, like the shattered preserves in the cupboard. An unfinished, badly sown patch for a quilt hints at Mrs. Wright's nervousness.

Perhaps most importantly, the clues of the birdcage, whose door has been broken, and the dead bird itself suggest to them what might have sparked the drama. They conclude that Mr. Wright, perhaps in a fit of rage, violently opened the door and wrung the bird's neck. The beautiful box in which they find the bird shows that Minnie Wright valued her pet very highly. Since Mr. Wright was strangled – his neck was wrung, so to speak – it is very likely that it was indeed his wife who killed him, taking revenge for his murder of her cherished companion.

But the image of the cage can also be read in another way. It might be understood as a symbol of the marriage in which Minnie was imprisoned, just like the bird. This analogy is supported by Mrs. Hale's recollection that her neighbor was very fond of singing in her youth. The broken cage might then also be interpreted as a sign of her liberation – even if her freedom has been achieved in a violent manner.

The drama goes even further, however. For the women realize that they themselves have contributed to Minnie Wright's isolation by not visiting more often – because of the husband's unfriendly manner, they found the atmosphere in the house unpleasant. "That was a crime! That was a crime!," Mrs. Hale comments (1935). One could say that it is the entire social organization of gender and family life in rural America at this point in time that destroys the Wrights' marriage. Because they understand this, the women do not think that Minnie Wright should go to prison or even suffer the death penalty for her deed. If they constitute "a jury of her peers," as the title of the short story version of the play proclaims, their verdict is "justifiable homicide." Therefore, they do not tell the men what they have found and even take the bird, the most incriminating evidence, with them.

From an intersectional perspective, one notices the centrality of heterosexuality in the play – it is one of the major factors that sets the drama in motion. Heteronormativity structures gender in *Trifles*, as do whiteness and class. For the nuclear family that proves to be Mr. and Mrs. Wright's undoing emerges as a distinctly white and middle-class formation in the nineteenth century. Inaccessible to enslaved African Americans, Native Americans, and working-class white people, the nuclear family and the idea of "separate spheres" for men and women, which is eminently visible in Glaspell's play, served as a sign of social distinction – but they rested on the subordination of the women of the house, the wife, daughters, and in many cases the domestic servants.

The latter, often racialized working-class women, suffered most. Where their class status, rights deriving from marriage, and frequently their whiteness gave wives and daughters certain privileges, not least of them the power to dominate and exploit servants, these were unavailable to the women who worked for them (Harris). *Trifles* also does not address the fact that the rural community it represents as the site of dysfunctional gender arrangements was established in the context of settler colonialism, and that, as Morgensen has shown, "modern" white US-American concepts of gender and sexuality form an integral part of this colonization.

A reading of the play informed by current research in Gender Studies thus illuminates the text's critique of heteronormativity and contemporary constructions of gender, while also noting its silence on matters of non-heteronormative sexualities and genders, as well as settler colonialism, "race," disability, and other forms of oppression.

Works cited

Butler, Judith. *Gender Trouble: Feminism and the Subversion of Identity.* New York: Routledge, 1990. Print.

---. *Undoing Gender.* New York: Routledge, 2004. Print.

Collins, Patricia Hill. "Some Group Matters: Intersectionality, Situated Standpoints, and Black Feminist Thought." *Fighting Words: Black Women and the Search for Justice.* Minneapolis: U of Minnesota P, 1998. 201–28. Print.

Crenshaw, Kimberlé. "Mapping the Margins: Intersectionality, Identity Politics, and Violence against Women of Color." *Standard Law Review* 43.6 (1991): 1241–99. Print.

Glaspell, Susan. *Trifles.* 1916. *The Norton Anthology of American Literature.* Shorter eighth ed. Ed. Julia Reidhead et al. New York: Norton, 2013. 1927–36. Print.

Halberstam, Judith Jack. *Female Masculinity.* Durham, NC: Duke UP, 1998. Print.

Harris, Trudier. *From Mammies to Militants: Domestics in Black American Literature.* Philadelphia, PA: Temple UP, 1982. Print.

Holmes, Morgan, ed. *Critical Intersex: Queer Interventions.* Burlington, VT: Ashgate, 2009. Print.

Lorde, Audre. *Sister Outsider: Essays and Speeches.* Trumansburg, NY: Crossing P, 1983. Print.

Mohanty, Chandra Talpade. "Under Western Eyes: Feminist Scholarship and Colonial Discourses." *Feminism without Borders: Decolonizing Theory, Practicing Solidarity.* Durham, NC: Duke UP, 2003. 17–42. Print.

Morgensen, Scott Lauria. *Spaces between Us: Queer Settler Colonialism and Indigenous Decolonization.* Minneapolis: U of Minnesota P, 2011. Print.

Rubin, Gayle. "The Traffic in Women: Notes on the 'Political Economy' of Sex." *Toward an Anthropology of Women.* Ed. Rayna R. Reiter. New York: Monthly Review P, 1975. 157–210. Print.

Spivak, Gayatri Chakravorty. "Can the Subaltern Speak?" *Marxism and the Interpretation of Culture.* Ed. Cary Nelson and Lawrence Grossberg. Basingstoke: Macmillan, 1988. 271–313. Print.

Stryker, Susan, and Stephen Whittle, eds. *The Transgender Studies Reader.* New York: Routledge, 2006. Print.

19 Queer and Transgender Studies

Beyond simple dualistic notions of
sexuality and gender

Bart Eeckhout

Although Queer and Transgender Studies have come to exert an appeal in many places around the globe and are being practiced today in a variety of culturally specific forms, the historical emergence of these two related fields is inextricably tied up with the English-speaking world, in particular the United States. It is worth reminding ourselves of the simple fact that "queer" and "transgender" are English words. The latter is a recent neologism that builds on the word "gender," which itself came to be used only in the second half of the twentieth century to reflect the ways in which cultural meanings are ascribed to a person's biological sex.

Positing a distinction between biological sex and gender was especially useful to shift the attention toward cultural, social, and linguistic processes underlying the opposition between masculinity and femininity in any given society. The addition of the prefix "trans" in turn made it possible to highlight how dominant norms of masculinity and femininity fail to make sufficient room for individuals whose gender identities and/or expressions do not comply with such norms.

The historical background of "queer" in the context of "Queer Theory" – and, increasingly, "Queer Studies" – is somewhat different. For centuries, the adjective was used in the sense of strange, odd, eccentric. But over time it came to be applied to particular people displaying such behavior, acquiring sexual associations in the process, until in the twentieth century it became one of many derogatory and insinuating labels for homosexual people (principally men). Although this insulting usage was on the wane again by the 1980s, "queer" as a sexual label was reactivated around 1990 in three different contexts: among activists, among artists, and among academics.

At that point in history, the word "gay" had become widespread as a positive label with which homosexual men and, to a slightly lesser extent, lesbian women in the United States chose to identify. But the AIDS crisis in the 1980s, breaking out especially among gay men, led to a social backlash in the form of governmental indifference and the rise of a fundamentalist Christian movement calling itself the Moral Majority. By the end of a polarizing decade, AIDS activists had come to resort to more confrontational tactics to make themselves heard. Among these was the assumption of the stigmatizing label "queer" as a term of self-reference. The slogan "We're here, we're queer, get used to it!" was chanted on protest marches, and one organization called itself Queer Nation. More or less simultaneously, the label New Queer Cinema came to be applied to a number of equally polemical independent films by directors such as Todd Haynes, Jennie Livingston, Isaac Julien, and Tom Kalin. Also around 1990, a handful of provocative academic publications reoriented the disciplines of Gay and Lesbian Studies, feminism, and Gender Studies in the direction of what was soon to be called Queer Theory.

Although it is Teresa de Lauretis who is generally credited with having launched the label in 1991, Queer Theory became especially synonymous with two books from the previous year that had an enormous impact: the philosopher Judith Butler's *Gender Trouble: Feminism and the Subversion of Identity* and the literary critic Eve Kosofsky Sedgwick's *Epistemology of the Closet*. What these two critical interventions shared, not just with each other but with a spate of publications associated with Queer Theory in the early 1990s, was a radically questioning attitude toward identity thinking. In developing their ideas, Butler, Sedgwick, and others drew inspiration from various sources, ranging from post-structuralist theory (principally Michel Foucault, Jacques Derrida, and Jacques Lacan; see Chapter 13) to traditions within lesbian feminism (such as the American anthropologist Gayle Rubin, who insisted on the need to distinguish carefully between gender and sexuality in Cultural Studies; see Chapter 18). One of the main ideas American queer theorists derived from such antecedents was a contestation of simplified dualistic thinking, whether in gender terms about men vs. women or in sexual terms about gay vs. straight. Instead, they proposed skeptical and dynamic perspectives in which sexual and gender identities – even sexual desire itself – are not treated as fixed notions or phenomena across time and space.

The critical thinking that has come out of Queer and Transgender Studies is characteristically multidisciplinary and many-layered. It forces readers to acknowledge complexities and contradictions without giving in to the psychic or political pressure to simplify and reduce. This means that queer and transgender theorists will ordinarily resist the kind of synthetic survey attempted in this brief chapter, or the didactic language in which I write, which sacrifices a certain amount of nuance and jargon to entry-level comprehensibility. Yet it also means, more positively, that critics working in the field love to draw case studies from the realm of Cultural Studies. After all, they share a conviction that cultural experiences and products are crucial to the construction of gender and sexuality, and thus need to be questioned constantly for what they express and achieve, often in unspoken or unconscious ideological ways. And so I propose to develop the rest of this chapter by sampling three internationally successful, Academy-Award-winning movies that might be said to be, schematically, about two gay (or perhaps bisexual?) men, three lesbian (or again bisexual?) women, and one transgender (or maybe lesbian?) person: *Brokeback Mountain* (dir. Ang Lee, 2005), *The Hours* (dir. Stephen Daldry, 2002), and *Boys Don't Cry* (dir. Kimberly Peirce, 1999).

All three case studies invite a reading that is alert to a complex combination of interacting elements. Chief among these are the contingencies of place and history (what in narrative theory is called the setting of the stories), and, against the background of these settings, the opacity of (self-)understanding when it comes to the sexual and gender identity of protagonists, the discourses of self-identification in which protagonists engage, and the overall treacherousness of sexual and gender categorization.

Brokeback Mountain: **Understanding sexuality in a homophobic setting**

Take our first example, *Brokeback Mountain*. Both the original short story (written by one of the most prominent US-American writers, Annie Proulx) and the film adaptation tell the tragic story of two young men, Ennis Del Mar (Heath Ledger) and Jack Twist (Jake Gyllenhaal). The two fall in love with each other and we follow their relationship over a period of nearly two decades, ending with the death of Jack and the solitude and desolation in which this leaves Ennis. Summed up heavily like this, the plot outline is merely conventional. Its tragic quality might seem to reside only in Jack's premature death in middle age. But as soon as we look closely at the setting, the narrative becomes much more specific and meaningful. We encounter Ennis and Jack first in their late teens in 1963. They live in the rugged state of Wyoming, part of the region in the American heartland generally designated as the West. About one third of the landscape here consists of prairieland, the other two thirds of the Rocky Mountains. Although Wyoming is larger than the United Kingdom, it has only about half a million inhabitants. People live in very small clusters, far apart and without connection to major cities. Proulx introduces her characters by telling us they were "raised on small, poor ranches in opposite corners of the state, [...] both high school dropout country boys with no prospects, brought up to hard work and privation, both rough-mannered, rough-spoken, inured to the stoic life" ("Brokeback" 1–2).

Time and place are major components of this story. We need to understand we are in a period before even the 1969 Stonewall Riots in New York City took place. (These would come to figure the beginning of gay liberation in the United States.) And we need to understand the enormous mental and cultural gap that separates life in the Rockies or on the prairies from that in the nation's cosmopolitan cities along the coasts. Thus, when the story takes us almost two decades further into the twentieth century, social conditions in Wyoming barely change; they are not affected by the tides of liberation rolling over New York or San Francisco. Throughout these decades, life in Wyoming remains a matter of primitive survival in tough surroundings. Economically as well as emotionally, it depends on the strength of the traditional family unit. An alternative homosexual lifestyle is not an option in this conservative environment, and pursuing it is likely to be punished by violence. Looking back on the story's reception, Proulx indeed protested that those who "dubbed it a tale of two cowboys" got it all wrong: To her it was "a story of destructive rural homophobia" ("Getting Movied" 130).

Filling in this kind of background helps us understand why another mainstream response likewise misses the point: When the film came out, some commentators sought to universalize the love story by drawing a parallel with Shakespeare's classic tragedy *Romeo and Juliet*. That story, too, ends in death because of a social obstacle that keeps the two lovers from being united: the feud between their respective families. But to call *Brokeback Mountain* a gay *Romeo and Romeo* is to elide the specific place of sexuality in the narrative. Ennis and Jack do not simply struggle with external opponents in the form of family expectations and obligations: They also and primarily have to fight internalized norms that prevent them from understanding and acknowledging their own desires, or from imagining the possibility of a sustainable relationship.

To a queer critic, this presents a fitting illustration of the historical and cultural contingency of sexualities. A person's sexuality is not a pre-established biological or genetic program; it does not precede that person's entrance into a cultural environment. Rather, as Queer Theory has insisted from the start, sexuality is a social and discursive construction impossible to separate from the time and place in which somebody lives. This is why discussions of *Brokeback Mountain* in terms of a gay *Romeo and Romeo* are misleading in yet another way: The label "gay" is inappropriate for the story's setting. In the early sixties, "gay" was only beginning to emerge as a term of proud self-identification, but this was still largely restricted to subcultural circuits in big cities. Growing up semi-literate and isolated in Wyoming, Ennis and Jack would not have understood this application of the word. When they meet in 1963, they only know terms of insult whose symbolic violence terrifies them and makes it impossible for them to attribute any positive quality to their affective and sexual bond. Throughout the summer on Brokeback Mountain when they first have sex, they refrain from talking about their feelings or sense of self, except on one brief, telling occasion when Ennis says, "You know I ain't queer," and Jack responds, "Me neither" (McMurtry and Ossana 20 in typescript). At this point, neither Ennis nor Jack is able to conceive of himself as legitimately attracted to the other, and they cannot imagine a future together as a loving couple. So they part ways after the summer and start heterosexual lives as married men and fathers before hooking up again years later. As in the rest of the story, Jack then proves to be the more open-minded character of the two, increasingly willing to imagine a life together, but for Ennis, traumatized by a childhood memory of a lynched couple of men, the taboo remains absolute and inviolable until the end.

When Proulx decided to give heterosexual lives to her protagonists, she wanted to "mirror real life by rasping [their] love against the societal norms that both men obeyed, both of them marrying and begetting children, both loving their children, and, in a way, their wives" ("Getting Movied" 132). Thus, the men come to live bisexual lives in practice, in which the fact that they are in denial about their homosexuality does not therefore disqualify their heterosexuality as mere self-delusion. A queer reading will rather acknowledge the complexity of their time-bound and place-bound sexuality as impossible to capture by the labels we so often stick on people in our urge to categorize.

The Hours: understanding fluid female desires

The difficulty of categorization in a context of seeming bisexuality returns in the otherwise very different literary and cinematic narrative presented by *The Hours*. Here the original version is by another major US-American writer, Michael Cunningham. As with *Brokeback Mountain*, both the novel and the film managed to become popular successes and garnered multiple prestigious awards. In an interestingly chiastic configuration, while the female Proulx composed a story about two men, the male Cunningham centered his narrative on the experiences of three women. *The Hours* interweaves three independent plotlines into a single narrative. One plotline is set in 1923, the second around 1950, the third around the turn of the millennium (the precise dates differ slightly between novel and film). All three narratives take place in a single, seemingly ordinary day that yet contains profound existential crises for the three women in question: The English modernist writer Virginia Woolf (Nicole Kidman) living in Richmond, just outside London, a young house-wife by the name of Laura Brown (Julianne Moore) in an anonymous Los Angeles suburb, and a middle-aged woman in a lesbian relationship living and working in New York City, Clarissa Vaughan (Meryl Streep).

In *The Hours*, the disparate settings, with their intentional contrasts in time and place, serve in some sense as contexts to be overcome. The narrative must look for coherence by establishing multiple connections and using various mirroring devices (subtle in the novel, conspicuous in the film). One of the risks taken especially by the film is that of merging the three women's lives until the resulting portrait comes close to suggesting a general feminine condition (perhaps only a Western, white, middle-class condition and applying only to the twentieth century, but still largely similar). A queer critic is likely to resist this impetus, in particular when it comes to putting a label to the three women's elusive sexualities. Yet this elusiveness seems to be itself intended. Both novel and film clearly draw inspiration from Woolf's characteristic insistence on a fluid worldview. So if the three interwoven narratives suggest a shared cultural condition of white middle-class women in the modern Western world, they do not therefore wish to spell out modern categories of sexual identity.

The queer resistance to categorizing labels is most relevant for the three same-sex kisses exchanged on screen. Here it is worth pointing to the cultural impact of these kisses. *The Hours* was one of the first Hollywood productions in which three leading actresses were allowed to take center-stage as the individual focus of narrative attention (so not principally in their relation to men). If such actresses are then depicted in the act of erotically kissing another woman, the scenes acquire considerable iconic force for a mainstream audience suddenly grappling with the implications of what they are watching.

A spectator inspired by queer-theoretical ideas is again likely to reflect on contextual meanings and to avoid foreclosing the discussion about sexualities. When the character of Virginia Woolf in the 1923 plotline presses a hard kiss on the lips of her departing sister, how are we to translate this? Is this a disclosure of Woolf's suppressed lesbianism in a confusingly incestuous manner? Is it a call to Vanessa to acknowledge her sister's distress in the suburbs and to take her back to the sexually liberated Bloomsbury group in London? Or is it an expression of Woolf's ability as a creative genius to surprise herself and others with powerful images of intensely ambiguous moments? Likewise, when Laura Brown melts for the story of her neighbor Kitty, who has to undergo surgery, and kisses Kitty softly on the lips, how are we to read this in a Los Angeles suburb around 1950? Clearly, Kitty is better at not letting the kiss signify too much, quickly pretending nothing has happened, while the depressed Laura, who feels so bad at performing the gender rituals of the heterosexual housewife, wonders about the implications and reads a kind of accusation in her little boy's fixed stare. The rest of the plotline will show us Laura planning to commit suicide, and reveal, much later, how she ultimately leaves her husband and two children to go live by herself, but even at that stage we never find out whether this has anything to do with her sexuality.

In contrast with the two previous kissing scenes, the intense kiss Clarissa exchanges with Sally at the end of the third plotline is unproblematic as an expression of sexual identity: The two are an emancipated lesbian couple in New York City by the turn of the millennium. But does this kiss also allow spectators retroactively to interpret the two previous scenes as equally lesbian, as if the same identity and sexuality applied across time and space? And how lesbian is it precisely in light of the kiss Clarissa exchanged as a young woman with her gay friend Richard – a memory she has been obsessing over during the day as the most perfect moment in her life?

Boys Don't Cry: understanding the uniqueness of transgender lives

Potentially confusing questions of the sort just listed are triggered also by our third and final case study, *Boys Don't Cry*. Inspired by a real-life story set in Nebraska (just east of Wyoming) in 1993, this movie introduces us to Brandon Teena (Hilary Swank), a twenty-one-year-old we would nowadays call transgender – though as in *Brokeback Mountain* such a term is not available then and there. Anatomically a girl, Brandon's gender identity seems to be that of a boy. Early in the film he denies being "a dyke" and dismisses sex-reassignment surgery as financially out of the question, while his preferred gender expression is clearly as a boy. But we should remain aware that there is a margin of instability in the relation between gender expression and gender identity: We should not automatically expect to find coherence and legibility in all respects. To live in his preferred gender as a boy, Brandon runs away from Nebraska's only minor city, Lincoln, to the very small town of Falls City, where he tries to enter the fantasy of a new life. The spatial transition serves to remind us that settings may be crucial in analyzing not only sexual identities but also gender identities, even sexual anatomies. In her ground-breaking work from the 1990s, furthermore, Judith Halberstam emphasizes another point: While "[m]etaphors of travel and border crossings" are everywhere in transgender discourses, we should beware of translating such metaphors into a "dialectic of home and border," with home as the place where "one finally settles into the comfort of one's true and authentic gender" (480, 483, 479).

Certainly in Brandon's story, the new "home" found in Falls City is a precarious and conditional one. It consists of a small, down-and-out group of new friends – one female (Candace), two male (John and Tom) – who know nothing about Brandon's birth gender. They are a temperamentally volatile bunch with no social prospects and given to substance abuse. The internal relations are further complicated when Brandon falls in love with Candace's sister Lana (Chloë Sevigny). During their first sexual encounter, Lana catches a glimpse of Brandon's female anatomy, but she chooses to go with the flow. The intimacy is sufficiently rewarding for her not to pull out of the relationship afterwards either. She is willing to join Brandon in his sexual fantasy and even rescues him at one point from the women's section in the local prison. Brandon's new supposed home is tragically ripped up, however, after the three other friends find out his anatomical secret. In a sequence of violent scenes, John and Tom force Lana to face up to her friend's "true" identity as a "lesbian" and go on to rape Brandon. When Brandon subsequently files a complaint with the police, the two young men chase him down, killing not just Brandon but also Candace.

Among many other things, this harrowing story invites us to complicate our understanding of what Halberstam calls the "relations between identity, embodiment, and gender" as well as the "differences and continuities between transsexual, transgender, and lesbian masculinities" (465). To conclude this chapter, let us look briefly at one example of a typically complicating interpretation by a famous queer scholar. In her discussion of the film in *Undoing Gender*, Butler reminds us, first of all, that "[t]he term 'queer' gained currency precisely to address [...] moments of productive undecidability" (142). "In the case of transgender," she writes, "there are various ways of crossing that cannot be understood as stable achievements, where the gender crossing constitutes, in part, the condition of eroticization itself." This is what she sees in *Boys Don't Cry*, in which

> transgender is both about identifying as a boy and wanting a girl, so it is a crossing over from being a girl to being a heterosexual boy. Brandon Teena identifies as a heterosexual boy, but we see several moments of disidentification as well, where the fantasy breaks down and a tampon has to be located, used, and then discarded with no trace. His identification thus recommences, has to be reorchestrated in a daily way as a credible fantasy, one that compels belief. (142)

Butler wonders whether the narrative allows us to qualify Brandon at all as a lesbian or a boy, even though it is clear that Brandon insists on "doing himself as a boy" (143). "Would it be any easier for us," she adds in her characteristically questioning style,

> if we were to ask whether the lesbian who only makes love using her dildo to penetrate her girlfriend, whose sexuality is so fully scripted by apparent heterosexuality that no other relation is possible, is a boy or a "boy"? If she says that she can only make love as a "boy," she is, we might say, transgendered in bed, if not in the street. Brandon's crossing involves a constant dare posed to the public norms of the culture, and so occupies a more public site on the continuum of transgender. It is not simply about being able to have sex a certain way, but also about appearing as a masculine gender. So, in this sense, Brandon is no lesbian, despite the fact that the film, caving in, wants to return him to that status after the rape, [...] returning Brandon, as the rapists sought to do, to a "true" feminine identity that "comes to terms" with anatomy. (143)

As spectators we had better avoid rushing to any categorical conclusions, Butler feels, especially if this means that either Brandon's body is turned into an instrument for affirming gender norms or his gender is turned into an instrument for understanding his sexuality. The narrative shows, rather, that "gender has its own pleasures for Brandon, and serves its own purposes. These pleasures of identification exceed those of desire, and, in that sense, Brandon is not only or easily a lesbian" (143–44).

We might wrap up this chapter in a similarly open manner by recalling that for Queer and Transgender Studies "many, if not most, sexual and gender identities involve some degree of movement (not free-flowing but very scripted) between bodies, desires, transgressions, and conformities" (Halberstam 468). At this point in history, American culture has come to present a conspicuously wide range of products and performances that invite us to keep that movement going.

Works cited

Boys Don't Cry. Dir. Kimberly Peirce. Perf. Hilary Swank, Chloë Sevigny, and Peter Sarsgaard. Twentieth Century Fox, 1999. DVD.

Brokeback Mountain. Dir. Ang Lee. Perf. Heath Ledger and Jake Gyllenhaal. Focus Features, 2005. DVD.

Butler, Judith. *Gender Trouble: Feminism and the Subversion of Identity*. New York: Routledge, 1990. Print.

---. *Undoing Gender*. New York: Routledge, 2004. Print.

Cunningham, Michael. *The Hours*. New York: Picador, 1998. Print.

De Lauretis, Teresa. "Queer Theory: Lesbian and Gay Sexualities." *Differences* 3.2 (1991): iii–xviii. Print.

Halberstam, Judith. "Transgender Butch: Butch/FTM Border Wars and the Masculine Continuum." *The Routledge Queer Studies Reader*. Ed. Donald E. Hall and Annamarie Jagose, with Andrea Bebell and Susan Potter. London: Routledge, 2013. 464–87. Print.

The Hours. Dir. Stephen Daldry. Perf. Meryl Streep, Julianne Moore, and Nicole Kidman. Miramax International, 2002. DVD.

McMurtry, Larry, and Diana Ossana. "Brokeback Mountain, the Screenplay." *Brokeback Mountain: Story to Screenplay*. Annie Proulx, Larry McMurtry, and Diana Ossana. New York: Scribner, 2005. 29–127. Typescript reproduction 1–97. Print.

Proulx, Annie. "Brokeback Mountain." *Brokeback Mountain: Story to Screenplay*. Annie Proulx, Larry McMurtry, and Diana Ossana. New York: Scribner, 2005. 1–28. Print.

---. "Getting Movied." *Brokeback Mountain: Story to Screenplay*. Annie Proulx, Larry McMurtry, and Diana Ossana. New York: Scribner, 2005. 129–38. Print.

Sedgwick, Eve Kosofsky. *Epistemology of the Closet*. Berkeley: U of California P, 1990. Print.

20 Age Studies

Godfather is aging

Philipp Kneis and Antje Dallmann

"From city to city, state to state, coast to coast, *The Godfather* is now a phenomenon," Paramount advertisements claimed in 1972 (qtd. in Lewis 34). With its sequels, *The Godfather* film trilogy still counts among the most influential popular texts even forty years after the first part's release. It continues to be discussed and analyzed – not least in scholarly publications and in university seminars – as film text "that captures the transformation of the American Dream into a nightmare of alienation and dissolution" (Quart and Auster 109).

The Godfather narrates the rise, reign, and fall of mobster Michael Corleone. Yet, one could argue, the series also deals with very general questions about human life beyond the discussion of an Italo-American mafia family. It is usually assumed to be about crime, the mafia, family, the immigrant experience, Italian-American culture, power, hypocrisy, fate, and many, many other things. I will attempt to look at the film text from yet another perspective.

At the end of *The Godfather: Part III*, the youngest son of mafia Don Vito Corleone, Michael Corleone, who is now an old man, is sitting alone in the decaying courtyard of his house in Sicily, accompanied only by two small dogs. He is deep in thought, reminiscing about a life that in hindsight seems failed, wasted. Then, old Michael puts his sunglasses on, almost so as not to have to see his past again and not to have to remember his life. He slumps down on his chair, falls, and dies, a death noticed only by one of his dogs.

This scene mirrors the death scene of Michael's father, but with critical departures. Vito had died in the garden of his estate in America, where he had planted tomatoes – a symbol for successful Italian immigration to the United States. Vito had been feared by many, and he had created a life for himself and his family out of nothing, the prototypical American Dream – albeit with more than just a touch of crime. In contrast, Michael dies after many failures, scandals, and tragedies have destroyed his family, tarnished his reputation, and after he had to return to Sicily. He seemingly returns from riches to rags in old age.

Theories as ways of seeing

Complementing the multitude of approaches to and readings of *The Godfather*, I propose yet another one that does not contradict but rather supplements, even if it occasionally revises, other ways of seeing the films. Different theoretical approaches, especially if they appear to go against the grain of conventional readings, can open up ways of seeing that may lead to a deeper understanding of the object of study. In a way, the field of theory thus works as a toolbox containing a variety of oftentimes complementary approaches that, not unlike a different camera angle or a different lens, might reveal new details, completing a picture.

The lens applied to the *Godfather* film series in this chapter is one that looks at it via the category of age. If we speak of Age Studies, we are concerned with an understanding of old age not as a medical problem or from the perspective of social demographic change, but as a question of the social and cultural construction of the meaning and dignity of individual lives. As Susan Wendell explains in *The Rejected Body*, the culturally constructed Western category of "humanity" normalizes "a young, adult, male, non-disabled paradigm" (19). Age Studies, like Disability Studies, together with, for instance, "postcolonial, queer, [and] feminist [...] studies require[...] a new reckoning with the forces that construct identity, especially as formed through physicality" (Chivers xxviii). Thus, Age Studies as a discipline within Cultural Studies is concerned with the social and cultural construction of age as a category of difference in modern Western society. In the following, I will provide a brief overview of basic aspects of Age Studies, before returning to a discussion of *The Godfather*.

Theorizing age

Frequently, the concept of "age" is used synonymously with "old age," youth tends to be discussed under the headings of childhood and adolescence, and middle age associated with a crisis of the realization of advancing age, which appears as a conflict between spirit and body (see Cole, *The Journey*). The topics of old age and aging can thus appear to be sources of a seemingly perpetual frustration in a Western culture that has been steeped in the duality of soul and body, which sees the soul or spirit as solely important and the body as merely a shell.

In pre-industrial societies, fewer people than today reached the stage of old age, particularly when they lived under risky conditions – like, for instance, seventeenth-century Chesapeake colonists whose average life expectancy was twenty-five (see Bronner).[1] The transformation of society through capitalism, from pre-industrial to industrial, however, has changed the significance and meaning of age and aging in far-reaching ways. French sociologist Michel Foucault has argued that from the eighteenth century on, "[d]ifferent power apparatuses are called upon to take charge of 'bodies' [...] to help and, if necessary, to constrain them to ensure their own good health. The imperative of health: at once the duty of each and the objective of all" (277). In capitalist industrialism, thus, which perceives the healthy human body as an economic factor that is normalized (a body that is understood as an illusory norm), old age consequently turns into a precarious condition, a burden not only for individuals and their families, but for society as a whole, and into a subject of "biomedicalization" (Estes 587).

One of the central tenets of pre-capitalist cultures was the respect shown to the old – at least within a broader cultural narrative, if not necessarily in individual experience – and the relative veneration by the young for the old as wise and knowledgeable (Thane 9). The capitalist re-structuring of society through the logic of an economy of wage labor – with the related social tools of regulated retirement, pension, and health care systems – have created, even while prolonging individual lives and providing a better standard of living, an arbitrary break in people's lives that distinguishes between a productive and an assumedly unproductive phase, a "roleless role" (Burgess):

> In short, the retired older man and his wife are imprisoned in a roleless role. They have no vital function to perform such as they had in rural society. [...] Nor are they offered a ceremonial role by society to make up in part for their lost functional role. (20)

In modern capitalist society, thus, age is a category of critical difference (Woodward x), and old age is perceived as a deficiency. Americanist Rüdiger Kunow argues in this context that "'old' people come to be defined by what they are not, rather than by what they are – an inscription of senescence as always other, not healthy, not normal, and never itself" (28). This focus on alleged deficiency is reflected in ageist attitudes, that is, in "the systematic stereotyping of and discrimination against older people, analogous to racism and sexism" (Cole, "The 'Enlightened' View" 34).

The perception of what it means to be old, furthermore, varies (and has varied in Western culture) depending on other categories of difference such as, for instance, gender. "Feminist age studies," age critic and theorist Margaret Morgenroth Gullette points out,

> is a [...] movement toward integrating "age" into theory-building as well as into research, politics, and practice – not only as a variable, but on par with gender, class, "race"/ethnicity, sexual orientation, religion, disability, and place. A critical cultural studies, its purview includes all ages of life, considered relationally, the institutions of the life course as differentiated for different subject positions, and intergenerational relations, in history and now. ("Age Studies and Gender" 12)

Age Studies, in fact, can reveal not only that age is culturally constructed, and that – using Gullette's term – individuals are "aged by culture." Age Studies also points out that constructions of old age are contingent on other categories of difference (gender, "race," class) and that age, in this sense, is a cultural field for whose discussion it is important to acknowledge the inter-sectionality of such categories. This is, clearly, also true for the relation between perceptions of old age and of disability. Ageism, in fact, is connected to ableism, which can be defined as

> a network of beliefs, processes and practices that produces a particular kind of self and body (the [bodily] standard) that is projected as the perfect, species-typical and therefore essential and fully human. Disability then, is cast as a diminished state of being human. (Campbell 44)

Old age and disability, as the othered within all categories of difference, are constructed as pathologized opposites of states of being that are imagined and propagated as the norm: white, male, heterosexual, middle-class, etc.

The aging godfather: natural(ized) age

Then, how do we re-"read" *The Godfather* films through an Age Studies perspective? Which new insights do we gain? The films set out to portray a world within a world, namely that of the Sicilian Mafia, the "Cosa Nostra" in America. In *The Godfather: Part III,* we encounter a male protagonist who is aging, yet whose aging, pointedly, is represented within the well-worn formula of jaded white male nostalgia that deplores the loss of influence, power, and prestige. Michael Corleone's death scene, thus, is not a critique of how culture ages – or others – the individual, but rather of how the individual fails if he is unable to live up to a culture's expectations, to the myths a culture creates, structured along a narrative of shock at the loss of white male entitlement.

On a related note, age is, in ambivalent ways, also used as an important ingredient within the film's re-negotiation of a mythical self-identification of the United States as "young nation." "Age," I am going to argue in the following, is thus appropriated as an ideology-laden sign in *The Godfather,* normalizing not only (and not even primarily) young age, but naturalizing – through recourse to the concept of aging that seems particularly human, a universal destiny shared by all and everybody – culture-contingent subject positions and troubled notions of an American national identity.

Cultural representations often associate the Mafia with a world view that could be called "traditional" in the sense that it enforces non-modern values such as the absolute authority of the pater familias, the rule of "law" as represented by mighty patrons who act like feudal lords and grant favors to their "vassals," and gender roles that stereotype women within a maternal role, only second to patriarchal warring men. In *The Godfather,* violence is not portrayed as the organization's aim, but rather as a (necessary) means of conflict resolution and a testing ground for men to prove their worth as warriors. Homage is paid to Roman Catholicism as a marker of Italianness and for providing a semblance of morality.

The Mafia system represents something that can be called the "Old Order" as opposed to the "New Order" of American democracy, rule of law, capitalism, and a strong civil society, in which violence is seen as pathological and as a function of the state, not of private citizens. While Vito Corleone appears to successfully maintain his version of the Old Order in America, Michael represents the next generation that tries to reconcile the two, and oversees the transformation from Old to New. He ends up succeeding in neither system.

The older Michael Corleone gets, the more he asks himself questions about his life – a process that psychologists call "life review" (Butler). This happens the more desperate he becomes to hold family traditions up. He is not alone in this: Other older men, his enemies Hyman Roth and Frank "Five Angels" Pentangeli, similarly engage in revisiting their pasts. Used as a narrative tool, the "life review" in this sense serves as a narrative technique of naturalization. Depicted as a "natural" process of self-reflection in older age, Corleone's life review not only revisits his own past, but also skeptically reflects broader social and cultural changes from "old" to "new." Thus, this review deplores, and calls its audience to commiserate by the use of the seemingly universal formula of the tragedy of human aging, with the decline of a male-dominated society of clear-cut gendered hierarchies, status and privilege through birth, violence, unchanging tradition, and unconditional submission to the existing law of the most powerful.

The Godfather series, arguably, can be read as a tragedy, and follows some of the rules of Aristotle in that there is a unity of plot that leads from a clear beginning to a clear end. The beginning of the first of the three movies shows Vito Corleone at the height of his power, while Michael has just returned from his military service and is at the sidelines. The tragedy of Michael is that he is pushed, over the years, into a life he never wanted and tried to escape, and that in the end, he has lost everything, becoming the reverse mirror image of his father at the time of the latter's death. It could be argued that the ending of *Godfather: Part III* is the logical outcome from the start, and is actually governing the entire plot. This is made visible by the recurrent theme of old age.

Thus, as we have seen, the topic of old age can be found in *The Godfather* films on several levels: (1) on the individual level, in the effects that aging and old age have on key characters, (2) on a social level, in the contrasting of traditional (Sicilian) society (the Old Order) versus modern society (the New Order), but also symbolically (3) on a geographic or local level, in the interplay between Europe (the Old World) and America (the New World).

Arriving at Ellis Island after having had to flee Sicily, Vito Andolini, renamed Vito Corleone by an immigration officer (after the name of his village), has to begin anew in the New World, starting both his biological family and forging his mafia family at the same time. The latter represents the traditional Old Order, which Vito is successfully adapting to the New World, situating it parallel to the modern New Order. This is the legacy he leaves Michael, hoping his son will continue what he has started. Michael is thus forced to follow his father's footsteps, but both his own hopes and dreams for life and the circumstances around him make Michael aim to pass from Old into New Order, into giving up those traditions that now, in an American modernity, are seen merely as criminal. Michael's murder of his brother Fredo is a breaking point; it is the moment that has him realize that Old Order and New Order are incompatible. He is pulled in to the traditional ways whether he wants to or not. While Vito is successful as a father, as a traditional "businessman," and as an immigrant in America, Michael's downfall is marked by his failure as a father when his daughter dies, even though he has succeeded as a businessman.

Age thus is a multifunctional paradigm throughout the filmic text. At a diegetic level, the level of the story itself, we find a seemingly universal story about aging. Michael Corleone himself is only able to realize his position fully once he has entered old age, probably because he then understands that he is too old to begin anew, and that none of the choices he had made as a younger man are reversible. This realization about the finite nature of life, about the importance of every single moment (as visualized in flashbacks), and about, in Michael's case, the impossibility to take it all back, contribute to how his death becomes a judgment over whether his life had been a good one or not. The entire narrative, ranging from *Part I* through *Part III*, is structured around this very question.

Yet referring to such seemingly general, fundamental, universal aspects of the life course itself, *The Godfather* fully normalizes white male subject positions. Thus, readings along the lines of age may not only shed additional light on the understanding of a particular text – they might also reveal a stance captured within this text toward specific cultural and social patterns, or myths. In *The Godfather*, age is in fact used throughout as a sign that takes up specific aspects of an American national mythology, pointing toward changes from traditional to modern societies in the (symbolic or metaphorical) terms of aging.

The American Dream is not challenged frequently, yet its most ardent support can be found in narratives that center on relatively young characters who have all their life, as they say, ahead of them. In following an Aristotelean structure, the film series shows a unity of plot, from the beginning to the end – and it appears that the perspective of a view from the end, from old age, provides license to depict failure, even in a drastic fashion. Famous texts, like Ernest Hemingway's *The Old Man and the Sea* or Herman Melville's *Moby Dick*, likewise present revisions of the American Dream through the narrative tool of the life review. It is precisely the perspective from close to the end of life, "The View in Winter" (Blythe), that might allow us to challenge affirmative notions of the American Dream and ask questions about results, about success and failure, about individual people and their lives.

In a metaphorical reading, Michael as a second-generation immigrant is caught between two worlds, and, failing to reconcile his conflict, he is shown as deeply disillusioned. Yet if his downfall is read as failure to realize his very own American Dream as a promise of enduring success, as critics often do (like Quart and Auster, whom I have quoted above, who read *The Godfather* as tale of the "transformation of the American Dream into a nightmare"), this entails urgent questions regarding the construction of this mythic category of "Americanness." For, what *The Godfather* deplores is the demise of tightly knit extended families captured through individual Italian immigrant families and the Cosa Nostra as an imaginary picture of South European social relations portrayed as archaic, yet more personal and therefore more just: social relations in which the old are supremely relevant because they carry with them the wisdom of the past; the only knowledge worth preserving. Pointedly, this is a society of clear-cut gender relations where different others, for instance Michael's mentally challenged brother Fredo, are depicted as dispensable. Thus, meaningfully, it is not through crime that *The Godfather*'s American Dream comes to fall. Released at a time of Women's and the Civil Rights Movements, *The Godfather* can rather be read as social-conservative reaction to progressive social transformations, as Sabine Haenni convincingly argues: "*The Godfather* almost seems to embody 'the wish for an all-white militant group'. An all-white male militant group" (250).

Texts that contain the perspective of old age, thus, may offer additional insights: into how culture ages individuals, how age functions as a symbolic category that is deeply naturalized, and at the same time, how age interlocks with other categories of difference. Critical readings of popular texts, like *The Godfather*, in the context of age, thus, might shed light on how hegemonic cultural positions are naturalized through an interplay of categories of difference, including age. For obviously, there is no universal, general, fundamental formula of aging since the way we perceive age, and are perceived in our own age, always depends on our positionality. Thus, I read the aging godfather not as exemplary, generalizable tale of aging. Rather, I interpret it as using a mythic formula that distorts the view on a multitude of culturally embedded narratives of aging, and on the incommensurable individual experience of age, privileging a male white subject position while effacing other positionalities. In this sense, looking beyond the white male paradigm of the nostalgic life review and its often problematic implications, exemplified by the godfather's story of old age, we will find a host of narratives, told from a multitude of perspectives, from which we can learn about how culture ages individuals.

Note

1 See Thane (9) for a balanced discussion of age expectancy as a statistical equation in which high infant mortality affects the average age expectancy.

Works cited

Blythe, Ronald. *The View in Winter: Reflections on Old Age.* New York: Harcourt Brace Jovanovich, 1979. Print.

Bronner, Simon J. "Old Age." *Encyclopedia of American Studies*. http://eas-ref.press. jhu.edu. Web. 18 Dec. 2014.

Burgess, Ernest W. *Aging in Western Societies*. Chicago, IL: Chicago UP, 1961. Print.

Butler, Robert N. "The Life Review: An Interpretation of Reminiscence in the Aged." *Psychiatry* 26 (1963): 65–76. Print.

Campbell, Fiona Kumari. "Inciting Legal Fictions: Disability's Date with Ontology and the Ableist Body of the Law." *Griffith Law Review* 10 (2001): 42–62. Print.

Chivers, Sally. *From Old Woman to Older Women: Contemporary Culture and Women's Narratives*. Columbus: Ohio State UP, 2003. Print.

Cole, Thomas R. "The 'Enlightened' View of Aging: Victorian Morality in a New Key." *The Hastings Center Report* 13.3 (1983): 34–40. Print.

---. *The Journey of Life: A Cultural History of Aging in America*. Cambridge: Cambridge UP, 1992. Print.

Estes, Carol. "The Biomedicalization of Aging: Dangers and Dilemmas." *The Gerontologist* 29 (1989): 587–96. Print.

Foucault, Michel. "The Politics of Health in the Eighteenth Century." *The Foucault Reader*. Ed. Paul Rabinow. New York: Vintage, 2010. 273–89. Print.

Gullette, Margaret Morganroth. "Age Studies and Gender." *Encyclopedia of Feminist Theories*. Ed. Lorraine Code. London: Routledge, 2003. 12–4. Print.

---. *Aged by Culture*. Chicago, IL: U of Chicago P, 2004. Print.

Haenni, Sabine. "*The Godfather* (1972)." *Fifty Key American Films*. Ed. John White and Sabine Haenni. London: Routledge, 2009. 158–63. Print.

Kunow, Rüdiger. "Chronologically Gifted? 'Old Age' in American Culture." *Amerikastudien/American Studies* 56.1 (2011): 23–44. Print.

Lewis, Jon. "If History Has Taught Us Anything ... Francis Coppola, Paramount Studios, and *The Godfather Parts I, II*, and *III*." *Francis Ford Coppola's* The Godfather *Trilogy*. Ed. Nick Browne. Cambridge: Cambridge UP, 2000. 23–56. Print.

Quart, Leonard, and Albert Auster. *American Film and Society since 1945*. Fourth ed. Santa Barbara, CA: Praeger, 2011. Print.

Thane, Pat. "The Age of Old Age." *The Long History of Old Age*. Ed. Pat Thane. London: Thames & Hudson, 2005. 9–29. Print.

The Godfather. Dir. Francis Ford Coppola. Perf. Marlon Brando, Al Pacino, James Caan, and Diane Keaton. Paramount Pictures, 1972. DVD.

The Godfather: Part II. Dir. Francis Ford Coppola. Perf. Al Pacino, Robert Duvall, Robert De Niro, and Diane Keaton. Paramount Pictures, 1974. DVD.

The Godfather: Part III. Dir. Francis Ford Coppola. Perf. Al Pacino, Diane Keaton, Andy Garcia, and Talia Shire. Paramount Pictures, 1990. DVD.

Wendell, Susan. *The Rejected Body: Feminist Philosophical Reflections on Disability*. New York: Routledge, 1996. Print.

Woodward, Kathleen. Introduction. *Figuring Age: Women, Bodies, Generations*. Ed. Kathleen Woodward. Bloomington: Indiana UP, 1999. ix–xxviii. Print.

21 Postcolonialism and American Studies

Beyond daffodils and blue eyes

Mita Banerjee

In the framework of American Studies, the study of "difference" has loomed large in a variety of ways. The study of "race," class, and gender differences, along with an attention paid to age and disability, has been foundational for American Studies research, and the social and political struggles of the Civil Rights Movement of the 1960s found their institutional reflections in the so-called "canon wars" of the 1970s, resulting in a new canon of American literature that included, to an unprecedented degree, women writers and authors from ethnic minority groups. As a key text for teaching this new canon of American literature, *The Heath Anthology of American Literature* with an editorial board spearheaded by Paul Lauter came to complement, and contest, the canon contained in *The Norton Anthology of American Literature* (see Baym), which had hitherto been central to American Studies education. If the canon had thus been changed and broadened to include different experiences of American history, society, and culture, a similar broadening occurred with regard to the methodologies that might best be employed to analyze, decode, and discuss such difference.

Among these methodologies, Postcolonial Theory has been of central importance. The work of postcolonial theorists Homi Bhabha, Edward Said, and Gayatri Spivak, whom Robert Young once called the "Holy Trinity" of Postcolonial Studies (163), became a central point of overlap between the Postcolonial Studies originally based in British Studies – especially in the study of the "new English literatures" emerging from former colonies such as India and Africa – and American Studies (see also Singh and Schmid). In the latter context, the work of Palestinian American critic Edward Said, whose seminal work *Orientalism* appeared in 1978, became especially influential. Drawing on Michel Foucault's post-structuralist approach, Said argued that European writings about the "Orient" – writings by canonical authors as diverse as Goethe and Flaubert – formed a discourse in which the "Oriental" subject was inevitably seen as bizarre and completely alien to the knowledge systems of the West. The Orient thus became part of a discourse that was entirely self-contained. This was a discourse, Said argued, that the "Oriental" subject was powerless to resist; his or her agency disappeared in the moment of being described by the Orientalist.

A number of images and ideas appear in Said's study of Orientalism that came to be central to Postcolonial Theory as a whole. First, the experience of the colonized subject is recorded in the language of the colonizer, who imposes on this subject his own system of signification. What, then, happens in the act of such an imposition? Colonialism, Said argues, is much more than an economic system; it is, above all, a system of ideas. As Said argued in his subsequent book, *Culture and Imperialism*, the empire was justified and hence perpetuated not only by economic or military means, but by way of cultural signification.

This idea has much in common with W.E.B. Du Bois's notion of "double consciousness." In a segregated society, Du Bois notes, African Americans were made to look at themselves through white eyes, through the gaze of a dominant culture to which African Americans were inferior. The African American subject hence came to be trapped in a schizophrenic split, looking at himself through eyes that were not his own. This is an image also famously captured by Frantz Fanon, a postcolonial psychoanalyst and theorist whose work *Black Skin, White Masks* (1952) quickly became one of the foundational texts of Postcolonial Theory.

As, especially, African American critics have argued, such double consciousness is present in minority communities to this day. Quoting Stuart Hall, African American feminist critic bell hooks has pointed out in her collection of essays, *Black Looks*, "[t]hey had the power to make us see and experience ourselves as 'Other'" (qtd. in hooks 3). Cultural Studies critic Stuart Hall, who in his turn bases his argument on none other than Said, thus reinforced the applicability of Said's Postcolonial Theory to an African American context.

The trajectory of Postcolonial Theory is hence twofold. First, it identifies the ways in which colonialism operates, especially with regard to its "brainwashing" of colonial subjects. Second, it looks for ways in which such "double consciousness" may be escaped and resisted. This twofold process of resisting colonial imaginaries is vividly illustrated in a novel by Jamaican writer Jamaica Kincaid. In keeping with Said's argument in *Culture and Imperialism*, Kincaid points out in her novel *Lucy* that the colonial education system was central in making the colonized subject doubt the legitimacy of her own culture and language. What ensues is a logic in which the colonized subject is doomed to learn to be British, thus imitating the colonizer to the best of her abilities.

Colonial mimicry in Jamaica Kincaid's novel *Lucy*

In Kincaid's novel *Lucy*, a young woman from the West Indies goes to England for the first time in her life. There, she sees the daffodils about which she had to learn poems throughout her entire education in the West Indies, yet without having an idea what these flowers, which had been commemorated in William Wordsworth's canonical poem, might look like. Kincaid writes,

I remembered an old poem I had been made to memorize when I was ten years old and a pupil at Queen Victoria's Girls' School. I had been made to memorize it, verse by verse [...]. After I was done, everybody stood up and applauded with an enthusiasm that surprised me, and later they told me how nicely I had pronounced every word [...]. I was then at the height of my two-facedness: that is outside I seemed one way, inside I was another; outside false, inside true. [...] I had forgotten all of this until [my employer] Mariah mentioned daffodils. (18)

This passage vividly exemplifies what Du Bois, in an African American context, calls "double consciousness": Being made to recite Wordsworth's poem "I Wandered Lonely as a Cloud" (1807), with the daffodils as one of its central metaphors, Lucy feels "two-faced"; yet, it must be noted that she is simultaneously aware that one of these faces is true while the other seems false.

In this passage, daffodils are much more than mere flowers; rather, they are a metaphor that encapsulates the entire absurdity of the colonial education system and, in some ways, colonialism itself. As the colonial official Thomas Macaulay wrote in 1835 in his "Minute on Education," education was seen by the British colonial empire as one of the most powerful tools for colonizing entire peoples. The power of colonialism, above all, lay in changing the way colonial subjects thought, in interfering with the very image they had of them-selves. As Bhabha writes in his discussion of Macaulay's "Minutes," "[a]t the intersection of European learning and colonial power, Macaulay can conceive of nothing other than 'a class of interpreters between us and the millions whom we govern – a class of persons Indian in blood and colour, but English in tastes, in opinions, in morals and in intellect'" (87). Thus, the "new" colonized subjects, which the colonial education system set out to produce, might *look* Indian or Jamaican, but they were supposed to be English in character.

For the peoples thus colonized, the perniciousness of this system could not have been greater. The power of the colonial rule lay in the attempt at making colonial subjects despise their own culture and, as Macaulay subtly hints in his minutes, the color of their skin. What ensued from this was what postcolonial theorist Bhabha has called a culture of "mimicry": In this logic, entire peoples would try to "mimic" British culture, yet they would never quite succeed. A trace of their own origin or upbringing would stubbornly remain; in this sense, mimicry was a futile attempt from the outset. Colonialism, then, was much more than a system of economic domination; it was also, first and foremost, a system of psychological and cultural rule.

Seen from a female perspective, such ideas of colonial mimicry are especially crucial for concepts of beauty. When Lucy first meets her British employer, Mariah, the latter seems "celestial" in the beauty of whiteness. Whiteness and beauty become synonymous here:

She looked so beautiful standing there in the middle of the kitchen. The yellow light from the sun came in through a window and fell on the

> pale-yellow linoleum tiles of the floor, and on the walls of the kitchen, which were painted yet another shade of pale yellow, and Mariah, with her pale-yellow skin and yellow hair, stood still in this almost celestial light, and she looked blessed, no blemish or mark of any kind on her cheek or anywhere else [...]. (Kincaid 27)

Kincaid clearly subverts the ideal of white beauty even as she is describing it from the perspective of her Caribbean protagonist. To Lucy, Britain itself is colored in the cream tones of pale yellow; the kitchen scene may be beautiful, but it is also artificial in its picture-book perfection. Nonetheless, it is this perfection to which Lucy herself can never hope to aspire; not only does her own skin have blemishes, but it is Black to make matters worse.

The project of decolonization, by the same token, starts with what African writer Ngugi wa Thiong'O has called "decolonizing the mind." As in Kincaid's novel *Lucy*, the challenge that the colonial subject has to face is to *unlearn* colonialism and to value, once again, her own skin and her own culture. It is this process of unlearning colonialism and of resisting its psychological brainwashing of its subjects that Indian writer Salman Rushdie has captured in a single image: the image of the empire "writing back" at the center. Taking his cue from George Lucas's *Star Wars* trilogy, Rushdie ("The Empire Writes Back") imagines a postcolonial world in which the tables have been turned, where the empire – the former colonies – "strike back" at the center, the former colonizer, which had euphemistically termed itself the colonies' "mother country." The way in which the colonies strike back at the center, however, is in writing: They "write back" at the erstwhile colonizer to tell him that his entire system of thought, not only in making West Indian students recite poems about English flowers, which they had never seen, was flawed.

It is in this sense that many postcolonial novels – from Kincaid's *Lucy* to George Lamming's *In the Castle of My Skin* and Rushdie's *Midnight's Children* – are coming-of-age novels. In these narratives, the lives of the young protagonists become metaphors of the postcolonial nation: Just as the colony needs to "grow up" and emancipate itself from the former "mother country," these young protagonists need to come into their own. In this process, they need to appropriate and take charge of the tools with which colonialism has left them, especially the English language itself, the pillar on which Macaulay's education system rested. In order to come up with a truly "postcolonial" system of thought, however, they need to bend the English language to suit their own, postcolonial needs. In this very act of linguistic and cultural appropriation, the English language itself becomes a new, hybrid form. Thus, what ensues from decolonization is not a precolonial status quo. The possibility of returning to an Arcadian reality before the advent of British colonialism will always remain an impossibility, a fiction. Rather, the potential lies in creating new cultural forms, new subjectivities, which incorporate the legacy of the empire and turn it into something productive, in which wrongs can be playfully and metaphorically righted, just as in Rushdie's idea of the empire writing back to the center.

In this process of reversal, entire literatures have emerged that have been termed "new literatures in English." These literatures produced by writers from the former colonies have profoundly altered the shape of the English language and the nature of the canon of English literature: Today, Rushdie and Kincaid are being read alongside Wordsworth. Through this process of reversion, British children may come to read about Caribbean flowers that they have never seen; and this lack of knowledge not only will appear as a reversal of the colonial process, but will point to something more than mere politics. It will attest to the power of literature to shape the way we embrace the world.

Internal colonialism: Toni Morrison's *The Bluest Eye*

What, then, would these considerations imply when applied not to a British, but a US-American context? As outlined above, Postcolonial Theories have been at their most productive when they have been related to the lives of minority communities in the United States. Toni Morrison's novel *The Bluest Eye* illustrates concerns that are highly similar to those voiced in Kincaid's *Lucy*. What this similarity implies, moreover, is that the subjugation of African Americans in the United States can be seen as a form of *internal colonization*. Having been forcibly brought to the United States from Africa as slaves, African Americans subsequently found themselves in a situation that was highly similar to colonial systems of rule. Similarly to the British colonialism described above, this internal colonization of African Americans was a form not only of economic exploitation, but also of psychological cruelty. As slaves, African Americans were not perceived as human. The system of slavery was one of "chattel slavery," with slaves being defined as animals and as property to be bought and sold at the white master's whim.

Once slavery had been abolished, the psychology of slavery persisted in the sense that African Americans were still seen as inferior to white Americans. Politically, socially, and legally, a system of segregation emerged that, however, prided itself on its own equality. Starting with the court case of Plessy v. Ferguson in 1898, facilities such as schools or restaurants were said to be "separate but equal," with African Americans being confined to spaces in which they would not "mingle" with white Americans.

As Anne Cheng has described in her book *The Melancholy of Race*, this logic of "separate but equal" was abolished only in 1954, in Brown v. Board of Education of Topeka. As Cheng shows, the argument, which was finally powerful enough to sway juridical and public opinion, was based on psychological studies that featured interviews, which had been conducted with African American school children. Psychologists found that these children held themselves to be inferior to white children. African American children were hence not only inferior to a white gaze, but in their own eyes as well. Psychologists concluded that such feelings of inferiority would invariably result in a stunting of the children's psychological and intellectual development, and its cost for the American social and economic system would be immense. While the 1954 Supreme Court ruling officially abolished the "separate but equal" doctrine, however, the psychological burden of this history – from slavery to segregation – persisted in African American communities.

It is this legacy of a system of internal colonization that is at the heart of Morrison's novel *The Bluest Eye*. In the novel, a young girl, Pecola, looks in the mirror and sees a face that she perceives as an ugly one, despising her own Blackness. Like her parents, Pecola becomes convinced of her own ugliness. As Claudia, the young narrator, describes this process of internalization,

> [y]ou looked at them and wondered why they were so ugly; you looked closely and could not find the source. Then you realized that it came from conviction, their conviction. It was as though some mysterious all-knowing master had given each one a cloak of ugliness to wear, and they had each accepted it without question. (28)

The master who has given Pecola's family the "cloak of ugliness to wear," then, is white society.

Beauty, in *The Bluest Eye*, is the beauty of whiteness; it is the beauty described in primers such as *Dick and Jane* readers in which school children, both Black and white, come to internalize the same white norm. It is this white norm that children like Pecola and Claudia seek to emulate. The children are obsessed with Mary Jane candies: Eating "Mary Janes," they at once try to ingest their beauty, "becoming" Mary Janes themselves.

More than anything, Pecola wants to have blue eyes. To her, blue eyes become the epitome of white female beauty, the beauty depicted on the wrapping of Mary Jane candies: "She eats the candy, and its sweetness is good. To eat the candy is somehow to eat the eyes, eat Mary Jane. Love Mary Jane. Be Mary Jane" (38). Just as to Kincaid's Jamaican protagonist Lucy, her white employer Mariah seems "celestial" in her whiteness, to Pecola, Mary Jane is the ideal of white femininity.

Like Kincaid's Lucy, who has been made to mimic a white British world she has never seen, Pecola tries to reinvent herself as white and, failing to do so, comes to despise her own skin. In Morrison's novel, the Black subject is trapped in a vicious cycle of make-believe and self-hatred. This trap leads to the trauma at the climax of the novel. Self-disgust is not only Pecola's burden, but it is also responsible for the plight of her father, Cholly Breadlove. Caught up in a cycle of violence and self-hatred, Cholly sees his young daughter standing in the kitchen, helpless and forlorn. In the warped psychology of his misguided feelings and due to the hopelessness of his own situation as a Black subject in a white world, Cholly proceeds to rape his own daughter, showing his love in a way that is clearly perverted. Cholly rapes his daughter when he sees in her eyes her unconditional love for him, a love that drives him into madness:

What could he do for her – ever? What give her? What say to her? What could a burned-out black man say to the hunched back of his eleven-year-old daughter? If he looked into her face, he would see those haunted, loving eyes. The hauntedness would irritate him – the love would move him to fury. How dare she love him? Hadn't she any sense at all? What was he supposed to do about that? Return it? How? (127)

Paradoxically, his rape of his daughter is the only way Cholly can find to "return" his love for Pecola. Like Morrison's subsequent award-winning novel, *Beloved*, *The Bluest Eye* revolves around a trauma brought about by the internal colonization of African Americans in the United States. Having been made to see themselves through white eyes and to mimic an ideal they will never attain, Morrison's Black protagonists – the young African American girl in *The Bluest Eye*, the slave mother in *Beloved* – transgress against their own humanity. Colonialism, Morrison implies, triggers a form of self-hatred that can only be conquered by "unlearning," by resisting the colonial logic itself.

American Studies and postcolonialism: Edward Said's *Out of Place*

Postcolonial theorist Said best illustrates the ways in which Postcolonial Studies have been closely intertwined with American Studies and with the United States as a global signifier. Said wrote *Orientalism* both as a critique of European "Orientalism" – criticizing the fictions that European canonical writers created of an Orient they themselves had invented – and as a reflection on his own location as a Palestinian American writer and critic. Thus, in his autobiography aptly titled *Out of Place*, Said recalls his childhood as a son born in Jerusalem of Palestinian parents, then living in Egypt with an American citizenship he had been able to acquire through his father. In Jerusalem, Said first attended the Anglican St. George's School in Alexandria; having been expelled from there as a "troublesome student," he proceeded to attend Northfield Mount Hermon School in Massachusetts. In *Out of Place*, Said describes his life as a Palestinian, whose English first name is seemingly at war with his surname: "[I]t took me about fifty years to become accustomed to, or, more exactly, to feel less uncomfortable with, 'Edward,' a foolishly English name yoked forcibly to the unmistakably Arabic family name Said" (3).

In Said's autobiographical narrative, the legacy of British colonialism is closely intertwined with the role held by the United States on a global scale. In this sense, Said's form of Postcolonial Theory is closely interrelated to what Shelley Fisher Fishkin has called Transnational American Studies. Fishkin argues that there are as many versions of American Studies as there are American Studies critics, with each critic bringing his or her own particular location to bear on his or her view of the United States as a nation-state. Moreover, what matters is a view of the United States not only as seen from within, but also from outside.

It is this twofold view of the United States that is reflected in Said's auto-biography *Out of Place*: He is recalling his childhood shaped by an American influence on the Middle East; and he is writing from his own present location, in 2000, as an American intellectual teaching in the English Department at Columbia University. Said's autobiography can thus be understood both as a postcolonial and an American autobiography.

It is in this sense that his autobiography brings together two sides of his oeuvre, which had previously seemed to run parallel to each other. In *Orientalism*, Said critiqued a European literary canon; in his other writings such as *Covering Islam*, however, he was concerned with the role of the United States for a global depiction of Islamic religious and cultural differ-ence. Said defined himself not so much as a postcolonial writer – even as his seminal work *Orientalism* helped shape the field of Postcolonial Studies as such – but as a Palestinian American specifically. His lifelong commitment was to peace in the Middle East, and to a balanced account, which would take into consideration the complexity of Arab culture and Islamic thought.

True to one of the dictums of fellow postcolonial critic Bhabha, Said was hence looking for a "space outside the sentence" (Bhabha 180). If, as has been outlined above with regard to Kincaid's and Thiong'o's notions of postcolonialism, language has been one of the essential tools of the colonizing process, colonialism may be resisted not only through language, but through finding spaces that exceed words. It is in music that Said found such a space outside of language. His conversations with Jewish composer and conductor Daniel Barenboim, published in 2004 (see Barenboim and Said), attest to the ways in which Said's vision encapsulated many perspectives at the same time, fusing his postcolonial history with his American location.

Works cited

Barenboim, Daniel, and Edward Said. *Parallels and Paradoxes: Explorations on Music and Society.* New York: Bloomsbury, 2004. Print.

Baym, Nina, ed. *The Norton Anthology of American Literature.* Eighth ed. New York: Norton, 2012. Print.

Bhabha, Homi K. *The Location of Culture.* New York: Routledge, 1994. Print.

Cheng, Anne. *The Melancholy of Race: Psychoanalysis, Assimilation, and Hidden Grief.* Oxford: Oxford UP, 2001. Print.

Du Bois, W.E.B. "Of Our Spiritual Strivings." *The Souls of Black Folk.* 1903. *The Oxford W.E.B. Du Bois.* Ed. Henry Louis Gates, Jr. Intr. Arnold Rampersad. Oxford: Oxford UP, 2007. 2–7. Print.

Fanon, Frantz. *Black Skin, White Masks.* 1952. Trans. Richard Philcox. New York: Grove P, 2008. Print.

Fishkin, Shelley Fisher. "Crossroads of Cultures: The Transnational Turn in American Studies – Presidential Address to the American Studies Association, November 12, 2004." *American Quarterly* 57.1 (2005): 17–57. Print.

Hall, Stuart. "Cultural Identity and Diaspora." *Colonial Discourse and Postcolonial Theory*. Ed. Patrick Williams and Laura Chrisman. London: Harvester Wheatsheaf, 1994. 392–401. Print.

hooks, bell. *Black Looks: Race and Representation*. New York: South End P, 1992. Print.

Kincaid, Jamaica. *Lucy*. New York: Plume, 1990. Print.

Lamming, George. *In the Castle of My Skin*. 1953. Harlow: Longman, 1988. Print.

Lauter, Paul, ed. *The Heath Anthology of American Literature: Concise Edition*. New York: Cengage Learning, 2003. Print.

Macaulay, Thomas. "Minute on Indian Education." 1835. *Revolutions in Romantic Literature: An Anthology of Print Culture, 1780–1832*. Ed. Paul Keen. Peterborough, Ontario: Broadview P, 2004. 313–15. Print.

Morrison, Toni. *Beloved*. New York: Knopf, 1987. Print.

---. *The Bluest Eye*. 1970. New York: Picador, 1999. Print.

Rushdie, Salman. "The Empire Writes back with a Vengeance." *Times* (3 Jul. 1982): 8. Print.

---. *Midnight's Children*. London: Penguin, 1980. Print.

Said, Edward, W. *Covering Islam: How the Media and the Experts Determine How We See the Rest of the World*. New York: Vintage, 1997. Print.

---. *Culture and Imperialism*. New York: Vintage, 1994. Print.

---. *Orientalism*. New York: Vintage, 1978. Print.

---. *Out of Place: A Memoir*. New York: Vintage, 2000. Print.

Singh, Amrijit, and Peter Schmid, eds. *Postcolonial Theory and the United States: Race, Ethnicity, and Literature*. Jackson: UP of Mississippi, 2000. Print.

Thiong'o, Ngugi wa. *Decolonizing the Mind: The Politics of Language in African Literature*. New York: Heinemann, 1986, Print.

Wordsworth, William. "I Wandered Lonely as a Cloud." *William Wordsworth: The Poems*. Ed. John O. Hayden. Vol. 1. New Haven, CT: Yale UP, 1977. 619–20. Print.

Young, Robert. *Colonial Desire: Hybridity in Theory, Culture, and Race*. London: Routledge, 1995. Print.

22 Critical Race Theory and Critical Whiteness Studies

Eva Boesenberg

What do *The Color Purple*, *The Great Gatsby*, and Barbie have in common? They can fruitfully be analyzed by using Critical Race Theory and Critical Whiteness Studies. Literature and culture do not arise in a social and historical vacuum. Rather, novels, films, and other cultural productions both reflect and reproduce historically specific social hierarchies, but they may also challenge them. In order to understand these processes, categories such as "race," class, and gender – as well as sexuality, dis/ability, age, etc. – are central for an analysis (not only) of North American culture. These categories are socially constructed, which means that they result from current as well as historical power relations between social groups. There is nothing natural about them. It is only the constant repetition of the assertion that some people are better than others that naturalizes and normalizes them, i.e., makes social hierarchies appear "natural" and "normal."

Critical Race Theory, then, examines specifically how "race" and ethnicity have been and continue to be construed in North America (here: the United States and Canada). One strand of Critical Race Theory is Critical Whiteness Studies, which investigate how whiteness operates. The word "critical" suggests that these forms of theory are meant to contribute to reducing racial hierarchies or even abolishing "race"[1] altogether.

Critical Race Theory

"Race" is not a quality of an individual or of social groups – it is not a biological feature people "have." Instead, "race" refers to a position assigned to people through a process called racialization. It is the dominant group – white middle- and upper-class people – that racializes or "others" social groups with less power. Since "race"/ethnicity is not the only system that establishes hierarchies in Western societies, the process of racialization differs depending on factors such as gender, sexuality, class, dis/ability, religion, age, etc. The experience of racism is different for a working-class Black lesbian and a straight upper-middle-class Black cis-man, for example (see Chapter 18). For a full understanding of "race," one thus needs an intersectional approach developed by scholars of color such as Kimberlé Crenshaw, Audre Lorde, or Patricia Hill Collins.[2]

With regard to North American culture, it is important to remember that both the United States and Canada arose as "settler colonies": Europeans and European Americans deprived Native Americans and First Nations of their land, claiming North America by settling there. Settler colonialism involved the construction of racial hierarchies legitimizing this conquest, which included particular constructions of sexuality (Morgensen). Likewise, slavery represented a central institution in the British North American colonies and later the United States until 1865 (Painter; Berlin). Contemporary concepts of "race" served to justify the enslavement of Native Americans and African Americans, defining them as inferior to whites.

Yet, African Americans and Native Americans are not the only ethnic groups targeted by racism in North America. What Edward Said has termed "Orientalism," a colonial discourse that lumps all cultures East of Europe together as "the Orient" and contrasts them unfavorably to a supposedly enlightened, modern, and democratic "West," led to the large-scale persecution of Asian Americans in the nineteenth and twentieth centuries, with the Chinese Exclusion Act of 1882 and the internment of Japanese Americans during World War II perhaps being the most egregious examples (Pfaelzer). Until the mid-twentieth century, Jewish Americans were also classified as "Orientals," suffering from pervasive Antisemitism (Brodkin; Dijkstra 348–91). The Ku Klux Klan, for instance, attacked both African Americans and Jewish Americans. Groups such as Chicanos/as and more generally Latinos/as as well as Muslims also suffer from racism – a form not necessarily based on notions of biology, but on an understanding of culture as something essential and unchanging. This is called "cultural racism."[3]

Because "race" remains pervasive in Western societies, it continues to affect knowledge production both in the university and elsewhere. In order to change this, scholars in Critical Race Theory seek to analyze the ways in which racial hierarchies resonate in academic research. Pioneers in this field have been academics of color such as W.E.B. Du Bois. In the late twentieth and the first decades of the twenty-first century, researchers such as Lorde, bell hooks, Gloria Anzaldúa, Patricia Williams, Henry Louis Gates, Jr., Gayatri Gopinath, Jasbir Puar, José Esteban Muñoz, Gayatri Spivak, Richard M. Juang, Roderick Ferguson, and many others have illuminated the workings of "race" and its interrelations with other categories by drawing on a variety of theoretical approaches. Some of them, most influentially perhaps Paul Gilroy, have called for the abolition of "race" as a concept altogether.

Reading literature through Critical Race Theory

How, then, can one use Critical Race Theory to understand and interpret North American literature and culture? I will suggest some approaches by looking at Alice Walker's novel *The Color Purple* (1982). It is important to note, though, that texts are not merely "objects" to be illuminated by "theory." Rather, literary works *contribute* both to Critical Race Theory and the construction of "race" as a category. My interpretation of *The Color Purple* will focus on three issues: the importance of slavery for understanding contemporary notions of "race"; the centrality of African American creative traditions and vernacular language; and finally the intersections of African descent with gender and sexuality.

Walker's novel highlights the significance of history for understanding the narrator-protagonist's story. Although Celie is not literally enslaved – the story is set in the early twentieth century – her situation resembles that of a slave because she has no control over her life and is deprived of all resources, even her bodily integrity. At thirteen, she is raped by the man she believes to be her father; she is forbidden to speak about this to anyone and is habitually beaten by him. He subsequently deprives her of her two children as well as an education (*The Color Purple* 4, 11). At this point, her condition resembles the "social death" that, according to Orlando Patterson, enslavement represented for its victims.

The story of Celie's eventual flight and her journey to self-determination has been called a "neo-slave narrative." A scene in which she is "inspected" by her future husband that resembles a slave sale makes the connection visible:

> He say, Let me see her again.
> Pa call me. *Celie*, he say. Like it wasn't nothing. Mr.– want another look at you.
> I go stand in the door. The sun shine in my eyes. He's still up on his horse. He look me up and down. [...]
> She good with children, Pa say. [...]
> Mr.– say, That cow still coming?
> He say, Her cow. (12)

Celie is exchanged between the two men without any regard for her own wishes – just like the cow she brings to the marriage. She is looked at and treated as an object, is denied access to language as well as "the gaze," the active power of looking. Her stepfather lists her qualities as one might those of goods to be sold. As with enslaved women, Celie's value consists in her labor power – the agricultural, domestic, and sexual work she will perform for her husband and his children. The major difference between Celie's predicament and that of female slaves lies in the fact that she at least enjoys the right of legal marriage to a man of her own social group.

The term "neo-slave narrative" also draws attention to the role of slave narratives as structural models for the novel. Scholars such as Frances Foster, Robert B. Stepto, and Augusta Rohrbach have established the centrality of slave narratives not only in African American literary history, but in US literary history in general – for instance their impact on the emergence of realism as a literary movement (Rohrbach). As in the slave narratives, literacy is essential for Celie's development; freedom is signaled by a change of place; and the text itself represents the crowning achievement of that freedom.

With Celie's exploitation at the hands of men, *The Color Purple* (like slave narratives by female authors, such as Harriet Jacobs's *Incidents in the Life of a Slave Girl*, 1861) also shows that Black women experience gender and sexual as well as racist oppression. By noting that racism affects African American men and women differently, the text emphasizes the intersections of "race" with gender and illustrates what Leslie McCall has called the "intracategorical complexity" of "race" (1773).

At the same time, the novel foregrounds the cultural resources Black women have historically used to combat racism and sexism. It shows how quilting serves as a medium of sisterly solidarity, linking Celie to her daughter-in-law Sofia and to Shug, her later lover. Celie subsequently uses her sewing skills to achieve financial independence as a designer of fashionable pants. But perhaps the most important resource for Celie is language. She draws on African American oral genres like "the dozens" (an insult game that usually targets one's opponent's mother) to stand up to her husband (170).

As she grows emotionally and intellectually, she refuses to abandon the Black English Vernacular she has spoken since her youth (183–84). Instead, she refines it. Her vivid, witty, flexible, and creative language proves both the value of Black cultural capital (Bourdieu) and her own talent as an artist. I would even argue, with Mikhail M. Bakhtin, that Celie's vernacular extends the expressive possibilities of US-American literature, creating a form that could be called "free direct discourse."

The text is structured by relationships between Black women at the level of content as well as form. For the most part, it consists of letters between Celie and her sister Nettie, adapting the genre of the epistolary novel, which came to prominence in eighteenth-century British fiction. Despite the fact that many men also expressed themselves in this genre, letters have traditionally been gendered female. The fact that the novel revolves around interactions among Black women suggests a "womanist" or Black feminist perspective. Walker defined "womanism" as a version of feminism dedicated to the fight against racism and class oppression as well as sexism (*In Search* xi–xii; see Chapter 17). Narrating the story from a Black lesbian perspective and affirming the value of African American female culture, the book itself can be understood as a womanist intervention in US-American literary history.

Other texts by writers of color employ very different strategies to criticize dominant constructions of "race." Thus Toni Morrison's short story "Recitatif" makes the process of racialization visible by stating that one of its protagonists is Black and the other white, while refusing to identify who is who. As a reader, you find yourself almost inevitably trying to figure out the characters' racial positions on the basis of clues that turn out to be unreliable. The reading process might thus lead one to recognize one's own reproduction of racial stereotypes, one's own entanglement in racist thought patterns.

Anzaldúa's analysis of "race" from a Chicana perspective draws attention to another set of aspects. Taking the changing historical location of the US-Mexican border as its point of departure, her text *Borderlands/La Frontera* undermines binary models of nationality, ethnicity, gender, and sexuality by emphasizing the hybridity that characterizes geographical and metaphorical "borderlands" in which different cultures interact and mingle (see Chapter 23). Such a dialogue of cultures and languages produces new, original cultural and linguistic forms as they manifest themselves for instance in Chicano/a literature. By combining autobiography, essays, and poetry, and by employing six Chicano/a languages (from TexMex to Pachuco and Spanglish), as well as American English and Mexican Spanish, the text showcases the value of hybridity at the level of form as well as subject matter. Even if, as some critics have argued, the term hybridity may have problematic effects, obscuring power relations and suggesting that there are in fact "races" that can "mix" (Nyong'o 5–6), the concept may still be useful in specific cultural and political contexts.

Critical Whiteness Studies

Whereas texts by writers of color tend to address "race" in a self-reflexive manner, this is not usually the case for works by white authors. Why? Because power operates, among other things, by passing itself off as "normal" to those who benefit from it – white people in terms of "race," heterosexuals where sexuality is concerned, upper- and middle-class people in class hierarchies, etc. Thus many white writers are not aware of their own racial position, even though it is logical that, if a society is structured by "race," there can be no "raceless" position.

Others may be unwilling to recognize their own whiteness and reflect critically on it. Realizing that one's own perspective and one's experience are very specific instead of "universal" or "just human" already signals a loss of power: One can no longer confidently generalize from such a vantage point. Further, whiteness is associated with a history of colonialism, slavery, and genocide – not a legacy anyone wants to inherit. Even today, whiteness means that one enjoys opportunities not open to everybody. Although white people might not ask for white privilege, as George Yancy points out, holding that position means being complicit in the exploitation of others – especially if one does not seek to understand how racism works and attempts to change one's behavior accordingly. One can reproduce racism without intending to, even despite one's best intentions. This is actually the primary way in which racism operates today.

The scholarly field that tries to clarify these mechanisms is called Critical Whiteness Studies. It is a branch of Critical Race Theory that looks specifically at the dominant or hegemonic racial position. Again, many of the leading scholars in this area are academics of color, Cheryl Harris, Steve Martinot, Yancy, and Morrison among them. Since the 1980s, white researchers such as David Roediger, Ruth Frankenberg, Richard Dyer, and Robin DiAngelo have also contributed important studies. I will draw on their insights to discuss whiteness in F. Scott Fitzgerald's most well-known novel.

Whiteness in *The Great Gatsby* (1926)

Whiteness is first of all noticeable in F. Scott Fitzgerald's book's color sym-
bolism. It stands for wealth, elegance, and status – whether in "the white
palaces of fashionable East Egg" (11), the dresses of upper-class women (14),
or Daisy's "little white roadster" (81). In fact, Daisy, the name of the central
female character who is so ardently desired by Gatsby, itself evokes a color
combination of white and yellow, or gold. (She is also called "the king's
daughter, the golden girl" 126; see also Chapter 15.) When the narrator Nick
Carraway goes into Manhattan with Gatsby,

> the city ris[es] up across the river in white heaps and sugar lumps all built
> with a wish out of non-olfactory money. The city seen from the Queensboro
> Bridge is always the city seen for the first time, in its first wild promise of
> all the mystery and the beauty in the world. (74–75)

The fact that this is an imaginary city – historical New York is clearly constructed from "olfactory" resources, money that smells – does not diminish
the brilliance and sweetness of this vision. But sweetness, that is sugar, was
also central to British colonialism and slavery in the Caribbean, and the language
employed here ("seen for the first time") recalls the rhetoric of European
conquest, revealing this image to be a white fantasy.

The representation of Tom and Daisy Buchanan shows how (upper-class
heterosexual) whiteness is gendered: Desirable women are complemented by
dominant men (some of whom, like Tom, explicitly advocate white supremacy,
see 19). Despite his scorn for Tom, Nick does not exactly question white
privilege either – he "laughs aloud" at the absurdity of three fashionably dressed
African Americans in a limousine who seem to think they can compete with him
and Gatsby (see 75). As Morrison has argued in *Playing in the Dark*, one distinctive feature of white US-American literature is its marginalization of what
she calls an "Africanist presence." Here, one can see how the Black characters
primarily serve to show the social superiority of the white narrator – even
though, in economic terms, they are obviously much more prosperous than he is.

Nick is also marked as white by his ambivalent relationship to Jay Gatsby
(160), whose claim to whiteness seems much less secure than his own. Even
though he admires Gatsby's drive and his capacity for self-invention, Nick
despises his taste. From the narrator's Old Money perspective, Gatsby's excessive
consumption – his flashy house, his gaudy car – identifies him as *nouveau riche*.
The questionable source of his money and his business partnership with Meyer
Wolfsheim, a Jewish American portrayed in an extremely racist manner (75–78),
also compromises Gatsby's whiteness. When it is finally revealed that his original
name was James Gatz (106), the question arises whether Gatsby himself is
Jewish and thus, in the logic of the 1920s' "scientific" racism, not quite white.

This does not mean that whiteness is necessarily morally superior in *The
Great Gatsby*. Tom and Daisy are among the most corrupt figures in the

novel. But Nick's eventual return to the Midwest, which is figured as a train ride through a winter landscape (182–83), reimagines the "real snow, our snow" (182) as a blank page on which he and the likes of him can "write" whatever they want – never mind that their "identification with this country" (182–83) is based on forcing Native Americans off their land in the context of settler colonialism.

In a similar rhetorical move, the ending of the text repeats a problematic collective American ideal by referring to "Dutch sailors'" first sight of the "fresh, green breast of the new world" (187), evoking the Eurocentric and sexist image of North America as "virgin land." Altogether, then, Fitzgerald's novel mythologizes whiteness (as well as hegemonic masculinity) instead of questioning it. Its criticism of the American Dream, limited as it is in its focus on the discrimination of the newly rich by Old Money families, thus risks reproducing most of the hierarchies that place this dream out of reach for a large majority of the US population.

... and Barbie?

Critical Whiteness Studies are also useful for analyzing the cultural effects of North American material culture, for example of toys like Barbie. One might start by looking at the production of Barbie dolls by young Asian women who labor under extremely exploitative conditions (Clark 194–225). Whiteness is here constructed in the context of transnational capitalism, both by the role of North Americans as consumers served by Asian producers and by the role of Mattel as a US-American company whose price policy results in awful working conditions. One can then follow the dolls into the toy store, a cultural space in which, as Christine L. Williams has shown, children learn to become consumers (137–74). In doing so, they are taught crucial lessons about class, "race," and gender – for instance through the way they are treated by the salespersons, through pricing, and the divisions of the stores into "boys'" and "girls'" sections.

Barbie dolls themselves come in a range of "ethnic versions" by now, but the blonde, blue-eyed, light-skinned, "white" doll remains the standard. As Ann duCille, Elizabeth Chin, and others have noted, "ethnic" (i.e., non-white) Barbies were at least originally cast from the same mold as the "white" one. Mattel uses a limited set of features to signify "race," basically skin tone, hair, names, and clothing, thus promoting a very superficial understanding of "race" as a social and cultural phenomenon. This is also a problem with regard to Barbies from the "dolls of the world" series that are supposed to represent different nations. Their portrayal is extremely stereotypical. Even if there are Black and white versions of the same Barbie, such as the 2013 "Mars Explorer," the package in which the Black Barbie is sold features only images of the blonde doll. The Black Barbie is outnumbered 4:1.

The whiteness Barbie represents is closely linked to consumption: Her clothing and accessories identify her as upper-middle class. Her consumption includes travelling to faraway countries such as India, which suggests that "the world" is there for her to explore. Such an attitude expresses white and class privilege and recalls a colonialist mindset. Barbie's whiteness is also gendered in problematic ways, whether through her unrealistic body shape, the preoccupation with shopping and conventional notions of beauty, or the fact that one of the few sentences the "speaking Barbie" was able to utter was "Math class is hard." With the presence of Ken, Mattel also places Barbie in a heteronormative romance plot.

In the end, however, the meaning of any cultural product depends on what its users make of it – what kinds of games they play with Barbie, what kinds of stories they invent for her. Erica Rand for instance has noted how some Barbie owners have "queered" her, in one instance even using her as a lesbian sex toy. Chin reports that the Black girls she worked with "did not allow their dolls to remain white" (172), braiding their blond hair and "making [them] live in black worlds" (173). Considering Mattel's advertising budget and the media it can employ, though, it remains questionable whether alternative understandings of the doll can challenge the image of whiteness the toymakers construct for Barbie.

Critical Race Theory in the classroom

Critical Race Theory cannot (and should not) only be employed to analyze literature and culture, it can also help to illuminate classroom dynamics. After all, the translation of scholarly work into everyday practices should begin where knowledge is produced and disseminated. Like any cultural space, the university is structured through "race" (among other categories of social differentiation). European universities are traditionally institutions of the elite. Despite all disclaimers, "elite" does not simply and innocently refer to meritocratic principles, but also to privilege (or, as Bourdieu would have it, social and cultural capital; see Chapter 15). In other words: European universities are structurally very white (and very male) dominated institutions. There are only few professors, administrators or even students of color (Eggers et al.; Schwarzbach-Apithy). Moreover, academics of color are frequently made to feel that they are "in the wrong place" (Kilomba 33–34). Their authority as scholars and/or learners is often challenged by white faculty and students alike.

Furthermore, many white teachers and students in the university are not aware of their own racial position, perceiving their perspectives as universal or "normal." Such an absence of self-reflexiveness is often coupled with or even caused by a lack of awareness that racism is a problem at all in European academic contexts (see also El-Tayeb). This obliviousness may express itself in exercising power by taking up more time and space in the classroom than appropriate and making vastly generalizing statements about other social groups. By using pronouns such as "we" or "all of us," white speakers intentionally or unintentionally claim to speak for the entire group, whether or not it includes people of color.

Here is a challenge on several counts. In order for the university to become a more democratic and inclusive institution, white teachers and students (including myself) need to pay attention not only to their language in the classroom – a case in point would be avoiding the n-word or any other racist term. I also need to learn to speak for myself and not for others. This clashes with the universalist ethos of much of academia. Critical Race Theory can teach instructors and students to question this very ethos. Even then, because of the crucial difference between intention and effect, something I say may be racist because I have not realized that my utterance transports racist meanings. In fact, this is almost inevitable, since I have been socialized in a society that is slow to acknowledge its racist underpinnings.

In actual classroom dynamics (in the form of heated debates), this problematic sometimes results in the angry and passionate protest: "I'm not a racist!" Why is this not a productive response? Because racism is sustained by specific utterances and actions, not qualities of persons. It may be better to postpone outrage, rethink what I just said and, if need be, alter my behavior and express things differently. While awareness of my speaking position as a white teacher or student and sensitivity about the reproduction of racism through language is an important step, ultimately European universities need to hire more people of color in all capacities, most especially as professors, and to enroll more students of color.

Promoting racial diversity is not only a matter of fairness and equal rights. Because social positions influence what researchers can see, the university as a whole will greatly benefit from as many different perspectives as possible. Seeing things from a new angle translates into new insights. Some of the knowledge European universities have historically produced has contributed to, and been marked by, fascism and colonialism. Any research that shows how this legacy resonates in today's forms of knowledge and that contributes to developing different knowledges and other ways of knowing is a great asset, not only for American Studies.

Notes

1   My putting "race" into quotation marks derives from my position as a white German for whom the term is inextricably tied to the Nazis' use of the German version of this word. I feel a need to distance myself from this construction, specifically the idea that humans can be divided into "races" based on biological or cultural characteristics. It may also be due to the fact that much of my academic socialization took place in the 1980s, when it was common to put the term into quotation marks to emphasize its character as socially constructed. Supposedly, this is no longer necessary today because this has become common knowledge. I am not so sure.

2 Noah Sow defines "people of color" as "a term for people who are not white, chosen by themselves. The concept [...] presupposes a shared experiential horizon of people not considered white in a white dominated society" (20–21, my translation). In the United States, membership in this group, which is based on self-identification, may include people as diverse as Chicano/as, Native Americans, Asian Americans, and African Americans; in Germany, Afro Germans, Asian Germans, and Turkish Germans, among others. The common denominator is the experience of racist discrimination.

3 Following DiAngelo, racism can be defined as "white racial and cultural prejudice and discrimination, supported intentionally or unintentionally by institutional power and authority, and used to the advantage of whites and the disadvantage of people of color" (87).

Works cited

Anzaldúa, Gloria. *Borderlands/La Frontera: The New Mestiza*. San Francisco: Aunt Lute Books, 1987. Print.

Bakhtin, Mikhail M. *The Dialogic Imagination: Four Essays*. Trans. Caryl Emerson and Michael Holquist. Ed. Michael Holquist. Austin: U of Texas P, 1981. Print.

Berlin, Ira. *Many Thousands Gone: The First Two Centuries of Slavery in America*. Cambridge, MA: Harvard UP, 1998. Print.

Bourdieu, Pierre. *Distinction: A Social Critique of the Judgement of Taste*. 1979. Trans. Richard Nice. New York: Taylor & Francis, 2010. Print.

Brodkin, Karen. *How Jews Became White Folks and What That Says About Race in America*. New Brunswick, NJ: Rutgers UP, 1998. Print.

Chin, Elizabeth. *Purchasing Power: Black Kids and American Consumer Culture*. Minneapolis: U of Minnesota P, 2001. Print.

Clark, Eric. *The Real Toy Story: Inside the Ruthless Battle for America's Youngest Consumers*. New York: Free P, 2007. Print.

Collins, Patricia Hill. *Fighting Words: Black Women and the Search for Justice*. Minneapolis: U of Minnesota P, 1998. Print.

---. "Gender, Black Feminism, and Black Political Economy." *Annals of the American Academy of Political and Social Science* 568 (2000): 41–53. Print.

Crenshaw, Kimberlé. "Mapping the Margins: Intersectionality, Identity Politics, and Violence against Women of Color." *Stanford Law Review* 43 (1991): 1241–99. Print.

DiAngelo, Robin. *What Does It Mean to Be White? Developing White Racial Literacy*. New York: Lang, 2012. Print.

Dijkstra, Bram. *Evil Sisters: The Threat of Female Sexuality in Twentieth-Century Culture*. New York: Holt, 1996. Print.

Du Bois, W.E.B. *The Souls of Black Folk*. 1903. New York: Bantam, 1989. Print.

DuCille, Ann. *Skin Trade*. Cambridge, MA: Harvard UP, 1996. Print.

Dyer, Richard. *White*. London: Routledge, 1997. Print.

Eggers, Maureen Maisha, Grada Kilomba, Peggy Piesche, and Susan Arndt, eds. *Mythen, Masken und Subjekte: Kritische Weißseinsforschung in Deutschland*. Münster: Unrast, 2005. Print.

El-Tayeb, Fatima. *European Others: Queering Ethnicity in Postnational Europe*. Minneapolis: U of Minnesota P, 2011. Print.

Ferguson, Roderick. *Aberrations in Black: Towards a Queer of Color Critique.* Minneapolis: U of Minnesota P, 2003. Print.

Fitzgerald, F. Scott. *The Great Gatsby.* 1926. Harmondsworth: Penguin, 1979. Print.

Foster, Frances. *Witnessing Slavery: The Development of Ante-Bellum Slave Narratives.* Madison: U of Wisconsin P, 1994. Print.

Frankenberg, Ruth. *White Women, Race Matters: The Social Construction of Whiteness.* Minneapolis: U of Minnesota P, 1993. Print.

Gates, Henry Louis, Jr. *The Signifying Monkey: A Theory of Afro-American Literary Criticism.* New York: Oxford UP, 1988. Print.

Gilroy, Paul. *Against Race: Imagining Political Culture beyond the Color Line.* Cambridge, MA: Harvard UP, 2000. Print.

Gopinath, Gayatri. *Impossible Desires: Queer Diasporas and South Asian Public Cultures.* Durham, NC: Duke UP, 2005. Print.

Harris, Cheryl I. "Whiteness as Property." *Harvard Law Review* 106 (1993): 1709–91. Print.

hooks, bell. *Writing beyond Race: Living Theory and Practice.* London: Routledge, 2013. Print.

Juang, Richard. "Transgendering the Politics of Recognition." *Transgender Rights.* Ed. Paisley Currah, Richard M. Juang, and Shannon Price Minter. Minneapolis: U of Minnesota P, 2006. Print.

Kilomba, Grada. *Plantation Memories: Episodes of Everyday Racism.* Münster: Unrast, 2008. Print.

Lorde, Audre. *Sister Outsider: Essays and Speeches by Audre Lorde.* 1984. Berkeley, CA: Crossing P, 2007. Print.

Martinot, Steve. *The Machinery of Whiteness: Studies in the Structure of Racialization.* Philadelphia, PA: Temple UP, 2010. Print.

McCall, Leslie. "The Complexity of Intersectionality." *Signs* 30.3 (2005): 1771–800. Print.

Morgensen, Scott Lauria. *Spaces between Us: Queer Settler Colonialism and Indigenous Decolonization.* Minneapolis: U of Minnesota P, 2011. Print.

Morrison, Toni. *Playing in the Dark: Whiteness and the Literary Imagination.* 1992. London: Picador, 1993. Print.

---. "Recitatif." *Confirmation: An Anthology of African American Women.* Ed. Amiri Baraka and Amina Baraka. New York: Norton, 1983. 243–61. Print.

Muñoz, José Esteban. *Disidentifications: Queers of Color and the Performance of Politics.* Minneapolis: U of Minnesota P, 1999. Print.

Nyong'o, Tavia. *The Amalgamation Waltz: Race, Performance, and the Ruses of Memory.* Minneapolis: U of Minnesota P, 2009. Print.

Painter, Nell Irvin. *The History of White People.* New York: Norton, 2010. Print.

Patterson, Orlando. *Slavery and Social Death: A Comparative Study.* Cambridge, MA: Harvard UP; 1982. Print.

Pfaelzer, Jean. *Driven Out: The Forgotten War against Chinese Americans.* New York: Random House, 2007. Print.

Puar, Jasbir K. *Terrorist Assemblages: Homonationalism in Queer Times.* Durham, NC: Duke UP, 2007. Print.

Rand, Erica. *Barbie's Queer Accessories.* Durham, NC: Duke UP, 1997. Print.

Roediger, David R. *The Wages of Whiteness: Race and the Making of the American Working Class.* London: Verso, 1991. Print.

Rohrbach, Augusta. *Truth Stranger than Fiction: Race, Realism, and the US Literary Marketplace.* New York: Palgrave, 2002. Print.

Said, Edward W. *Orientalism.* New York: Pantheon Books, 1978. Print.

Schwarzbach-Apithy, Aretha. "Interkulturalität und anti-rassistische Weis(s)heiten an Berliner Universitäten." *Mythen, Masken und Subjekte: Kritische Weißseinsforschung in Deutschland.* Ed. Maureen Maisha Eggers, Grada Kilomba, Peggy Piesche, and Susan Arndt. Münster: Unrast, 2005. 247–61. Print.

Sow, Noah. *Deutschland Schwarz Weiß: Der alltägliche Rassismus.* München: Bertelsmann, 2008. Print.

Spivak, Gayatri Chakravorty. "Can the Subaltern Speak?" *Marxism and the Interpretation of Culture.* Ed. Cary Nelson and Larry Grossberg. Urbana: U of Illinois P, 1988. 217–313. Print.

Stepto, Robert B. *From Behind the Veil: A Study of Afro-American Narrative.* Champaign: U of Illinois P, 1979. Print.

Walker, Alice. *The Color Purple.* New York: Harcourt Brace Jovanovich, 1982. Print.

---. *In Search of Our Mothers' Gardens: Womanist Prose by Alice Walker.* San Diego, CA: Harcourt Brace Jovanovich, 1983. Print.

Williams, Christine L. *Inside Toyland: Working, Shopping, and Social Inequality.* Berkeley: U of California P, 2006. Print.

Williams, Patricia J. *The Alchemy of Race and Rights: Diary of a Law Professor.* Cambridge, MA: Harvard UP, 1991. Print.

Yancy, George. *Look, a White! Philosophical Essays on Whiteness.* Philadelphia, PA: Temple UP, 2012. Print.

23 Border Studies and Hemispheric Studies

Rethinking America

Gabriele Pisarz-Ramirez

One of the most long-standing myths in American cultural history is the myth of the Frontier. The conflict between settlers and Indians, between "civilization" and "savagery" as well as the association of the Frontier with "empty" spaces providing unlimited opportunity and adventure was romanticized in countless dime novel Westerns and films. Frederick Jackson Turner, in his lecture on "The Significance of the Frontier in American History" in 1893, perpetuated this myth, arguing that the Frontier and Western expansion were crucially important for the creation of American values such as democracy and individualism (see Chapter 6).

Especially the idea of an "empty" West had long been opposed by those population groups who had lived in the region before it was settled in the process of US-American expansionism, predominantly Mexican Americans and Native Americans. Beginning in the 1970s, scholars of Mexican and Native American history began to unearth texts and artifacts that documented the complex history and culture of the region, including the history of the 2,000 miles long border between the United States and Mexico and the territories north and south of this border. Their critical voices were joined by those of historians and literary critics such as Patricia Limerick and Annette Kolodny who pointed out the limitations of the Frontier myth and argued for a revised conception of the Frontier as a "meeting ground" (Limerick 269) or a space of "ongoing first encounters" (Kolodny 13) and for the necessity to incorporate the voices and perspectives marginalized by Turner. Border Studies emerged from this critical engagement with the Frontier myth and from the awareness that people living at the US-Mexican border – today the most densely populated border space worldwide and the site of a considerable theoretical and cultural production – are often rooted transnationally and at the intersection of different cultures, languages, ethnic, and racial groups. In his 1996 movie *Lone Star*, film director John Sayles presents us with a contemporary view of the border at the turn to the twenty-first century.

The border in John Sayles's *Lone Star*

The movie opens as two men find human bones and a weathered sheriff's star in a dusty desert landscape. The scene is set in Frontera, Texas, a fictional border town, and the bones belong to Charlie Wade, a notoriously cruel and racist sheriff who ruled Frontera in the 1950s before he disappeared one day as did ten thousand dollars from the county funds. When Frontera's current sheriff Sam Deeds arrives on the scene, it becomes clear that a crime needs to be solved.

Although, as Kimberly Sultze (20) has pointed out, all important components for a Western are there – desert scenery, a dead man, a crime, and a sheriff willing to resolve it – something is amiss right from the start. Instead of a spectacular mythic landscape typical of classic Westerns – such as Monument Valley in a John Ford film – the camera lingers at low angle, giving us a view of cacti and shrubbery. One of the two men wears a polo shirt and shorts and reads out plant names from a book – he is a nature lover; the second man, a collector of old metals, wears headphones and a metal detector. These two unheroic figures are then joined by Sheriff Sam Deeds who does not even carry a weapon. The camera does not look up to him, presenting him as a larger-than-life figure, but rather invites the viewer to look down on him as he is shown crouching on the ground looking for pieces of evidence.

Viewers also need to listen closely to what the characters are saying – another feature untypical of a classic Western where voices are usually very clear. And while in most Western movies we have only a few central characters, Sayles's film presents us with over fifty different characters, some of whom only appear in one or two scenes. This is sometimes confusing, as we do not know immediately what the function of some of these characters and what they say for the plotline is. Moreover, the film includes many flashbacks that shed a light on episodes several decades previous to the current events, without clear cinematic signals that it is moving back in time. The element of confusion created by these cinematic strategies is of course intended, conveying a sense of the interrelations of past and present and of the complexity of Frontera's border history.

An indicator of this complexity is the Spanish name of the place, which points to the fact that the territory – Texas – used to be Mexican before its incorporation into the United States in 1845. The movie – unlike many Westerns – presents us with a view of the town's history that gives a voice to the people who call the border home. However, this history is not presented to us in one piece. It emerges gradually in the course of Sheriff Deeds's investigation of the murder case and has to be assembled from information he gathers from the townspeople – little fragments of memory, hearsay, casual remarks – and old documents. In the course of the movie it becomes clear that there are a multitude of stories in Frontera. But not all of these stories are equally accepted. Some linger unexplored and invisible beneath the "official" version of Frontera's history, some are present only as rumors, some are publicly denied. The movie unravels Frontera's history on several levels, as characters in the movie explore the history of the town or their own history and that of their parents. The image that emerges sheds a light not only on the events surrounding the death of Charlie Wade, but also on the many boundaries that fracture the community of this town – boundaries of "race," class, language, and historical perspective.

In a scene at the beginning of the film, high school teachers and parents are engaged in a heated discussion about which version of history is to be taught to the children and how far the textbook version should be followed. Some of the parents and teachers are Anglo-Americans, but at least half of them are of Mexican American descent. While some parents argue that the winners of history should decide about this, and that the textbook version should be taught because it reflects the "winners'" viewpoint, others point out that the majority of inhabitants of Frontera are Mexican Americans, Blacks, and Native Americans and that their children have a right to learn about alternative versions. While one Anglo teacher thinks that the tolerance for difference should only apply to food and music, another suggests that it is important to present a more inclusive picture. What becomes clear in this scene as in the entire film is that the issues at stake at the border are centrally issues that are also at stake in the nation – or, as Chicano critic José David Saldívar put it in a seminal book in 1997, that "border matters" for the nation. Critically interrogating traditional narratives of "American" identity and national paradigms of culture that proclaim a monocultural and monolithic version of history, and that have regarded the border region as peripheral and negligible, Saldívar argues that the transnational culture of the borderlands constitutes a social space in which new imaginaries, hybrid cultures, and theoretical productions emerge. In *Lone Star*, Texas operates for Sayles as a microcosm of America, as he himself has stated: "One of the reasons I chose Texas for this thing is because the state of Texas has a compressed history that is like a metaphor for the history of the United States" (Smith 232).

One of the plotlines in *Lone Star* circles around sheriff Deeds's father, the legendary Buddy Deeds who replaced Charlie Wade as sheriff after Wade's disappearance. Official town lore still presents Buddy Deeds as a hero and benefactor of the town. After the remains of Charlie Wade have been found, Buddy Deeds becomes a prime suspect as he had opposed Wade early on. Most of Frontera's citizens do not want to believe he is a murderer, unlike his son Sam who has resented his father ever since he broke up Sam's high school love relationship with a Mexican American girl, Pilar. Sam, who left town as a young man and has only recently returned to Frontera, becomes the main driving force in trying to uncover the mystery about Charlie Wade's disappearance. He assumes his father to have been a racist like his predecessor, but after listening to the stories told him by different people in town, he needs to revise his image of his father. As it turns out, Buddy Deeds was not the murderer of Charlie Wade, and he was respected in town because, while he used politics to foster his own personal interests and that of his friends, these friends were Black, Anglo, and Mexican Americans alike.

It is significant how borders are presented in the movie. While some protagonists (like former Sheriff Charlie Wade) try to keep borders clear and definite – especially those that demarcate "race" and class hierarchies – the unraveling plot makes clear that these borders have always been permeable, if only unofficially. This becomes visible in the plotline that concerns the story of Sam's high school girlfriend Pilar and her parents, Mercedes Cruz and her husband Eladio who was killed by Charlie Wade while trying to bring Mexican friends of his across the border. While Pilar, now a teacher at the local high school, tries to convey to her students a more accurate version of history than the textbook presents, her mother Mercedes, a successful local businesswoman, advocates an assimilationist stance, prohibiting her employees from speaking Spanish at work and calling the police when she sees people trying to cross the Rio Grande from Mexico to the United States. In a later flashback however, it becomes clear that Mercedes herself came to the United States as an undocumented immigrant and that she is denying her own history. Moreover, as it turns out, she was conducting an affair with Sam's father Buddy Deeds after her husband's death, and Pilar is actually not Eladio's daughter, but Buddy Deeds's, and thus Sam Deeds's half-sister. This detail is found out by Sam after he has resumed his romantic relationship with Pilar and as he investigates the murder case.

In one scene Sam crosses the border into Mexico to question a former friend of Eladio Cruz, a local tire dealer in Ciudad León. As the tire dealer makes clear to him, for many Mexican Americans the border at the time of Charlie Wade's rule was just a "line in the dust," an arbitrary boundary drawn by those in power after the occupation of Mexico in 1848. In his narrative, Eladio Cruz died because he was "giving some friends of his a lift in his *camión* one day – but because he's on one side of this invisible line and not the other, they got to hide in the back like criminals." For Charlie Wade, Eladio Cruz was committing a transgression, and the ensuing violence indicates the power hierarchies in place at that border.

John Sayles's *Lone Star* was a commercial success and an Oscar nominee (for best screenplay). This is quite remarkable if we consider how provocative the movie is not only in its revision of border history, but even more in its depiction of an incestuous relationship that takes the issue of borders and border-crossing on yet a different level. After Sam has told Pilar what he has found out – that they are siblings – they decide to ignore the incest taboo and stay together. As Kim Magowan has convincingly argued, "Sayles combines incest, society's most ubiquitous taboo, with miscegenation in ways that simultaneously nod to cultural tradition and break from it" (20). Interracial relationships for a long time in American history were outlawed and yet practiced, especially in the American South by slave owners who sexually exploited their female "property." While Sayles moves the scene from the binary racial setting of the slavery South to the realm of the Texas border region, it becomes clear that the taboo of racial mixture played an important role in the history of Frontera, even if it was often transgressed. Interracial relationships are a frequent phenomenon in the Frontera community, generating much of its population. If the miscegenation taboo has been ignored, Sayles seems to argue, it might be possible to choose to ignore the incest taboo, too. Since both taboos are cultural constructions they are both negotiable (Magowan 22).

As we can see in this reading of the movie, the concept of the border refers not only to a geographical location but is also used metaphorically to interrogate boundaries between culturally constructed categories such as "race" or ethnicity. An author who has famously addressed constructions of gender and sexuality as well as spirituality in her use of the term "border" is Chicana writer Gloria Anzaldúa.

Gloria Anzaldúa's *New Mestiza*

In her landmark *Borderlands/La Frontera: The New Mestiza* (1987), a hybrid text that mixes autobiography, poetry, and theory, Anzaldúa has theorized the border from her subject position as a Chicana feminist and a lesbian of color – a position that, as she points out, is linked to the experience of multiple exclusions. Growing up in South Texas in the 1940s and 1950s, she was confronted with racism and oppressive poverty, but also felt excluded from her own ethnic community both as a woman and as a Chicana lesbian. In the poem opening the book, Anzaldúa describes the border as a

> 1,950 mile-long open wound dividing a *pueblo* a culture,
> running down the length of my body,
> staking fence rods in my flesh,
> splits me splits me
> *me raja me raja* (2)

In this brief passage we can already discern several important ideas that run through the book. Anzaldúa refers to the border both in a geographical and in a metaphorical way. It is a line that divides Mexicans in Mexico and Mexican Americans in the United States but it is also the psychic state of living in the borderlands, in-between different ethnic groups, between genders, between cultures and languages. This life of in-betweenness inflicts wounds, actual and metaphorical ones, and Anzaldúa metaphorizes these wounds as the rods of the border fence being driven into her flesh. As the image of the wound shows, she describes this experience as extremely painful, which is significant as many postmodernist theorists of hybridity have tended to envision in-betweenness and hybridity as a playful state, neglecting the power relations involved.

The notion of being split is a returning image in the book. Anzaldúa's experience of living among people of divergent worlds led her to refuse to pledge allegiance to one particular group, belief system, political idea, or geographical location – as she felt was constantly required of her. In the chapter "Fear of Going Home: Homophobia" she describes the difficulties of being lesbian in a traditional Catholic Mexican American community: "For the lesbian of color, the ultimate rebellion she can make against her native culture is through her sexual behavior" (19). Responding to those who regarded Mexican American women who were lesbians as "traitors" to the community and who see homosexuality as something "alien" to Mexican American culture, she states: "I feel perfectly free to rebel and to rail against my culture. [...] Not me sold out my people but they me" (21).

One way in which in-betweenness becomes graspable in the passage above is language. Just like the title of the book, *Borderlands/La Frontera*, it shows how Anzaldúa brings in different languages and thus different perspectives. The book is written in a mixture of Standard English, working-class English, Náhuatl, Standard Spanish, Chicano Spanish, and Spanglish, crossing linguistic borders constantly and giving monolingual English speakers a difficult reading experience. Sometimes the Spanish passages (like in the above section of the poem) are translations of the English (*me raja* = splits me), but often Spanish passages remain untranslated, producing "gaps" for the monolingual reader. This strategy is of course intentional in view of the various exclusionary practices that have marginalized those US-Americans who have not grown up with English as their native tongue. But it also reflects the linguistic reality of the borderlands where many people grow up speaking Spanish or mix English with Spanish in their everyday language practice.

This form of code-switching often implies switching between different world views and epistemological perspectives, an aspect that Latin American critic Walter Mignolo has described as "border gnosis" or "border thinking." What he refers to are ways of thinking that acknowledge the multiple sites from which knowledge is produced, thus deconstructing binary ways of thinking as well as logo- and ethnocentric global hierarchies of knowledge production. This is another important way in which Border Studies are significant for American Studies: They help us consider the United States not from its center(s), but from its margins and its gaps, from the areas neglected by mainstream history books, and they force us to take into account different viewpoints, and non-Eurocentrist models of world explanation.

From the situation of multiple exclusions and of seeing herself caught between different "camps" – as a Texan, Mexican, Chicana, Indian, as a feminist, and a lesbian of color – Anzaldúa develops her theory of the "new mestiza." The "new mestiza" is a woman who positions herself at the crossroads of all these "camps."

> The new *mestiza* copes by developing a tolerance for contradictions, a tolerance for ambiguity. She learns to be an Indian in Mexican culture, to be Mexican from an Anglo point of view. She learns to juggle cultures. She has a plural personality, she operates in a pluralistic mode – nothing is thrust out, the good the bad and the ugly, nothing rejected, nothing abandoned. Not only does she sustain contradictions, she turns the ambivalence into something else. (79)

Anzaldúa sees the "new mestiza" as a figure for the future of America, as embodying the end of binary thinking and a source of new energy and creativity. Other border writers have articulated the decentralized, multiply rooted identities of intercultural subjects in the borderlands in concepts such as "frontera imaginary" (Saldívar xii), "Queer Aztlán" (Moraga 145–74), and "Nepantla" (Mora). All these concepts do not only offer critical interventions into previous more essentialist conceptions of ethnic identity, they also interrogate traditional narratives of "American" identity and exceptionalist notions of the United States' role on the continent. These writers participate in a wide network of theoretical discourses that have, since the beginning of the 1990s, re-explored the concept of nation.

Border Studies since its inception in the 1980s have developed in various directions. One important critical field is the emerging Comparative Border Studies that includes not only the Mexican-American border but other borders and other constellations of national and transnational forces – such as the cross-border military expeditions the United States is undertaking in the fight against terrorism – and that explores the interrelationships between, e.g., the US-Mexican border and the "Af/Pak frontier" (Feldman), the Israel/Palestine boundary or the US-Canadian border (see Sadowski-Smith Introduction; "The Centrality of the Canada-US Border"). Another development has been the beginning of an intersection and overlapping of Border Studies with other disciplines, such as Comparative Literary Studies, Latin American Studies, and Inter-American Studies to form the new field of Hemispheric Studies (see Sadowski-Smith and Fox; Bauer).

From the border to the hemisphere

Hemispheric Studies enlarge the perspective from the US-Mexican border to the entire American continent. They explore the ways in which the United States has throughout its history been economically, politically, and culturally entangled with other parts of the Americas, be it through the slave trade, be it through the United States' nineteenth-century expansionist ventures in the Caribbean and Central America, or its more recent military involvement in various Latin American countries. Early hemispheric approaches to American history were developed by Herbert Bolton in the 1930s ("The Epic of Greater America") and in an essay collection edited by Lewis Hanke entitled *Do the Americas Have a Common History?* (1964). In 1990 Gustavo Pérez Firmat edited a collection asking *Do the Americas Have a Common Literature?* Scholars also have begun to analyze canonical texts from American literature in an inter-American framework. To give just two examples, Eric Sundquist has read Herman Melville's novella *Benito Cereno* as a restaging of the Haitian revolution and Vera Kutzinski links William Faulkner's South in *Absalom, Absalom!* with its immediate surroundings, the Caribbean and Latin America, describing the southernmost parts of the United States as cultural "rimlands of the Caribbean" (61).

A brief look at the beginning scene of Martin Delany's *Blake; or the Huts of America*, a novel about an escaped slave who prepares a transnational slave rebellion and a text that speaks directly back to Harriet Beecher Stowe's *Uncle Tom's Cabin* (1852), shows how we can make the hemispheric approach productive for our study of literature. This novel was published serially in the *Anglo-African Magazine* in 1859 and the *Weekly Anglo-African* in 1861 and 1862. The first book edition was published in 1970 by Beacon Press in Boston, edited by Floyd Miller. Entitled "The Project," the first chapter of the novel, which comprises only two paragraphs, describes a meeting of six gentlemen, four Americans and two Cubans, on a day of presidential elections in Baltimore. The men pay little attention to the elections, however, but are rather "absorbed in an adventure of self interest": They discuss the refitting of an old ship. After they have reached an agreement on the main point of discussion – the question whether the ship is to be refitted in Baltimore or on Cuba – they leave.

We cannot make much sense of this scene and might ask ourselves why Delany begins his novel with such an apparently insignificant incident, until we read the scene in the context of US involvement in hemispheric economic relations in the 1850s. What is actually at stake in the scene, i.e., the "project" the gentlemen are pursuing, is the refitting of an American slave ship as a Spanish ship, a method practiced by American slave traders to circumvent the 1807 federal law that prohibited the importation of slaves to the United States. The way American traders were able to continue their participation in the trade was by sailing under cover – in this case, by using vessels that did not legally belong to Americans but were owned by Portuguese and Spanish nationals.

The scene thus sheds a light on the economic investments Americans had in the Caribbean and the profits they drew from the region, both as slave traders and as owners of plantations on Cuba. The reason why they were able to pursue their economic goals with relative impunity was that these goals were in line with national politics: There had been several unsuccessful attempts by the United States to buy Cuba from Spain, and in public discourses of the antebellum period the view prevailed that Cuba would eventually fall into US hands due to Spain's dwindling influence on the American continent and the inability of Cuban Creoles to rule the country. This view is also reflected in the novel when one of the gentlemen from Chapter 1 later declares that "Cuba must cease to be a Spanish colony, and become American territory. Those mongrel Creoles are incapable of self-government, and should be compelled to submit to the United States" (62).

Blake reveals the hollowness of republican ideals of liberty and democracy that dominated nationalist US rhetoric in the view of a system that tolerated and enabled slavery. Significantly, the novel's protagonist organizes a slave revolt that involves slaves both in the United States and Cuba, creating a hemispheric context for Black liberation. As Andy Doolen has argued, Delany thus removes African Americans from a nationalist discourse that automatically referred their appeals for racial justice back to a failed white revolutionary project.

An understanding of the connections between the different regions of the American continent helps us to reveal the constructedness of many binarisms that have, as Ralph Bauer remarks, "burdened American Studies" – binarisms such as nature/culture, self/other, Europe/America (242) – not least the notion of an "America" that often stands to represent not just a nation but an entire continent. Referring to the continent, more recent studies therefore more appropriately speak of "the Americas," acknowledging their hemispheric frame of reference.

Works cited

Anzaldúa, Gloria. *Borderlands/La Frontera: The New Mestiza*. San Francisco: Aunt Lute Books, 1987. Print.

Bauer, Ralph. "Hemispheric Studies." *PMLA* 124.1 (2009): 234–50. Print.

Bolton, Herbert Eugene. "The Epic of Greater America." *American Historical Review* 38.3 (1933): 448–74. Print.

Delany, Martin Robison. *Blake; or the Huts of America*. 1859. Boston, MA: Beacon P, 1970. Print.

Doolen, Andy. "Be Cautious of the Word 'Rebel': Race, Revolution, and Transnational History in Martin Delany's *Blake; or, The Huts of America*." *American Literature* 81.1 (2009): 153–79. Print.

Feldman, Keith P. "Empire's Verticality: The Af/Pak Frontier, Visual Culture, and Racialization from Above." *Comparative American Studies* 9.4 (2011): 325–41. Print.

Hanke, Lewis. *Do the Americas Have a Common History? A Critique of the Bolton Theory*. New York: Knopf, 1964. Print.

Kolodny, Annette. "Letting Go Our Grand Obsessions: Notes toward a New Literary History of the American Frontiers." *American Literature* 64.1 (1992): 1–18. Print.

Kutzinski, Vera M. "Borders and Bodies: The United States, America, and the Caribbean." *CR: The New Centennial Review* 1.2 (2001): 55–88. Print.

Limerick, Patricia. *The Legacy of Conquest: The Unbroken Past of the American West*. New York: Norton, 1988. Print.

Lone Star. Dir. John Sayles. Perf. Chris Cooper, Elizabeth Peña, and Stephen Mendillo. Columbia Pictures, 1996. DVD.

Magowan, Kim. "Blood Only Means What You Let It." *Film Quarterly* 57.1 (2003): 20–31. Print.

Mignolo, Walter. *Local Histories/Global Designs: Coloniality, Subaltern Knowledges, and Border Thinking*. Princeton, NJ: Princeton UP, 2000. Print.

Mora, Pat. *Nepantla: Essays from the Land in the Middle*. Albuquerque: U of New Mexico P, 1993. Print.

Moraga, Cherríe. *The Last Generation: Prose and Poetry*. Boston, MA: South End P, 1993. Print.

Pérez Firmat, Gustavo, ed. *Do the Americas Have a Common Literature?* Durham, NC: Duke UP, 1990. Print.

Sadowski-Smith, Claudia. "The Centrality of the Canada-US Border for Hemispheric Studies of the Americas." *FIAR* 7.3 (2014). Web.

---. "Introduction: Comparative Border Studies." *Comparative American Studies* 9.4 (2011): 273–87. Print.

Sadowski-Smith, Claudia, and Claire F. Fox. "Theorizing the Hemisphere: Inter-Americas Work at the Intersection of American, Canadian, and Latin American Studies." *Comparative American Studies* 2.1 (Spring 2004): 41–74. Print.

Saldívar, José David. *Border Matters: Remapping American Cultural Studies.* Oakland: U of California P, 1997. Print.

Smith, Gavin, ed. *Sayles on Sayles.* London: Faber & Faber, 1998. Print.

Sundquist, Eric J. *To Wake the Nations: Race in the Making of American Literature.* Cambridge: Cambridge UP, 1993. Print.

Turner, Frederick Jackson. "The Significance of the Frontier in American History." *Rereading Frederick Jackson Turner: "The Significance of the Frontier in American History" and Other Essays.* New York: Holt, 1994. 31–60. Print.

Index